DEVELOPING NATION
NEW PLAY CREATION IN ENGLISH-SPEAKING CANADA

DEVELOPING NATION
NEW PLAY CREATION IN ENGLISH-SPEAKING CANADA

Edited by Bruce Barton

Playwrights Canada Press
Toronto • Canada

PLAYWRIGHTS CANADA PRESS
The Canadian Drama Publisher
215 Spadina Avenue, Suite 230, Toronto, Ontario, CANADA M5T 2C7
phone 416.703.0013   fax 416.408.3402
orders@playwrightscanada.com • www.playwrightscanada.com

The publisher acknowledges the support of the Canadian taxpayers through
the Government of Canada Book Publishing Industry Development Program,
the Canada Council for the Arts, the Ontario Arts Council,
and the Ontario Media Development Corporation.

Cover image: Martin Julien, participating in the session of Nightswimming's "Pure
Research" led by Cathy Nosaty in 2006 at the Glen Morris Studio, University of
Toronto. Photo by Laurel MacDonald.
Cover Design: B. Barton & JLArt   Production Editor: JLArt

Library and Archives Canada Cataloguing in Publication

Developing nation : new play creation in English-speaking Canada /
Bruce Barton, ed.

Includes bibliographical references.
ISBN 978-0-88754-593-1

1. Playwriting. 2. Drama--Technique. 3. Canadian drama (English)--21st
century--History and criticism. I. Barton, Bruce, 1958-

PN1661.D47 2009   808.2'0971   C2009-901463-7

This book
was printed
on 100%
recycled stock.

First edition: May 2009
Printed and bound by Hignell Book Printing at Winnipeg, Manitoba.

For Pil and Lily,

who never let me forget to create

Table of Contents

Acknowledgements

I offer my thanks to the excellent research assistants on the Creative Spaces research project who were instrumental in the original literature review: Natalie Corbett, Barry Freeman, Christopher Jackman, Patrick Robinson, Birgit Schreyer Duarte, and Aktina Stathaki. Likewise, my gratitude goes out to all the fine writers and publications that have made their important material available to this venture. I would like to thank graphic designer Jodi Armstrong for her always fine artistic touch and professionalism, as well as the folks at Playwrights Canada Press: Annie Gibson, for her encouragement and patience, and, in particular, Angela Rebeiro, whose enthusiasm, guidance, and considerable manual labour were all major contributions to this collection. I would also like to thank the Graduate Centre for the Study of Drama, University of Toronto, for their ongoing support to the Creative Spaces project, and to the Social Sciences and Humanities Research Council for funding the activity in the first place.

All essays and interviews included here are published with the permission of the copyright holders. For full bibliographical information see Appendix 1: Works by Author.

Bruce Barton

Introduction:
Creating Spaces
by Bruce Barton

A new work of art is a conspiracy… (Paula Danckert)

At the beginning of her contribution to this collection, Yvette Nolan states, with relief, "At least we're not still trying to define *what is dramaturgy*." And while this is, to a degree, accurate, it should be noted that this shift is not really a recent development nor the result of there being a clear or commonly held definition. As I move through the more than two decades worth of articles included in this volume I cannot help but be struck by the consistent investment in keeping such definitions at bay. The "conspiracy" that Danckert refers to, above and in her contribution, is repeatedly confirmed, protected, and celebrated throughout these pages. Monique Mojica, quoted in Diane Roberts's 1996 article on dramaturgy at Toronto's Nightwood Theatre, proposes the following:

> When I think of what dramaturgy is, I think it's like being on a wave— you're on a current, and you try to do everything you can to keep that current going. You're grabbing thoughts that come from other levels and trying to connect them. When there is a vital germ, an essential vitalness [sic] to something a writer or performer is trying to discover, or uncover, a dramaturge helps the creator to identify it and form it. (22)[1]

The power in this description (as in so much of Mojica's expression) is inseparable from its abstraction, from its refusal to be tethered to logic or pragmatism while it nonetheless grasps towards utility and application.

Repeatedly, throughout this collection, dramaturgy resists the mantle of stable definition and instead insists on perpetually redefining itself in relation to its context: the people, projects, and parameters it operates upon and within. Yet, as other entries in this collection demonstrate, this wary elusiveness concerning definitions in no way precludes concrete description and analysis of its "working parts." As Kate Lushington proposes in the same article, "[T]here is a specific craft to dramaturgy, to dramaturgical skills. Skills and knowledge" (23). Further, in the fifteen years I have worked as a professional dramaturg and playwright in Canada (which makes me a relative newcomer compared to many of the contributors to this collection), I can attest that it is the contrast between a fluid and adaptable *understanding* of dramaturgy and the perception of an all too common "one-size-fits-all" approach to its *practice* that emerges as one of the most frequent topics of discussion. The machinery of dramaturgy has been a remarkably popular topic of debate, in personal exchanges and in published criticism, for several decades. Some of the most noteworthy positions and personalities from that conversation have been gathered here to be revisited and reassessed with an eye to the future.

Searching for "Creative Spaces"

For clarity: arriving at a fixed definition of dramaturgy was never a motivation behind this collection. As I suggest in the second of my two contributions,

> The range of possible definitions of [dramaturgy] is practically as broad as the number of its practitioners is great, and most contemporary discussion on this topic has productively moved beyond attempts to categorically determine and fix its "correct" objectives and/or techniques into a consideration of its effective variety and potential. ("Navigating 'Turbulence'," 103)

Rather, the inspiration for this collection emerged directly out of a large-scale research project entitled "Creative Spaces: New Play Development in English-Speaking Canada" that my collaborators and I are currently conducting at the University of Toronto. Generously supported by SSHRC (Social Sciences and Humanities Research Council), "Creative Spaces" focuses on the material conditions of professional, institutional new play development activity. For our purposes, "material conditions" refers to the *people* (personnel and participants), *contexts* (spaces and places), [2] *duration* (time and timing), *processes* (strategies, techniques, tools), *products* (relationship to performance) and *support* (funding and resources) that comprise specifically *text-based*, new play development across the primarily English-speaking regions of this country.

In their introduction to *Staging Coyote's Dream: An Anthology of First Nations Drama in English* (Playwrights Canada Press, 2003), editors Mojica and Ric Knowles assert that "Among the things that Native theatre artists must contend with that can 'contain' their work and limit the possible evolution of new forms are material conditions, economic, organizational, and cultural, that determine which types of work are produced and which are not" (viii). Without challenging or in any way attempting to diminish the formidable obstacles that Aboriginal dramatists and practitioners encounter on a daily basis, the "Creative Spaces" project takes as its starting point the perception that the "organizational, processual, and professional bottles into and out of which everything must be poured" (viii) are, to a significant degree, conditions encountered by virtually *all* playwrights attempting to work within the commercial theatre industry in Canada. As Beth Herst, writing more than a decade ago, straightforwardly puts it in her contribution, "[T]he way theatre is made has a determinant effect on the kind of theatre that results, and that way is never ideologically neutral. We cannot separate the 'how' from the 'what,' the means by which theatrical meaning is, literally, produced and that meaning itself" (47). Yet, somehow, this understanding today retains the status of "common knowledge," supported by extensive anecdotal exchange but little integrated or systematic study. "Creative Spaces," then, was designed to examine the ways in which Canadian developmental dramaturgy can be seen to reflect the complex set of economic, industrial, political, and aesthetic conditions that combine to determine, within flexible but finite parameters, what is "possible" in Canadian professional theatre.

At the time of this writing (early 2008) our team has conducted a detailed, nationwide survey of producing and developmental theatre organizations. This will be followed, over the coming months, by numerous on-site case studies, including interviews, which will focus on a range of conventional, alternative, and self-consciously oppositional approaches to professional developmental dramaturgy. The global objective of the research is to discover a set of "best conditions" (as opposed to "best practices") for new-text-based play development in Canada, based on the experiences of a broad spectrum of professional theatre practitioners.

The first stage of the "Creative Spaces" project, however, consisted of an extensive literature review of virtually every article on new play development published in Canada over a twenty-year period. The opportunity to view these pieces as a whole has yielded often surprising confirmations *and* contradictions; the insights offered and the questions raised are clearly key to an understanding of the broader dynamics and the future potential of our theatre practice, both nationally and internationally. Of course, the necessarily limited selection of articles included in this collection—the tip of the proverbial iceberg—is hardly "representative." My hope, however, is that it evokes the complexity of the institutional new play development situation in this country with unprecedented complexity.

Choices and Contexts

Our literature review combed a wide variety of popular, professional, archival, and academic resources. The final selection for the current volume was based on an intersection of criteria, including regional and cultural representation, historical continuity and coverage, thematic diversity, and cumulative "thoroughness" of focus. This last criterion is, of course, as impossible as it is worthy in a volume of this size, and this collection is far from comprehensive. However, guiding principles for selection can be found in a desire to include only articles that 1) specifically address the material conditions of new play development (people, places, and processes); 2) prioritize practitioner experience and perspective; and 3) provide scholarly contextualization that directly addresses developmental circumstances and activities.

In particular, the desire for thematic diversity and thoroughness of focus has resulted in a quite varied collection of articles, involving a considerable range of documentation practices. Inevitably, this has led to some standardization in terms of presentation, formatting, and punctuation. However, in this respect, I have in most cases attempted to err on the side of fidelity to the original documents. Appropriately, I believe, the more scholarly pieces have been vetted and occasionally revised to adhere to current academic citation practice. However, these guidelines have been applied with more restraint to the essays drawn from other contexts. Similarly, key terms have *not* been standardized across the entries (you say "dramaturge," I say "dramaturg"), although some dated usages (e.g., "on-line," "list-serve," etc.) have been updated.

In its inception, the ambitions for this collection included considerably more academic writing with the intention to more deeply contextualize the developmental dialogue. But as the scope and sheer size of the volume grew, important contributions by a number of Canada's key theatre scholars were nudged into the Further Suggested Reading section of the current publication. Nonetheless, it is difficult to underestimate the direct significance to the subject matter of this volume of observations by theatre researchers concerning the conflation of two overriding and interrelated historical trends: the pursuit of a Canadian "National Theatre" *by means of* the establishment of a Canadian "Dramatic Canon." As Denis Salter has argued, this twinning of objectives shapes a popular understanding of theatre practice as a *literary* exercise calling forth a *literary* mode of interpretation (the logical extension of which, in a chicken-and-egg relationship, is a literary mode of composition and development).[3] Writing of the powerful, early influence of cultural mandarins such as Vincent Massey, Alan Filewod asserts the restrictive impact of such a tight correlation between nationalism and creative practice in the lingering colonialism of mid-twentieth century Canada:

> [For Massey,] [t]o do a play is to do a nation. But plays, like nations, are built on principle, or else they reduce to meaningless "popular entertainments" (or materialist republics). These principles, for both drama and nation, are found in forms validated and preserved by historical usage. Tradition is the practice of adherence to historical forms; uniforms are the display of subjective position within the practice of tradition. In dramaturgy, this translated into a suspicion of the avant-garde and an abiding loyalty to a concept of classic form. ("Performing" 40)

Knowles has pursued this argument even further, pushing the implications of *canonicity* into late twentieth-century practice:

> The establishment of the canon is seen by many as a sign of Canadian drama's coming "of age," its reaching a turning point in what the vocabulary of prefaces and introductions reveals to be a Darwinian belief in an "evolving tradition." In the context of this discourse, work outside the current mainstream is accommodated, if at all, as "avant-garde," a military metaphor that accepts as potentially valuable plays that "develop out of" current forms and aspire eventually to take their places in the established canon. Plays that fail to qualify as part of the mainstream or of the avant-garde are either dismissed as failing to reach standards to which the may not aspire, or classified as "alternative" theatre, a label that serves to affirm the centre rather than the possibility of re-centring. ("Voices (off)" 92)[4]

Reflecting closely related observations, Filewod has convincingly challenged this opposition between "mainstream" and "alternative" theatre practice, at once recognizing the mythological nature of the history that supports this binary *and* that mythology's very real ideological and industrial impact.

Critical orthodoxy of the alternative theatre in English Canada locates the period of the late 1960s to the mid 1970s as a point of historical crisis during which the mainstream regional theatre system was challenged and overshadowed by the emerging alternates. The regionals are usually characterized by conservative repertoires, a mistrust of Canadian drama, middle-class audiences, and a marked tendency to prefer foreign, usually British, artistic directors. The alternates are the heroes in this cultural drama: nationalistic, committed to Canadian playwrights, young, radical, and self-consciously experimental [...] [However] [t]his entire mainstream/alternative paradigm progresses with no explicit reference to class or audience. It constructs the audience not as an active presence but as an ahistorical mass that is acted upon, a target for subscription drives and publicity campaigns. The terms are employed with virtually no reference to the cultural formation of the theatre as an expression of community. ("Erasing" 202)

In the same vein, however, Chris Johnson has tackled the assertion of canonicity in the creation, attendance, and educational dissemination of Canadian theatre, portraying both composition and reception as decidedly moving (and thus mobile) targets:

Canadian theatres do not support through their repertoire the notion of a Canadian canon, and recent criticism and analysis is so heavily concentrated on work outside the mainstream that the old canon's identity is shifting, contributing, again, to a porosity so extreme that the canonical authority of this "canon" is called into question. (47)

Johnson's observations effectively provide *context to the context* established through Salter's, Filewod's, and Knowles's arguments—a process that has continued in the wake of these well-established scholarly perspectives (which, ironically, now represent the basis of a critical "canon" of sorts). There is no question that contemporary Canadian playwrights and dramaturgs work within both explicit and implicit traditions: ideological, political, cultural, and aesthetic. And it would be naive to underestimate the overt and subtle operations of nationalism in the structures and processes of producing and non-producing theatre organizations—as in the public and private institutions and individuals that fund them. Yet these operations are rarely fully predictable, systematic, or stable. The shift from nationalism to multiculturalism to interculturalism and internationalism in Canadian theatre practice and scholarship is a direct reflection of this increasing diversity in terms of artist intentions and increasing complexity in terms of critical response. The Further Reading section of this volume attempts to steer readers to particularly relevant efforts by both practitioners and researchers at articulating the contemporary situation and further contextualizing the discussion represented in the pages of this collection.

Making Meaning: Table(s) of Contents

A distinguishing characteristic of this collection is the fact that it offers, in addition to the main Table of Contents (TOC), three alternative ways of organizing the included essays. These additional documents are intended to suggest a variety of ways to "make meaning" out of this congregation of voices. The first TOC appears in the traditional manner at the front end of the collection; the three alternative structurings appear as appendices at the end of the collection. The main TOC offers the articles in chronological order, organized by date of publication. The main appendix lists the contributing authors alphabetically, along with full bibliographical details for each entry; the second groups the entries into regional categories; the third is arranged by thematic focus and emphasis. Each of the alternative structurings come with its own advantages and complications; my hope is that the strengths *and* limitations of each will be mutually enlightening. Readers are thus encouraged to set their own priorities and make their ways through this material in the manner that seems most logical or specifically beneficial.

Table of Contents: *Chronological*

The chronological main TOC affords a strong sense of the decidedly *non*-Darwinian evolution of inquiry, concern, and emphasis in the public discussion of developmental dramaturgy over the last two decades. A number of intriguing trends are quickly evident upon even the most cursory survey of this progression; deeper inquiry yields yet more complex activity. It is no coincidence that the two decades surveyed in this collection begin in 1986—the date of *Canadian Theatre Review* (*CTR*)'s first special theme issue on new play development. Significantly, no fewer than five of the eight articles included in this volume that were published between that year and 1996 explicitly address the possibilities and—most emphatically—the potential pitfalls in developmental *workshops*. One after another, Elliott Hayes, Jan Selman, Sandra Tomc, Kathleen Flaherty, and Herst effectively locate this central aspect of new play dramaturgy within specific aesthetic, ideological, and material circumstances, clearly building upon accumulating experience with increasingly critical and theoretically informed analyses. This same period produced two studies of Vancouver's New Play Centre, the first by Jerry Wasserman and Denis Johnston, the second by James Hoffman. While distinct in terms of attitude, approach, and anticipated audience, each effectively initiates a focus on developmental organizations as key institutions within new play development. And Mayte Gómez's insightful assessment of Cahoots Theatre Projects' "Lift Off! 93" new play festival sets the stage for subsequent cultural and intercultural inquiry (while also adding a vital twist to the discussion of developmental workshops).

In 1996 *CTR* published its second theme issue on developmental dramaturgy, and the chronological TOC of this volume clearly reflects that issue's appearance. Yet the sudden diversity of approaches to new play development that is evident in these selections suggests that *CTR* was largely responding to, rather than initiating, this surge of interest and expression. While Deborah Cottreau's interview with Urjo Kareda of Tarragon Theatre offers ample exposure to a well-established set of new play development conventions, Sky Gilbert (Buddies in Bad Times Theatre), Lois Brown (St. John's Resource Centre for the Arts), and Roberts (Nightwood Theatre) effectively stir up the developmental "pot" in unorthodox, even intentionally provocative ways. When Gilbert's process-as-product orientation is juxtaposed with Bob White's overtly product-as-process formula, and Peter Smith and Lise Ann Johnson introduce Playwrights' Workshop Montréal's "extended workshop," the degree to which the developmental horizon was expanding becomes all too apparent.

The next decade (which witnessed the appearance of *CTR*'s third dramaturgy issue in 2004) demonstrates several dominant points of focus. Cultural specificity and the potential for intercultural plurality insistently enter popular discourse (Marty Chan; Alison Sealy-Smith, Djanet Sears and Knowles; Shannon Hengen). Traditional geographic and institutional structures are scrutinized (Barton; Shelley Scott). Renewed, increasingly sophisticated attempts are made at practical definitions and material frameworks (DD Kugler; Peter Hinton). Finally, the most recently published material brings with it a shift in gaze to physically-based and interdisciplinary practices (Barton; Rachel Ditor; Brian Quirt; Pil Hansen)—a move "beyond the text" in order to return to text-based dramaturgy equipped with an enlarged set of techniques and strategies and an enlivened palette of perspectives. The volume then concludes with a series of short entries appearing here for the first time: highly personal and insightful snapshots provided by key figures in developmental dramaturgy from across the country (Ben Henderson, Jenny Munday, Nolan, Quirt, and Rory Runnells).

Appendix 1. *Alphabetical*

This appendix is meant to reflect the fact that the world of developmental dramaturgy in Canada boasts a number of high-profile practitioners and critics with long-term investment and presence. Arranging all authors alphabetically provides immediate access to recognizable personalities while offering a systematic introduction to less familiar contributors. As noted, this initial ordering also provides full bibliographical information for each entry. One of the most conspicuous pieces of information this latter aspect yields is the predominance of included material that was first published in the pages of *Canadian Theatre Review* (*CTR*). There is no question that since its inception in 1974 *CTR* has played a key role in facilitating professional, critical, and scholarly dialogue about Canadian theatre. In particular, it is that journal's inevitably imperfect but always noteworthy efforts to communicate *across* these disciplinary divides and foster exchange between practitioners, presenters, audiences, reviewers, and academics that guarantees its centrality in this field. It is impossible to imagine this anthology without *CTR*'s inclusion in its pages.

At the same time, however, near-monopolies always deserve close scrutiny and critical assessment. Just as the "creative spaces" of new drama and theatre are directly shaped by the commercial and industrial "places" in which they are created, developed, and performed, so too is popular theatre discourse directly shaped by the vehicles that deliver it and the forums in which it unfolds. A clear reminder of this at the outset of this collection is, therefore, of considerable importance—as is the careful contextualization of this dominant "voice" through the inclusion of multiple additional (and largely scholarly) perspectives. Admittedly, the decision to foreground practitioners' voices means that there is a considerable range of expression here in terms of formality of language and structure, professional insight and experience, theoretical awareness and application, sophistication of argument, and creative licence. However, this is, I think, as it should be.

Appendix 2. *Regional*

It is likely still impossible to offer a "national" overview of new play development in English without addressing regional distinctions; thus the inclusion here of a geographically organized listing. Certainly, there is no questioning the reality of regional differences—aesthetic, historical, cultural, economic, ideological—and fixed boundaries afford clarity in terms of self-definition and the recognition of others. Yet while such categories are relatively accessible, upon closer examination the concept of "region" can be seen to be as elusive, in some senses, as "dramaturgy" itself. The regional categories in this listing are, in most cases, permeable distinctions, granted by virtue of critical mass rather than firm or absolute borders. In its highly collaborative nature, theatrical practice is unavoidably "cross-pollinated" through the unchecked mobility of practitioners, projects, and processes across regional divides. This by no means precludes manifestos of determined "otherness" from St. John's (Brown), or unique fiscal challenges brought on by Atlantic Canada's pan-provincial developmental activity (Barton; Munday), or the highly productive process-to-product working relations of Alberta Theatre Projects and the Banff Centre (White), or Vancouver's remarkably long history of commitment to new play dramaturgy (Wasserman & Johnston; Hoffman). At the same time, however, one look at Ontario's undeniably and productively messy cultural diversity (choose your author) reminds one how important it is that such overt regional differences do not overwrite inner tensions, shared issues, and exchanged experiences. In this spirit, it is the fourth and final listing (Appendix 3) that perhaps affords the most effectively focused and productive approach to "making meaning" out of this body of collected writings.

Appendix 3. *Thematic*

The act of organizing a body of essays into areas of thematic emphasis surely exhibits as much about the reader as about the pieces read. Any number of editors might thus recognize quite different preoccupations than those I have isolated. This caveat duly noted, however, the fourth listing proposes a number of generalized points of related concern that serve to foreground both those issues that remain relatively (even remarkably) consistent and those that emerge, recede, mutate, and evolve.

i) Forging Definitions

> "The dramaturge is an artist who intimately walks into the imaginations of others, knowing how softly or boldly to tread." (Hinton 5)

When one compares Mojica's suggestive "like being on a wave" (quoted at the beginning of this introduction) with Danckert's assertion that "Dramaturgy is the cartography of drama," the diversity of efforts towards "forging definition" (to borrow Hinton's expression) becomes clearly evident. As Hinton muses, "I have always been curious why a position that should be central to what we do consistently proves so hard to describe, is rarely perceived as necessary and so often is made invisible by our colleagues when compared to the more familiar and obvious disciplines of production" (6). Yet this "invisibility," according to Kugler, is a key element of his dramaturgical practice, a direct result of his relationship to the developmental process and to *the playwright's* product: "Oddly enough, I have always felt that one of my strengths as dramaturg was that I had no claim to ownership of any 'product.' What could I possibly own? Not the script, that's the playwright's. I bring my aesthetic to the service of the process. [...] 'My dramaturgy,' whatever that is, is utterly invisible" (50). Danckert's contribution exemplifies these efforts to circle around dramaturgy while deferring specific descriptions, continuing a lengthy tradition and simultaneously confirming and contradicting Nolan's contention that the desire for definitions has passed:

> Dramaturgy is argument, it is psychology, it is imagery, it is research, and it is design. It is the means for building fiction. It is how we arrive at interpretation. Dramaturgy is a reference point for every part of the writing process. It is the alleyways, the backroads, the uncharted terrain of the story.

ii) Treating "Workshopitis"

Hayes, in his 1986 contribution, introduces a dynamic repeatedly revisited through-out the next twenty years of criticism when he coins the term "workshopitis":

> Many Canadian theatres, confronting the criticism that they are not producing enough Canadian plays, conduct workshops in order to demonstrate their sensitivity to the problem. While such workshops are invaluable to our playwrights under the right circumstances, they also can be detrimental for, invariably, they contribute to a "masterpiece mentality" in Canadian actors and in our audience. The "masterpieces" are worth producing, or watching; other plays "need work." (36)

Remarkably, almost two decades later, Hinton offers the following mirror reflection:

> I am often amazed, when working on a classical text, by the lengths to which all involved will go to honour (let's say) Shakespeare's intent to make a five-hundred-year-old joke about the possible threat of Spanish invasion work for an audience today; while on a new play, a difficult emotional transition is challenged and questioned, and sometimes a rewrite is demanded. (7)

Equally significant is Hayes's observation, "In the final analysis, contemporary Canadian theatre reflects the state of the economy far more than the state of the arts" (39). As Flaherty explains, "The process is determined to maximize resources of time, space, and personnel. The available resources are determined not by artistic needs but by available funding. And the available funding is determined more and more by a corporate model of theatre production in which a play must pay its own way in a market-driven economy" (28). In Hayes's estimation, the result of this "workshop ghetto" is that writers stop writing or move to another discipline. However, in her contribution, Tomc astutely pursues a more subtle and insidious influence on a playwright's practical and aesthetic choices:

> While a playwright may not consciously set out to conform to the dominant set of expectations, many of the theatres involved here have discreetly justified their practices with a formulation of the playwrights "needs:" his need for privacy and isolation, for example, or her need for professional rather than public response. How is a playwright to avoid internalizing such formulations and escape producing them in a particular aesthetic? The playwright's "need" for isolation may too easily find fruition in the writing of a play that doesn't really need to be performed. (81)

Multiple solutions to this unproductive disconnect between development and pro-duction are explored here, each "radical" (Gilbert's adjective) *and* commonsensical in its own way. Located midway on the continuum between the Rhubarb! Festival's trial-by-fire approach to staged development—"opportunity without interference" (Gilbert 25)—and ATP's philosophy of "[a] script becomes a play in the crucible of production" (White 15), we find Playwrights' Workshop Montréal's "extended workshop." With its emphasis on prolonged development involving one or more production design components, the extended workshop was intended to "offer a unique passage for each play, our belief being that each project defines its own needs" (Smith and Johnson 11). It is easy to see the legacy of this model in Quirt's stated priorities for his contemporary developmental practice: "Choreographers, perform-ance artists and visual artists must be welcomed into our theatres to remind us of the vitality of other disciplines and how much they can offer to the theatre. By insisting on presenting the work of our writers on-their-feet, we will, I hope, commit to play and plays rather than readings." Perhaps the most "radical" response, however, is found in Herst's 1995 entry, where she endorses the workshop as a decisive instrument for undermining what she describes as the entire "director-led," concept-driven, meaning-suffocating process of mainstream theatrical production:

> Potentially at least, the workshop can make "meaning" a problem rather than a premise, a plural and unstable construction to be investigated rather than a fixed and manifest "truth" to be discovered. It can create a space for multiplicity, encouraging, even demanding, a self-consciousness about theatrical mediation and its effects that "the process", by definition, can scarcely allow. (51)

iii) Organized Labour

The institutionalization of new play development in Canada takes many forms and represents multiple motivations and investments; the articles included here observe, critique, and participate in those agendas. The two entries that address the past and (then) present activities of Vancouver's New Play Centre approach their subject from markedly different angles. Wasserman and Johnston offer a largely celebratory history lesson while Hoffman attempts a systemic—and rather less celebratory—analysis; yet both manage to convey a complex network of intentions, activity, and affects. Tarragon's Kareda, in conversation with Cottreau, reflected that theatre's deep Western heritage when he offered his now famous explanation that "What I look for is a writer with a very distinctive, individual voice. That you can identify within twenty pages as you're reading it" (7). Conversely, Hengen marks the same weight of tradition as a focus of opposition in her discussion of "The De-ba-jeh-mu-jig Method," subtitling her article on that Aboriginal theatre company's dramaturgical practice "The 'Four Directions' creative process moves script development beyond the European model" (35). Lois Brown describes the "sense of urgency to recover, to create, or to perish" (29) that galvanized Newfoundland theatre practitioners within the framework of the Resource Centre for the Arts in St. John's. Ironically, my exploration of the regional Playwrights Atlantic Resource Centre (PARC) focuses directly on that organization's response to the problematic ambiguity generated by the same trope of "community" in the Maritimes: "[B]y offering increased flexibility in the new play development processes made available, PARC seems alert to the potential for generating linkages—indeed, communities—defined by affinities of form and technique, rather than simple geography, between practitioners throughout the region" (45). Scott, for her part, moves beyond both traditional producing and non-producing organizations in search of effective developmental models—and finds many of the same possibilities *and* challenges operating in the Fringe festival circuit:

> I would argue that the Fringe circuit in Canada has great potential to play an important role in new play development. It is already, to some extent, a source for new Canadian plays, but this role could be enhanced if the Fringe were promoted as a viable, low risk venue for exploratory productions of plays in some stage of dramaturgical development. [...]

[H]owever, there is one particular obstacle to this potential: the tendency of the local media to emphasize familiarity as the highest virtue. (229)

Combined, these entries offer key insights into the diversity *and* commonalities of the institutionalized contexts in which developmental dramaturgy is housed: the "places" in and *by* which creative "spaces" are formed.

iv) Dramaturgy and/in Identity

While contemporary cultural criticism may consider identity politics somewhat passé, related issues have defined a large part of Canadian theatre practice and criticism in the past twenty years. Not surprisingly, developmental dramaturgy has been a primary focus of many of these concerns. Gómez's prescient analysis of the Lift Off! 93 festival effectively presages the current surge in intercultural criticism, particularly in its critique of dominant dramaturgical skills, venues, and practices: "I would argue that while the content of many of the plays presented subverted to a large extent the ideology of acculturation, the form of the dramaturgical development chosen in the workshops served to reproduce it and embrace it, a contradiction which was also present in most of the festival's conditions of production" (45–46). Intriguingly, however, Chan's contribution, written almost a decade later, seems to describe the reverse imbalance in expectations: "I began to suspect that I would never enjoy the same freedoms as non-minority writers. I worried that I would always be stereotyped as the Chinese-hyphen-Canadian writer. I feared I would land in an ethnic artist's ghetto, where my voice would be considered valid only if it had a Chinese accent" (15). In terms of specific dramaturgical practices, however, Chan's comments indirectly mirror Gómez's. While he reports anticipating "major differences" between his workshop experiences and those of a Caucasian writer, he notes, to his surprise (and with considerable irony), "I found no difference at all. Workshop participants treated him with the same tenacity and cruelty as they treated me" (13).

Sears, in her joint contribution with Sealy-Smith and Knowles, explains a developmental strategy she employed in the development of her play *Harlem Duet* to find balance within this uneven terrain:

> Now because *Harlem Duet* dealt with contentious issues around race, I wanted to be on the edge. I got two women, Diane Roberts, a Black director and dramaturg, and Kate Lushington, a white director and dramaturg. I'd have them respond to drafts with questions, and I'd take those home and sit with them. I found that helpful, because sometimes they didn't have a similar opinion, and it made sure that I had to decide where I needed to go to make the edge razor sharp. (24)

When these issues of race and ethnicity are combined with articles related directly or indirectly to gender (Herst, Roberts) and sexual orientation (Gilbert), it becomes clear that self-appointed authority and resourcefulness are requisite characteristics of identity-based agency within institutional new play development.

v) Beyond Text—And Back Again

A common focus within several of the most recently published articles included in this volume relates to the relationship between text-based dramaturgy and the development of movement-based or interdisciplinary works, and other modes of performance in which text is not the central or initial "core" in terms of process or product. Specifically, several of these articles address the potential benefits of exploring non-text-based dramaturgical principles and practices that may then be transferred or adapted to text-based work. Discussing Nightswimming's Pure Research program, which by definition allows artists to explore experimental, performance-based theatrical questions outside of the development of specific projects, Quirt asserts,

> Pure Research has encouraged Nightswimming's development process, to be more adventurous and more open to instinct and serendipity. Through Pure Research, I have developed a great tolerance for the unknown. I have embraced patience as a tool. I have come to value performance research as both an end in itself (as in Pure Research) and as a starting point for creation. (41)

As Ditor concedes, however, the exchange between text-based and movement-based theatrical forms is not always or necessarily reciprocal. While her dramaturgical process of "questioning the text" provided strong positive results in her work on a text-based classical play (Ibsen's *Hedda Gabler*), the same tactic yielded a distinctly different outcome when applied, largely unmodified, to the development of a new work with a physical theatre company:

> In *Flop* [created by the Vancouver-based Electric Company] the act of questioning the text appeared to accomplish the opposite—reducing the world of the play and highlighting old and new [...] dysfunctions in the group dynamic. [...] In searching for clarity we created an environment in the rehearsal hall that didn't promote emotional risk and honesty, and this was evident in the show. (40)

However, in my own experience, while such setbacks are familiar they are also more than compensated for by fruitful connections across dramaturgical contexts, precisely because of what I identify, in my second contribution to this volume, as a heightened openness to dramaturgical inquiry and exploration already operating in much physically-based creation:

> [M]y experience suggests that effective dramaturgy in a physically-based devised context is less about radical new strategies than it is about

a consciously altered orientation to the work—an orientation that more accurately focuses and accentuates a dramaturgical function that is, arguably, inherent in much physically-based creation. (114)

Ultimately, Hansen's exchange with a group of prominent Toronto dramaturgs suggests that the institutional divide between traditionally perceived text-based concerns and strategies and those more commonly associated with performance and production may be more discussed than respected in much contemporary developmental practice:

> In the cases chosen by the dramaturgs as the bases for our conversations, development did not only involve playwright and text. Rather, it could also occur in a field between multiple artistic disciplines where the dramaturg's task is to navigate the process, rather than offer expertise in, for instance, dramaturgical structures. This shift in function gives rise to a shift of object—from text to creative process and exchange. Once this shift is made, elements of staging and devising are introduced into the processes of play development. Thus, on closer examination, the often repeated divide between developmental and production dramaturgy may be both inaccurate and (to the extent it hinders further integration) counterproductive. (*Developing Nation* 170)

vi) Snapshots

The final grouping in the thematically organized article listing consists of short, newly commissioned entries from some of Canada's most experienced and widely recognized dramaturgs. Individuals from across Canada who hold key developmental positions were invited to contribute. Some, such as Iris Turcott (Ontario), were unable to participate due to competing obligations; others, such as Kugler (British Columbia) and Danckert (then Quebec, now Ontario), opted to be represented here through previously published material. However, dramaturgs from Saskatchewan (Henderson), Manitoba (Runnells), Ontario (Nolan, Quirt), and Atlantic Canada (Munday) all agreed to offer contemporary perspectives from (while not necessarily *on*) their places in the country.

Each of these dramaturgs was asked to consider two common questions. While all were given full freedom to deviate, should other subject matter seem more pertinent or urgent, most attend in general terms to the following queries:

1) What, from your perspective, has been the most significant development (or developments) in new play dramaturgy in Canada over the past ten years? Please describe the development(s) and explain the significance.
2) What should be the priorities for new play development in Canada today? Feel free to address issues of support, personnel, practice, or other aspects you feel deserve mention.

Not surprisingly, the results are highly illuminating.

Despite her aversion to definitions, Nolan is clear regarding her assessment of the dramaturg's primary responsibility:

> If we are blessed, if there is trust between the playwright and the dramaturg, as the dramaturg knows the play more intimately, the more she is empowered to speak for the play. Ay, there's the rub. Her primary allegiance is to the play. Not the playwright, not the producer, not the director, who may have a different vision of what this play will be. The dramaturg who knows the play is the advocate of the play, in the rehearsal hall, in the theatre.

For his part, Henderson echoes a commitment—repeatedly advocated throughout this collection—"to see new plays by our country's writers produced on our stages. That is the ultimate objective for all of us. No matter how much strong work we develop, until we can ensure that the work can go the final stage into production we are still failing." Munday writes that "one of the most significant and beneficial recent occurrences in play development has been the formation of what has become an informal Network of Playwrights' Development Centres (PDCCs) across the country." A source of mutual support and cooperation, this network is clearly facilitating increased exchange of artists, resources, ideas, and experience. Runnells picks up on both of these topics—production and national exchange—in his contribution: "The theatres must continue to produce new plays and recognize that the local playwright is part of the national fabric. Each must make the playwright in its community a national force." And as, perhaps, Canada's most active and influential dramaturg (in part through his tenure as president of the Literary Managers and Dramaturgs of the Americas), Quirt is given the "last word" in this collection. His brief entry outlines "four priorities" for Canadian developmental strategy: 1) "continued focus on diversity," 2) emphasis on "on-the-feet workshops," 3) the shift of play development back "to our theatres and [...] out of rehearsal halls," and 4) increasing "director training and internships."

These final entries demonstrate considerable differences of style, training, and aesthetic preference, and there are important insights to be gleaned from the degree to which each self-identifies with the issues specifically related to his/her location (geographic, cultural, industrial). Notwithstanding such differences, however, shared passion and common commitment are abundantly evident throughout. It is particularly intriguing that these qualities regularly emerge through expressions of a tenacious, service-based "otherness": the dramaturg as advocate, defender, negotiator, conciliator, caregiver. This is, of course, to a degree a conscious strategy, both personal and professional. It is also, to a degree, an inevitable, vocation-defining reality. Among other things, dramaturgy can be a thankless job; these individuals— and those represented by all the articles in this volume—are owed a considerable debt of gratitude.

Postscript

In November 2006, a delegation of Canadian theatre practitioners was invited to attend a five-day Workshop on New Play Development for Dramaturges from Canada and Germany. Held in Berlin, the event was organized through a partnership between the Canadian Embassy in Germany and the International Theatre Institute Germany (ITI–Germany). Invited guests included a large group of high-profile dramaturgs and playwrights from both countries[5] and the week was organized around a series of presentations, focused discussions, readings, and performances. Although my time at the event was limited due to other commitments, my strong impression—supported by all reports[6]—is that the event was animated, instructive, and productive in terms of mutual understanding, ongoing dialogue, and collaboration. For my part, I was asked to give a short opening talk, in my hybrid capacity as a practitioner and theatre researcher, on new play development in Canada. This was to be matched by opening presentations by Eva Behrendt, the editor of Berlin's *Theater heute*, and Albert-Reiner Glaap, a German academic who has been tireless in his advocacy of Canadian theatre in Germany.[7]

Not surprisingly, as I look back over the content of my necessarily yet unnervingly brief presentation at that event, I am gratified to see that many of the issues I considered noteworthy are well represented in the pages of this volume:

- the legacy of the pursuit of a national theatre via a dramatic canon;
- the increasingly flexible but nonetheless nationalist and/or localist agendas of funding organizations;
- the powerful influence exerted at the intersection of dramatic publishing and post-secondary education;
- the functions of organizations such as the Playwrights Guild of Canada and LMDA in establishing political, legal, industrial, and aesthetic standards and frameworks;
- the multiple, often—and often not—complementary intentions and motivations associated with new play development within producing organizations;
- the ongoing organizational, fiscal, and identity challenges experienced by non-producing developmental bodies;
- the emerging benefits related to the Network of Playwrights' Development Centres;
- the rapid growth of cross-, multi-, and intercultural creation, development, and production;
- the increasing exchange between text-based and physically-based dramaturgical processes and the generally enhanced role within script development of a broad range of "on-the-feet," performance-oriented dramaturgical strategies.

At the same time, however, I am also reminded just how "streamlined" and accessible these distinct elements seemed during my few minutes of "airtime"—and how each of us around the table, in his or her own way, could not help but juxtapose that clarity with first-hand experience of the actual complexity, inter-connectedness, and plain rowdiness of professional new play development in this country. Ultimately, it is my hope that the Creative Spaces research project will significantly contribute to the process of inquiry, clarification, analysis, and knowledge on this many-sided topic. However, I am also confident that this fittingly rowdy and many-sided collection goes some way towards capturing and respectfully exhibiting the density of voices, attitudes, opinions, and perspectives at work (and play) here in our "developing nation."

(2008)

Works Cited (articles *not* included in this essay collection)

Filewod, Alan. "Erasing Historical Difference: The Alternative Orthodoxy in Canadian Theatre." *Theatre Journal* 41 (May 1989): 201–10.

———. "Performing Canada: The Nation Enacted in the Imagined Theatre." *Canadian Theatre Review* 114 (Spring 2003): 72–74.

Glaap, Albert-Reiner, ed. *Voices from Canada: Focus on Thirty Plays.* Trans. Nicholas Quaintmere. Toronto: Playwrights Canada, 2003.

Glaap, Albert-Reiner and Sherrill Grace, eds. *Performing National Identities: International Perspectives on Contemporary Canadian Theatre.* Vancouver: Talonbooks, 2003.

Johnson, Chris. "Wisdome Under a Ragged Coate: Canonicity and Canadian Drama." *Contemporary Issues in Canadian Drama.* Ed. Per Brask. Winnipeg: Blizzard, 1995. 26–49.

Knowles, Ric. *Reading the Material Theatre.* Cambridge and New York: Cambridge UP, 2004.

———. *The Theatre of Form and the Production of Meaning: Contemporary Canadian Dramaturgies.* Toronto: ECW, 1999.

——— and Monique Mojica, eds. *Staging Coyote's Dream: An Anthology of First Nations Drama in English.* Toronto: Playwrights Canada, 2003.

Knowles, Richard Paul. "Voices (off): Deconstructing the Modern English-Canadian Dramatic Canon." *Canadian Canons: Essays in Literary Value.* Ed. Robert Lecker. Toronto: U of Toronto P, 1991. 91–111.

Salter, Denis. "The Idea of a National Theatre." *Canadian Canons: Essays in Literary Value.* Ed. Robert Lecker. Toronto: U of Toronto P, 1991. 71–90.

---

[1] All page numbers given in this introduction refer to the location of quotations in the original published documents. Full bibliographical information for titles not included in the Alphabetical Table of Contents can be found in the "Suggested Further Reading" section of this volume.

2   In *The Theatre of Form and the Production of Meaning* (1995), Ric Knowles proposes that the competing forces of containment and innovation in Canadian theatre practice can be effectively analyzed through an application of Michel de Certeau's distinction between *place* ("the established positions from which the currently dominant *strategically* defend their authority, resisting the temporal dimensions of chance and change" [160–61]) and *space* ("the undefined geographies through which the disempowered *tactically* shift ground, seize the moment, respond improvisationally to whatever they are presented with, and resist the solidification of time in an unchanging and stable spatial realm of universal structures and values" [162]). This discursive framework for assessing, on the one hand, the gravitational pull of structural inertia and resistance to change and, on the other, oppositional forces that resort to the "perversion" of existing forms and practices in a perpetual attempt at either iterative or catastrophic change, provides an equally fitting theoretical context within which to consider the characteristics of Canadian new play development. In a sense, all developmental dramaturgy contains within it the explicit competing discourses of, on the one hand, creating distinct *spaces* of creativity and innovation and, on the other, the reassertion of the authority of the *place* that contextualizes (and exerts influence through) these spaces.

3   For the details of this argument, see Salter.

4   For the complex extension of this early argument, see Knowles's subsequent publications *Theatre of Form* and *Reading the Material Theatre*.

5   Canadian participants included Paula Danckert, Lise Ann Johnson, Nadia Ross, Bruce Barton, Tim Carlson, Martin Faucher, Jonathan Garfinkel, Brian Quirt, Richard Wolfe, and Birgit Schreyer. German participants included Eva Behrendt, Barbara Christ, Stephanie Gräve, Andrea Koschwitz, Ute Scharfenberg, Anke See, Oliver Bukowski, Albert-Reiner Glaap, Thomas Frank, Frank Heibert, Christoph Lepschy, Armin Petras, Kristo Sagor, and Johannes von Westphalen. The event was coordinated by Andrea Zagorski of ITI–Germany and Gabriele Naumann-Maerten, the Cultural Attaché–Performing Arts of the Canadian Embassy.

6   The most detailed account is Birgit Schreyer's "a somewhat subjective Report on the Workshop on new Play development for Dramaturges from Canada and Germany in Berlin, Nov 27–Dec 2, 2006," which was commissioned by the event organizers.

7   See, for instance, his *Voices from Canada* and *Performing National Identities*.

Stasis: The Workshop Syndrome
by Elliot Hayes

Stasis comes from the Greek word meaning "to stand" and, in pathological terms, it refers to the stagnation or stoppage of any of the body's fluids, especially the blood. In dramatic terms the life-blood of the theatre must surely be the play text. Therefore, to merge these images by saying that the Canadian theatre is in stasis is to imply that theatres in Canada are not producing enough Canadian drama to sustain a healthy flow. Canadian theatre is in a state of stagnation.

Many Canadian theatres, confronting the criticism that they are not producing enough Canadian plays, conduct workshops in order to demonstrate their sensitivity to the problem. While such workshops are invaluable to our playwrights under the right circumstances, they also can be detrimental for, invariably, they contribute to a "masterpiece mentality" in Canadian actors and in our audience. The "masterpieces" are worth producing, or watching; other plays "need work." A generation of Canadian actors has learned how to "work" on a new script, not how to perform one; they read a script and take for granted that it will be revised and rewritten. Consequently, Canada appears an interpretive society rather that an expressive one, excelling in the performance of masterpieces while demonstrating an ironic disrespect for the living playwright who is treated like a Victorian child, seen and not heard. Our playwrights, educated in the rudiments in an austere environment, are coerced into a begrudging gratitude for productions or their substitute—the "practical gifts" of workshops.

The essential danger of workshops lies in the fact that the work is often talked about, not spoken aloud. While this can be illuminating if the right people are doing the talking, because the emphasis is on process and not production, a unique problem arises. It is natural that the playwright puts his or her personal idiosyncrasies into creating the work; the actors' idiosyncrasies are another matter, however. Too often an actor will bring his or her personality into the interpretation: "This character couldn't say that" often means, "I couldn't say that." This can be very misleading for a playwright already disheartened by the workshop's emphasis on weakness and faults. Rarely is the written work allowed to reach the state of resonance that we associate with a tried-and-true text. Collaborative vision may illuminate the text but it also can dull an individual voice and flatten a work of art. While a good workshop can function like an out-of-town try-out without the pressure, it still can be a frustrating experience if the play does not go into rehearsal and production within a reasonable amount of time. It is understandable that "workshopitis" is a descriptive noun now in the vernacular of the Canadian playwright.

Workshopitis is often used in reference to the Stratford Festival, which has not produced a Canadian play on one of its main stages (exclusive of an adaptation of a classic) since 1980. Richard Epps's *Intimate Admiration* will finally break that pattern in 1987, but in the meantime a workshop program has evolved which is exclusively devoted to script development. Though seen as little more than a glib gesture to Canadian drama or the most virulent form of workshopitis in some people's minds, it nevertheless has some validity and arose from honest concern. In

1984, Explorations, the new play development program, was supported entirely by a private donation. In 1985 it was funded entirely by the Ontario Arts Council; in 1986 it was funded by the Canada Council; and, in 1987, it will finally be run out of the theatre's operating budget.

Stratford's Explorations workshops have no production values: no more than suggestive props; on-off lights; no music. Sometimes the play is blocked minimally or read from lecturns. But whatever the format, the workshop culminates in a public reading in which I read the necessary stage directions. The audience accepts the convention quite readily.

Stratford's workshops are text-oriented: whether a one-time-only reading or a two-week session, they attempt to establish an atmosphere of creative discussion. If there is a director other than myself, I work as the playwright's advocate in cases where he or she is adamant with good reason, and as interpreter of criticism when there is clearly something wrong. Of course the process becomes subjective, and occasionally tense, but ultimately the writer is deferred to, since the workshop is intended as an examination of the text—not as a performance. With few exceptions the actors have been very generous in this respect. They enjoy the opportunity to work on a new text and respect the fact that the workshop can be an emotionally charged experience for the playwright.

Out of twenty-five new play workshops and readings I've conducted at Stratford over the last three years, only one ended as a negative experience. While all of the usual problems acted against it—rehearsals, matinee performances and last-minute casting according to availability—what really made this particular workshop fail was a combination of the writer's lack of playwriting experience and, ironically, expectations based upon previous workshop development of the same play. Having heard other actors read the roles, the playwright was unwilling to discuss the problems the Stratford actors were having with it—and there were quite a few. The director, who had already worked on the script, also was uninterested in further analysis of the text and, instead, tried a mock staging of the play in the twenty-or-so hours available. While the result demonstrated the director's ingenuity and the actors' performance technique (frequently a mixed blessing of new play workshops), the problematic play remained virtually unaltered and the writer left saying that the workshop had been a failure. The play did not—could not—develop under those circumstances and that set of expectations. The writer would not listen to the actors and dismissed their comments, reversing the traditional danger of workshops. The playwright's insistence that Stratford actors were unhelpful and resistant did not take into account the fact that the actor's opinions were devalued by the workshop process.

Workshops are nothing new at Stratford, and though the recorded history is subjective, it appears that of the countless workshops which have been conducted at Stratford over the last thirty-four years, only a handful of new plays have actually gone on to be produced on the professional stage. These include: John Herbert's *Fortune and Men's Eyes*, workshopped in 1965; Larry Fineberg's *Devotion*, workshopped in 1978; *Only Generals Die in Bed*, workshopped in 1982; Kenneth Dyba's *Lilly, Alta.,* workshopped in 1984; and Peter Donat's *Sherlock Holmes and the Shakespeare Solution*, 1985. But the most alarming fact is that only two plays have been produced at Stratford: Larry Fineberg's adaptation of *Medea*, workshopped in 1975, produced in 1978; and my own *Blake*, workshopped in 1982, produced 1983.

For many people these statistics will confirm the futility of workshops, which, they argue, have become a fob that far outweighs its usefulness. Without pursuing the argument, one sees that whether or not individual workshops are positive or negative experiences, they have had a profound influence on the Canadian theatrical psyche. Many playwrights have stopped writing or, at least, stopped writing for the stage; others are stifled by deep cynicism or blocked by seasoned frustration at the fact that workshops and warehouse spaces seem to be the only outlets available for Canadian drama in our major institutions under the current means of public funding. This frustration pervades despite the fact that theatres across the country such as the Arts Club, Theatre Network, Phoenix Theatre, Prairie Theatre Exchange, Magnus, Theatre Passe Muraille, the Tarragon, Toronto Free Theatre, Blyth, Mulgrave Road, CODCO, and others somehow consistently manage to produce Canadian plays. Understandably, it is these theatres that most resent the funded workshop which does not lead to production, for in any other country in the world these theatres would fill a central function of workshops—providing new plays for the major stages. In any other country in the world these companies would be seen without question as the lifeblood of the theatre; yet in Canada they represent the ghettoization of indigenous drama, for the works they develop rarely move beyond their own network: the system of production breaks down between the small theatres which produce Canadian plays and the large theatres which rarely produce them. These small theatres, thus categorized, also contribute to the stasis in Canadian theatre simply because they exist on limited budgets supported by comparatively small audiences in theatres seating less than three hundred. While in producing Canadian plays they act as our conscience, the very fact that they exist means that they must bear the responsibility of contemporary Canadian theatre. That the major institutions absorb most of the available arts funding, while only very rarely drawing upon the artistic successes of the smaller theatres to enhance their repertoires and establish the careers of Canadian writers in the international arena, gives them due cause for anger. What one might call the classic Canadian play is rarely allowed to evolve through this system. Indeed, the Canadian play continues to be precluded in a discussion of the classics, the third and often major C of all repertoires: classic, contemporary, and Canadian.

In the final analysis, contemporary Canadian theatre reflects the state of the economy far more than the state of the arts. In this vicious circle, large theatres are so dependent on box-office income that they feel they must please audiences with tried-and-true products, rarely taking a risk on the great unknown, the Canadian play. In this situation, the government should be encouraged to establish Canadian dramatic literature as politically correct and financially rewarding, allotting as part of the operating grants of the major theatres sums of money solely for the production of Canadian plays, thus ensuring that the production of Canadian plays becomes essential to the financial health of the theatre via a quota system. This offends some people, of course—people who do not object to the Art Bank because they have not heard of it, or who were only vaguely aware of the CRTC restrictions over the last decade which dramatically coincide with the blossoming of the Canadian music industry.

Public funding has never been, and never will be, the answer to problems concerning the expression of original thought. Art expresses the values of the individual first. The playwright, as visionary, should dictate the trends of the theatre, not as a slave to fashion but as an intoxicated clairvoyant who inevitably stumbles onto the truth, and who has shed enough inhibitions to tell it—consequences be damned. Yet, as Jane Buss, executive director of the Playwrights Union of Canada, says, "We are a lazy country, always willing to buy another ethic by going for the tried-and-true product of another country." For those of us who know that the product is here, a thriving theatre scene will only develop when we break out of the workshop syndrome and the studio spaces to parlay the small successes of our smaller theatres into larger successes in our larger spaces. If there is a light at the end of the tunnel, it is economic health based upon self-generated income: the flow of red-blooded cash.

(1986)

Workshopping Plays
by Jan Selman

At the Playwrights Union of Canada "Workshop Workshop" last August the statement was made that playwrights are not integral to the structure of Canadian theatre, and that they should be. Such a statement could be made for all the freelance artists who support theatre production in this country. Actors, directors, and designers, as well as writers, suffer such alienation unless they are on long-term contract to a theatre organization. The point is an important one, and certainly addresses some of the problems I have experienced in workshop situations.

Many theatre companies that are trying hard to assist in the development of new plays find themselves forced to scramble for every workshop dollar. Naturally, they try to get the "most for their money": actors are hired, so they'd "best be in rehearsal"; directors feel they must "use every minute"; dramaturgs are working on several plays at once. And because freelance directors are only available on the contract start date, the consultation between the playwright and dramaturg necessary during the workshop process is squeezed in or shortchanged, etc. It is no wonder that playwrights and many others in the theatre community question the viability of the workshop process.

What can be done? The purpose of this article is to examine principles that are basic to effective play workshopping. The starting point is a belief that workshops can be useful if the playwright wants one and if certain conditions exist. But, ultimately, the success of a workshop can only be measured in terms of the degree to which a powerful and engaging theatrical event eventually emerges.

1/ The Workshop Process. Given the current structure of Canadian theatre, there are approaches to each stage of workshopping that can help the process to play a vital role in script development.

At the PUC workshop, the playwright-director/dramaturg relationship was given a great deal of attention, it being acknowledged as the beginning element of the process. The playwright in the relationship was described as everything from friend to marriage partner to mail order bride. Much was made of the playwright-director "marriage" concept. Many of the participating playwrights, directors, and dramaturgs felt that trusting, tested relationships were very much required in successful workshopping. Certainly in the case where a playwright and director have a strong relationship, the theatre bureaucracy should find a way to bring them together. As dramaturg Jackie Maxwell said during the workshop, such a situation should not be considered a luxury.

While I have no argument with this, I nevertheless have found myself in "blind-date" situations that have worked very well. There are many more "unmatched" playwrights and directors across the country than "happily married" ones. Michael Springate, artistic director of Playwrights' Workshop Montréal, made the important point that artistic directors and dramaturgs need to put more attention and energy into finding appropriate partners. But, of course, even the best marriages can go stale. Vancouver playwright Peggy Thompson, in a very provocative contribution to the PUC discussions, pointed out the need for writers to break with old patterns (and partners) at times. Just as writers and directors look to effective partnerships, the play itself needs to be considered in the "matching up." Style and subject matter also should influence choice of director. A new voice, a different voice, can be what is needed to make the workshop effective.

One of the clearest points made during the playwrights' deliberations about workshopping was that writers need to know what they want from a particular workshop. As playwright Raymond Storey suggested, "The most important thing to know as a playwright before you go into a workshop is what you expect to take out of it when the workshop is over." Many used other words to say the same thing. When playwrights have a clear objective, they will get more from the experience. The same goes for directors: they need to enter into the process with a strong sense of what elements in the play need exploration.

Ideally, the playwright guides the pre-workshop decision-making process. What does the playwright immediately need to explore in the play's development? Why is he or she entering into a workshop at this time? It is the director's role to assist in the process of identifying these elements, a point that Calgary playwright and director John Murrell emphasized:

> I think that writers often know that they need to improve their work and I think you can get into danger as an artistic director [...] thinking that you have the best ideas for the playwright [...] If you dig for it and you wait for it, I think the playwright himself or herself offers the best clue to what the play needs most of the time [...] As a general rule we avoid saying "How do we help the playwright to fumble his way along the dark corridor of dramaturgy?" (The playwright) is the guide.

But there is another side to these deliberations. One also needs to assume that part of the function of the workshop process is to bring fresh ears, hearts, eyes and minds into the process. The beginning of that process, the stage of director-playwright consultation, inevitably involves an element of negotiation. Perhaps in an ideal world the two partners would meet, agree on their objectives, and enter the rehearsal hall as a cohesive unit. In practice, however, the director must first establish a trusting and respectful relationship with the playwright: usually, it doesn't just happen. The two need to plumb the play together and come to common understandings about what will be explored within the upcoming workshop. This is negotiated. It is also the director's role to use the workshop to explore and open up to scrutiny areas of the play with which the playwright might currently be satisfied. This is (not so easily) negotiated.

During the workshop an open atmosphere is important but its accomplishment is easier said than done. Understandably, workshops are a time of great trial for most playwrights: the minute discussion of a play is opened to a group of actors, a director, a dramaturg, and whoever else may be sitting in; in such a situation, the average playwright snaps into a protective, if not downright aggressive, stance. Frank Moher, a strong playwright and dramaturg, claims there are two kinds of playwrights: those who feel they must answer every comment and defend their play, and those who just take it all in. In my experience, both kinds are under high stress.

A few things can help create a productive atmosphere, however. One is strong chairing by the director. The parameters of the discussion need to be clearly stated so that both the playwright and the actors know what is "on the table." In some cases, it is helpful to suggest that the playwright not respond immediately to comments: the brainstorm atmosphere—everything is okay to say, everything is recorded, nothing is discussed—is useful at certain stages of a workshop so that everyone has a chance to speak. But often the playwright and the director also need a chance to take all the comments in and to reflect upon them. And inevitably points come up that are not particularly helpful: so why discuss them exhaustively at this point? Discussing everything right way can give certain ideas too much focus or provide nothing but frustration. And once one sparring match has happened, it is hard to re-establish a relaxed atmosphere.

Conversely, the director as chairperson sometimes needs to focus discussions, to help the workshop team delve into a particular aspect of the play and prevent conversation from becoming too diffuse. Because people have their own observations regarding specific aspects of the play, the process can benefit if everyone sets aside their points at times and digs into one specific element. The continued exploration of one character's development and relationships, for example, may be much more useful to the playwright than giving "equal time" to each: actors may be able to feed in to a variety of points, particularly from the perspective of the character each is reading. It is the director's role to choose the right time to zero in, when to ask for that narrowing of focus.

The director also can play a useful role by acting as a "neutral questioner": refocusing or moving discussions forward, leaving a dead end, or getting off an area where the playwright would rather be left to his own devices, are a director's responsibility. One of the most straightforward ways to do this is to ask a new question of the group. The end of the previous conversation must be signalled— "Thanks for everyone's comments on that point"—then the new question should be made as specific as possible. And it should be an open, as opposed to a loaded, one: "What are your reactions to...?" is a better form than "Don't you think that...?", for the neutral, open-ended question affirms that everyone's comments are important. It also re-energizes the group. While one area of discussion is complete or "off limits" for the time being, another area is open to explore. An atmosphere is thus created in which everyone's ideas are valued and where there is a sense of progress.

The creation of an improvisational quality also can be useful to some stages in the workshop process. If the playwright and director enter the workshop with a sense of experimentation and an interest in exploration, everyone will be more at ease. "Let's try it"; "Great, I'll think about it"; "Tell me more"; or "Show me how that could work" are all-important responses. As with improvised theatre, the mood must be energized, fast-paced, and enthusiastic. When this mood is established, it communicates an underlying message: this idea matters so let's explore it now, and later it can be either thrown out or kept—whatever the playwright chooses.

I wish I could offer some great insight into the best balance between talking about the play versus playing it. I can't because I quickly come up against the varying needs of each play and each playwright. My sense is that there is a tendency during workshops to go overboard on talk, and thereby undervalue the reading and playing stage: the playwright—and all the workshop participants for that matter—will learn new things about the play by working it. Perhaps, then, the most significant function of a workshop is to lift the play off its pages, which would mean, as Paul Thompson said at the PUC workshop, "The actors should show the playwright scenes." The playwright is likely to act on something that he or she can see or feel. On the other hand, as director Stephen Heatley also said at the PUC meeting, in response to comments that actors should not talk about the play, "We will talk about *Ghosts* when we're producing it. We will talk about the characters, we will talk about the relationships between those characters…." Both are important.

As I write this, much of it seems self-evident. Then I remember that I've come to these conclusions through negative as well as positive experiences. What should be most self-evident is often most overlooked; consequently, an obvious idea, like the playwright and director need time together, is often forgotten by the workshop organizer. But if a playwright and director are workshopping a play for the first time, they need time both to build trust and to explore the play. The director needs time to read the playwright's earlier work, and he needs access to that work: he should be helped with arrangements, and should be paid for this important research. If development of the play is truly the objective, the process must not be short-changed. Theatre companies must take more responsibility for building an ongoing consultation between the playwright and director that begins before the workshop and continues after.

This brings me to time allotment. Much discussed and fussed over before, during, and after every workshop, it must be accepted to vary with every play and every playwright: there are enough unknowns at the planning stage that no schedule will ever be perfect. A luxury situation—one that probably should be pursued more widely in Canada—occurs when the actors and director are "on call" for long periods of time. The Banff Playwrights Colony, discussed elsewhere in this issue of *CTR*, clearly creates this situation for it removes a major area of counter-productive pressure. As Stephen Heatley explained at the PUC discussion, "Workshops become dangerous when they become pressure-cooker situations where the writer is unwriting or rewriting a play too quickly because six people all claim they know what it is about." The playwright who is writing madly in order to bring back major script overhauls to a hungry workshop team is often writing at the cosmetic level. Time pressure can simply push a playwright to quick fixes.

On the other hand, the creation of deadlines is one of the major contributions that workshops can make to new play development, if it is handled properly. Writers, like most of us, get bursts of energy as the deadline of day one of a workshop approaches. Copies of a new draft, hot off the press, arrive with the cast's first cup of coffee. New scenes burst forth for the following day. Massive cuts to cherished but overlong pieces are announced. Workshop organizers must aim to create a very flexible schedule that can respond to the playwright's changing needs and, at the same time, allow the playwright and the director/ dramaturg to create their own deadlines during the process.

2/ The Workshop Series. Workshop organizers often try to deal with the logistical and financial problems created by the necessity for writing time within the workshop schedule by arranging to work on a number of plays simultaneously. While the workshop series, now very familiar in Canadian theatre, is a good response to contractual requirements and to the need to make the most of actors' time while under those contracts, the series format presents many organizational choices that can help or hinder a workshop's effectiveness.

The major pitfalls of workshop series result from overzealousness on the part of the organizer regarding the use of contract employees' (actors, directors, dramaturgs) time. Complex scheduling of every minute of the workshop can easily stretch the workshop dollar but it also can inhibit the development of the play. Consequently a few rules of thumb are worth taking into consideration. The director/dramaturg needs time to consult with the playwright both after each session and intermittently during any writing period of more than a day or two. To facilitate this, the director must not be over-committed to other plays, whether as an actor or director. As a result, I am tempted to propose that a director/dramaturg be responsible for only one play in a series, although there certainly are situations where this is not possible or necessary—when, for example, there are long stretches of writing scheduled between a play's workshop sessions. Nevertheless, the principle remains: director/dramaturgs and writers need consultation time throughout the workshop series just as they do in individual workshops.

From the point of view of organization, one of the best experiences I have had as a director in a play workshop series was at Toronto's Young People's Theatre's new play development series in 1985. Four plays were workshopped over a period of two weeks, with one director per play and one dramaturg for the series. Six flexible actors completed the workshop team. Writers attended the other plays' workshop sessions if they wished, although generally they were away writing; directors attended all the workshops unless a meeting with "their" writer was required; the actors worked on all plays. Consequently, there were no simultaneous workshops. In addition to the four main plays, four others that were nearer completion were given a half-day each so that the writers could hear them read and briefly discussed. There were several positive results of this series. Eight playwrights heard their plays; four plays underwent major development; directors and playwrights had sufficient time to develop good working relationships and to process the input on an ongoing basis; director/dramaturgs had an opportunity to observe others' approaches to the same tasks.

Another aspect to consider when organizing a workshop series is the opportunity to create a healthy give-and-take atmosphere. If there is "buzz" about several plays rather than only one, a playwright can feel part of a process which includes, but is not solely focused on, him or her. Everyone's energy is obviously focused on the creation of better plays, not "dumping on my play." This atmosphere can be helped by inviting everyone to an "opening event" which can be as simple as having coffee and introducing everyone, or as elaborate as introducing each play through talk and/or readings. Although not always practical, the model where the acting company works together on all the plays (as opposed to being split up into a variety of working groups which are working concurrently in various locations) helps create a positive atmosphere through a sense of community and common focus.

Indeed, focus is the central issue to the successful organization of a workshop series. Writers need time to focus on what the play needs: they should not feel pushed to "sell" the piece to the workshop team. Director/dramaturgs need the opportunity to focus in-depth upon the playwright's needs and working methods: they should be contracted to do so on a full-time basis during the workshop. Actors need an opportunity to focus on revealing the play to the playwright, to show the writer his or her play.

3/ The Public Reading. To go public or not to go public? The point was discussed by the playwrights and directors at PUC's "Workshop Workshop." Inevitably, the majority point of view was that the choice should depend on the needs of the play and the playwright. While this comment appears to be a motherhood statement, it has several implications and prompts a number of questions. Who defines the "needs of the play"—or the "needs of the playwright," for that matter? How is the public reading going to be "used" by the playwright?

If the decision to hold a public reading is made, there are a number of factors to take into consideration. The first is that the actors need time to prepare for it: too often the actor's situation is not considered fully enough in a workshop process. In all fairness, their reputations are affected by the public nature of the event as well as the playwright's. They should be given some time to work with the script. Consequently, directors need to set deadlines for script revisions and to put a hold on discussions of the latest changes. At the minimum, they should allow the actors to read the new elements into the script, receive a few specific notes, and read the play again. If the reading is staged, then even more time is required.

Should the reading be staged? Any decision must consider a number of factors. Very simply, what is the focus of the workshop? What are the playwright's and director's objectives? If the playwright needs to see the work on its feet or if there are "staging problems" in the current draft that need to be addressed, then staging will help. If the play relies heavily on visual or physical elements, then it also should be staged. But remember that if the audience's response is truly important, they must be given all the necessary visual information—the staging must be complete enough to be a credible test of the play.

The third aspect to consider when undertaking a staged reading is an introduction to the event. The audience should be given an indication of what they are going to hear and see: is this a "finished" play? Is it in process? They need an indication of what their role is to be. Will they be asked to comment afterwards? If so, what is the desired purpose or focus of their discussion? Will it be formal (chaired) or informal (over coffee in the lobby)? If the reading is not staged, the audience also should be given a hint about the setting of the play.

What is the audience's role in workshopping plays? Participants at the PUC workshop generally dismissed the value of formal discussion after public readings. Writer

Murray McCrae put many people's feelings into words when he said simply, "The experience can be devastating." Greater value was placed on sensing the audience's response throughout the reading and eavesdropping on lobby conversation afterwards.

I'm not so quick to dismiss the value of a well-chaired post-reading discussion, however. If the parameters of the discussion are clearly laid out and if the chairperson keeps the discussion focused on personal reactions rather than on dramaturgy, there is much to be learned.

Finally, if a public reading is presented, scheduling must include time for playwright-director/dramaturg consultation after the reading. The playwright needs an opportunity to process both his own and the audience's reactions; and everyone needs a chance to put these reactions into perspective. A real danger of the public workshop is that the audience, particularly one which is not experienced in seeing plays in progress, can become very entranced with the process of the whole event. And particularly if the play is funny, the "success" of the reading can cloud larger issues, which may well have been forgotten in the excitement of the event. As a result, a "where to from here?" discussion is essential.

The organizational principles that I have attempted to draft in this article can go a long way to creating conditions under which a play workshop can succeed. Within this framework, it remains for the actors, director, dramaturg, and the writer to make the efforts pay off. We need good play workshops in this country. We need artists who are trained in the process. Acting programs, universities, the professional associations, funding bodies, workshop organizations, and experienced professionals all have parts to play in the development of sounder, more effective workshopping. Despite the frustrations and difficulties that come with workshopping plays—or, perhaps *because* of them—we must consider workshops more carefully and respect the fact that they can vary enormously depending on the care we give to them.

(1986)

The Laidlaw Report
by Sandra Tomc

Since its establishment in 1981, the Laidlaw Foundation's Arts Program has contributed several million dollars to the development of new Canadian plays. The foundation's policy has been to cultivate "those pockets or niches of artistic development which, though worthwhile, are generally underfunded or ignored by other granting bodies,"[1] and the vast majority of its funds have gone toward the support of workshops, staged or directed readings. Laidlaw has made a point of nurturing Canadian plays and playwrights rather than theatre companies. The Foundation distributes funds on the basis of individual projects only, and any theatre, large or small, mainstream or alternative, theoretically has equal access to Laidlaw grants. Yet despite these good intentions, Laidlaw each year has inevitably given its heftiest grants to a small phalanx of established Toronto theatres: Factory, Tarragon, Theatre Passe Muraille and Toronto Free.

Last year, Nathan Gilbert, Laidlaw's executive administrator, began to feel that the Foundation was supporting these four at the expense of lesser-known companies doing substantially more innovative work. In the spring of 1987 he therefore set out to redress this problem, conducting a series of interviews with over sixty playwrights, artistic directors and associated members of Toronto's professional theatre community. Gilbert's admirable idea was to approach the issue of grant distribution by investigating the play development process itself—by working from the ground up, as it were—assessing financial need on the basis of the quotidian and painstaking business of constructing a piece of theatre. He distilled the interviews and compiled a report, which recommended to the Laidlaw Board and Committee that the current criteria for grant distribution be significantly altered.

There is no question that Gilbert's report is important, and not just because it recommends a redirection of Laidlaw funds. The report brings into relief the central part played by Laidlaw in developing the contours and directions of Canadian theatre. As in the past, the Foundation's renewed commitment to innovation and to close involvement with the play development process will inevitably, if indirectly, determine not only which playwrights are sponsored by theatre companies, but also the sorts of plays that playwrights will decide to write.

The Laidlaw Foundation, prior to this year, has loaned most of its support to workshops on the assumption that they were the most important aspect of the development process. What emerges in Gilbert's report, however, is that workshopping as practiced by many of the Toronto theatre companies supported by Laidlaw is of little value to playwrights. Indeed, many interviewees feel that a "workshop ghetto" has been created, a kind of nightmarish circuit in which a single play travels from one theatre to the next being endlessly "developed." The general feeling is that workshops are misused and overused, and are not serving the purpose for which they were originally intended, which is to help develop a play to the point where it's ready for production. While most companies are perfectly willing and even anxious to workshop a play, few are willing to actually commit themselves to its production. Most theatres, says the report, "generally acknowledge that they have a 'stable' of writers who write exclusively for their audience," which implies that such companies are workshopping plays without the smallest intention of producing them.

This gratuitousness of the workshop syndrome is, in many cases, equalled by its shallowness. The most popular and prevalent kind of workshops are those expressly oriented toward the literary dimensions of a play. This hardly comes as a surprise when one understands that theatres have little, if any, commitment to seeing the play produced. One virtue of stressing the literary is that a theatre can do so with relatively little expense. Of course, for playwrights whose work is not limited simply to words and gestures, the system is bound to be both frustrating and unhelpful.

As might be expected, therefore, the burden of Gilbert's recommendations for change falls on the workshop process. The implicit (though unstated) assumption of the report is that those theatres now receiving the best grants are not necessarily putting them to the most fruitful uses. Gilbert strongly urges that Laidlaw "play a strong, nurturing role for the new generation of theatres" whose work, he explained in an interview, seems more promising and exciting than the work being done by Toronto's established companies. The implication is that the newer theatres are exploring and exploiting the many dimensions of theatre in ways that their more traditional counterparts are not. The aim of Gilbert's recommendations, here as elsewhere, is to close the gap between the workshop and production phases of play development, to encourage companies either to produce the plays they workshop, or else to incorporate elements of the production phase—lighting, design, music, etc.— into current workshop curricula. He recommends that the Laidlaw Board and Committee give preference to companies with a "track record in developing plays which successfully go on to production," and suggests that applicants now be requested to submit with their proposal "a complete list of all new plays developed by the company, describing the nature of assistance—as well as a production history, planned or past, of each new play, produced either by the company of elsewhere." The goal, obviously, is to stamp out "workshopitis," and to give fledgling playwrights a chance to move up and out of the limbo between the imagining of a play and its actualization.

Gilbert's report was circulated among Board and Committee members in November 1987. According to Gilbert, his recommendations were accepted, if not to the letter, then at least in spirit. It is too early yet to quantify the report's ramifications, but Gilbert did confide that already this year the Foundation for the first time had turned down the application of a theatre it had always heavily supported. If this unprecedented event is any indication, the report will have a fairly profound effect on the Toronto theatre community.

But what I find most interesting about the Laidlaw report, however, is not the solutions it proposes but the questions it fails to address. Neither Gilbert nor any of the people he interviewed speculates as to how the workshop problem came about in the first place. Why, in the last few years, have Toronto theatres perpetuated this work-shop ghetto? How are we to account for the existence of a play development system that often is useless to playwrights and time-consuming for theatres? Who does such a system benefit? And, finally, is Laidlaw, as a major source of funding for workshop projects, implicated in the problems which Gilbert's report hopes to correct?

Until this year, according to Gilbert, Laidlaw preferred to take responsibility only for that part of play development that fell clearly within the bounds of Laidlaw's commitment to "research and development," the part between the writing of a script and its production. The policy of the Foundation was to fund the development of any one script only once. Thus companies which had received a grant to workshop a specific play could not apply for money to have the same play produced. As far as Laidlaw was concerned, its obligations to the playwright stopped after the first workshop. This helps to explain, at least partially, why so few of the plays on the workshop circuit were picked up for production. Moreover, since Laidlaw habitually supported the "new works" programs sponsored by the major Toronto theatres without fussing about their content, it explains how the same play could crop up in one series after another and never move beyond the workshop stage.

But this still doesn't explain how an overcrowded circuit of overworked plays came into being in the first place. Theoretically, at least, the theatres involved had little to gain in its development: since Laidlaw's money was granted only on the basis of individual projects, it would presumably have made little difference to a company's regular functioning to have dispensed with this or that workshop, especially at the point where workshops were becoming tedious to everyone concerned. But, of course, as Gilbert admitted, a portion of the money from Laidlaw grants inevitably bleeds into other areas—the salaries of the crews and theatre staff, for instance. While this is not strictly legitimate, neither is it really cheating, since the theatre's crew and staff do contribute, however indirectly, to whatever project the theatre undertakes. In a recent article in *Theatrum 9* (Spring 1988) ("Tarragon: Playwrights Talk Back") Michael Devine rather maliciously hints that every year Tarragon somehow absconds with about $30,000 of Laidlaw funds granted specifically for its Playwrights Unit. What Devine doesn't take into account is that the money from Laidlaw also helps Tarragon stay alive, that it probably contributes to the salaries of members of the Tarragon staff who are necessary to the theatre's functions and who also spend part of their time assisting with the Playwrights Unit. We have to accept the fact that even the established Toronto theatres exist in a perpetual state of financial uncertainty. One can hardly blame them for strategically channeling and painstakingly redistributing what little money they get. Yet it is precisely the financial vulnerability of these theatres that makes their curricula susceptible to pressures which have little to do with aesthetic or artistic considerations. Theatre companies need Laidlaw's support; consequently they design projects that will be attractive to Laidlaw's decision-makers. When the Foundation announced its intention to support "research and development," the workshop, I suggest, became an important and desirable commodity, regardless of its usefulness either to playwrights or theatres.

The histories of the Factory Theatre and Theatre Passe Muraille provide a good example of the way in which the concept of the workshop has developed over the last few years in accordance with the changing economic situations of these two theatres. When Laidlaw established its arts program in 1981, Passe Muraille and Factory were among the four theatres, along with Tarragon and Toronto Free, doing what Laidlaw considered the most innovative and original Canadian drama. At that time, neither Factory nor Passe Muraille had a workshop program that could be regarded separately from its public productions: For example, the Factory's "Works" festivals showcased new plays with as many accoutrements of a fully elaborated production as the theatre could afford. But as both theatres became more established and began catering to different audiences, they developed workshop programs that had an increasingly smaller role to play in their regular seasons. Factory continued with its "Brave New Works" series, but the production style of these presentations was no longer stressed. Passe Muraille's "New Works" series, developed in the early 1980s, was almost exclusively devoted to dramaturgical critique. Staged workshops were relatively few and far between. Both companies, moreover, got a lot of money to do this. Laidlaw's grants to Passe Muraille in 1984–85 came to a total of $57,000; Laidlaw's grants to Factory from 1983 to 1985 came to $60,000. Whether the money was put to good use is immaterial: the point is that when these theatres began cultivating new and more conservative audiences, development, experimentation and innovation no longer had a critical relation to their regular productions. But neither theatre apparently could afford to relinquish "innovation" and, as a result, a discrete compartment was created for "the development of new works," a compartment in which "development" was no longer a means but an end in itself. What began as an effort to make experimentation continuous with commercial output evolved into a segregation of the two and, hence, the creation of the "workshop ghetto" perceived by so many of the playwrights Gilbert interviewed.

Interestingly, the very isolation of such compartments has come to be regarded by some as part of their usefulness. One of the things stressed by the representatives of Factory in the Laidlaw report was the potentially harmful effects of an audience for the fledgling playwright. Jackie Maxwell, Bob White and Neil Munro all agreed that an audience only interfered with the flow of creative productive energies buzzing back and forth among playwrights, actors and directors. Now, considering that Factory has always made a point of the public presentation of its workshops, the change of attitude, intentionally or not, would seem to be an attempt to justify an already existent gap between the workshop, figured here as a purely private process (a closed dialogue between theatre and playwright), and the public venue, now regarded, oddly enough, as dangerous to the delicate aesthetics of the development process. It is worth noting by contrast that Nightwood Theatre, a relatively young "alternative" theatre that emphasizes the collective construction of its scripts, came out in strong support of public attendance at workshops, while Buddies in Bad Times, another "alternative" company, has preferred to forgo the concept of the workshop altogether in favour of the small low-budget public productions presented at the "Rhubarb! Festival." The idea of separating a play's development from audience response, or of neatly dividing the textual from the theatrical, has not entered into the estimations of theatres like Nightwood and Buddies, whose innovative efforts are still very much a part of their public presentations.

Ironically, Laidlaw's funding policy between 1983 and 1987 encouraged this compartmentalization. Those companies proposing workshop projects invariably got the largest grants. Laidlaw, we have to remember, makes a point of not sponsoring a theatre's regular season and [its] "research and development" policy pre-empts the consideration of major productions as suitable candidates for grants. In fact, of the theatres which received Laidlaw grants from 1983 to 1987, less than a third proposed projects which involved a fully mounted production, and out of this third only one theatre in the entire five-year period received above $5,000; in most cases it was considerably less. Clearly it has been in the interest of theatres to set up workshop series and development projects, if only for the fact that these seem to command the biggest grants.

It is interesting to speculate how this has affected the landscape of Toronto theatre over the past few years. Obviously the system I've described prefers the textually oriented play, the kind that most easily lends itself to development on the page only. But more than that, this system also encourages authors to write the kind of plays that workshop programs find acceptable, for authors are as integral to the network as theatre and funding bodies. While a playwright may not consciously set out to conform to the dominant set of expectations, many of the theatres involved here have discreetly justified their practices with a formulation of the playwrights' "needs": his need for privacy and isolation, for example, or her need for professional rather than public response. How is a playwright to avoid internalizing such formulations and escape reproducing them in a particular aesthetic? The playwright's "need" for isolation may too easily find fruition in the writing of a play that doesn't really need to be performed.

By the same token, the isolation of process from production inevitably presupposes certain "needs" on the part of the theatre audience. Implicit in the argument for keeping workshops separate from public performances is the notion that audiences somehow have a lower tolerance to experimentation than playwrights and directors, that the public requires a product whose rough edges have all been assiduously scraped away. Unfortunately, such attitudes create as much as cater to the consumer ethic that many of these theatres originally set out to combat. It may be true that Toronto's more established theatres aim their work at what might be termed a "middle class" audience. But what sort of snobbery is it that assumes these people's uniform impatience with anything but the stalest perfection? By denying the public a share in the development process of new Canadian works, Toronto theatres are not only unjustly affirming and revalidating the notion of the viewer as consumer, they are unfortunately committing themselves to the sort of mediocrity consumers are supposed to like.

If the last few years are any indication, Laidlaw's response to "workshopitis" will doubtless reverberate in the quality and kinds of theatre we'll be seeing in Toronto over the next few years. In accordance with Gilbert's recommendations, one might logically predict an increased emphasis on theatrically as opposed to textually oriented plays, a broader insistence on the value of public performances and increased patience with work-in-progress. But we can't lose sight of the fact that this readjustment may engender its own problems, that experimentation may become an end in itself, or that a literary aesthetic may unjustly be relegated to inferior status. Ideally one would hope that Laidlaw's renewed commitment to interaction with the artists it patronizes will once again help check the unwitting blindness to which both partners in this sort of marriage are inevitably prone.

(1988)

---

[1] "The Play Development Process: A Needs Assessment for the Laidlaw Foundation" (July 1987), a report written by Linda J. Suss from interviews conducted by Suss and Nathan Gilbert. This report is the object of my article and has been my major source of information on the Laidlaw Foundation. In addition, I draw on an interview with Gilbert, conducted 7 June 1988, and on the Foundation's grant distribution reports, 1 January 1983–31 December 1985 and 1986–1987. Information concerning specific theatres was gained from interviews with Diane English of Factory Theatre, Urjo Kareda of Tarragon Theatre, Jerry Doiron of Theatre Passe Muraille, and Simone Georges of Buddies in Bad Times Theatre.

The New Play Centre: Twenty Years On
by Denis Johnston and Jerry Wasserman

As Vancouver's New Play Centre (NPC) celebrates its twentieth anniversary, Western Canada's premier play development organization can't decide whether to revel in its substantial accomplishments or worry about its ongoing identity crisis. On the plus side it has plenty to celebrate. Two decades of script development and, to a lesser extent, new play production have helped nurture a thriving theatrical culture in British Columbia and given first exposure to plays and playwrights of national reputation.

Play critiques and workshop services have been the heart and soul of the NPC since its inception in 1970. Currently receiving two hundred to two hundred and fifty scripts a year, the NPC offers BC writers one or more of the following dramaturgical options: (1) Critique Service—the script is read and critiqued by two theatre professionals; (2) One On One Workshop—a director/dramaturge works individually with the playwright for anywhere from hours up to three days; (3) Actors Workshop—a full cast and director work with the writer for four hours to a week, with all participants including the writer paid eight dollars an hour; (4) Public Reading, sometimes staged; (5) full production, or sometimes only a workshop production. In 1989 a popular screenplay critique program was added to the playwriting services.

On the production side, the 1989–90 season saw David King's screwball comedy *Harbour House* break NPC attendance records. The season also balanced new plays by NPC veterans Tom Cone (*love at last sight*) and Ian Weir (*Bloody Business*) with four one-acts by writers never before professionally produced.

Other activities include the Young Playwrights Search, a competition for high school students run annually in conjunction with Carousel Theatre; a library service featuring an extensive collection of Canadian scripts, published and unpublished; the Playwrights Unit, ongoing workshops for six writers selected to work with a senior playwright (this year John Lazarus); and thrice-yearly programs of writing classes for stage, screen and TV. Government and corporate funding is relatively healthy and firmly in place. Finally the NPC's secure tenancy in the Waterfront Theatre, on popular Granville Island near the downtown core, must be considered a major bonus in a city with a critical shortage of performance space.

But as it enters the 1990s, the New Play Centre faces nagging questions about its very nature, as well as growing competition on both the development and production fronts. The past five years have seen the inception of a number of alternate companies and two festivals that encourage new work—Women in View and the Vancouver Fringe Festival. Even mainstream theatres like the Arts Club are increasingly developing their own new plays. "The original mission was to try to get local material on the stages," says Pamela Hawthorn, NPC artistic director from 1972 to 1989. "That was accomplished. The question now is where do you go from there?"

Some would question whether that original mission was truly accomplished; others wonder how successfully. Vancouver playwrights have not by and large been a dominant force in Vancouver's own theatres. Grumblings about stylistic tameness and naturalistic bias have dogged the NPC, and the often conflicting demands of developing versus producing plays, always on a limited budget, have never been fully reconciled. With the notable exceptions of Margaret Hollingsworth and Betty Lambert, women have been under-represented among NPC playwrights, despite the prominence of women in its administrative and directorial ranks. Visible minorities and Native writers have been, in fact, largely invisible.

But back in 1970 the problem was more basic: how to get professional playwriting started in British Columbia. The only company producing new plays in Vancouver in the late 1960s was its regional theatre, the Playhouse, which had scored noteworthy hits with Eric Nicol's *Like Father, Like Fun* in 1966, George Ryga's *The Ecstasy of Rita Joe* in 1967, and Ryga's *Grass and Wild Strawberries* in 1969. Alternative theatre was blooming in such companies as Savage God, led by John Juliani, and the collective Tamahnous Theatre, founded by such now-familiar artists as Larry Lillo and John Gray. But at that time, alternative theatres were focused on young Canadian actors and directors rather than on new Canadian playwrights. The need for something like the New Play Centre was first recognized by Douglas Bankson, a creative writing instructor at UBC, and Sheila Neville, a reference librarian who had long been involved in Vancouver's then vibrant amateur theatre community. Neville, a governor of the Dominion Drama Festival (DDF), enlisted Bankson's support in a proposal that the DDF sponsor a string of regional play development centres across Canada. When the DDF failed to act on their proposal, Bankson and Neville decided to start such a regional centre themselves. In May 1970 they received five hundred dollars in seed money from the Koerner Foundation, and the New Play Centre was born.

Bankson established the policy that every script submitted to the NPC would receive two written critiques. Initially he read and appraised every submission himself and for a second opinion approached members of Vancouver's growing professional theatre community, including such young directors as John Juliani, Ray Michal and Jace Van der Veen. The most promising scripts were given a public rehearsed reading and discussion, most often held in the lounge of the Arts Club Theatre on Seymour Street. In the NPC's first 18 months, Bankson processed about thirty scripts in this way, held a half-dozen public readings and uncovered, he estimated, seven or eight writers of promise. He also found that professional directors were very excited at the prospect of reading new scripts, and that professional actors were eager to take part in the readings, even on a volunteer basis.

By the end of 1971, on the eve of Canada's national explosion of new dramatic writing, Neville and Bankson decided that the NPC needed to expand beyond its part-time capacity. For the position of managing director they approached Pamela Hawthorn, a Trail, BC native who had gone on from UBC to take an MFA in directing at Yale. Hawthorn took the job, initially at no salary, and remained with it for 17 years. As Bankson later said, "The New Play Centre wouldn't have gone anywhere without Pam."

Bankson and Neville never intended the NPC to be a producing organization. They felt the role of the NPC ought to be to critique new plays and to bring the best of them to the attention of producing groups, amateur and professional. Hawthorn wanted to extend the development process to include production. In August 1972, the company held its first public performances, at the old Vancouver Art Gallery, with a one-week run of Sharon Pollock's first play, *A Compulsory Option*, directed by Hawthorn. The following week came a program of two one-acts also developed at the NPC, *The Helper* by Tom Grainger and *Dandelions* by Cherie Stewart-Thiessen. The next year, two more programs of one-acts were offered, one at the Arts Club and another at the Playhouse, including new works by Leonard Angel, Margaret Hollingsworth and Leon Rooke.

The rising profile of the NPC soon became linked with that of the Vancouver East Cultural Centre, a former church on the city's east side which reopened as a theatre in 1973. There the NPC established its reputation as a producing company with its annual du Maurier Festival of new Canadian plays, beginning in 1974. Through this festival, the NPC also developed an identifiable stable of playwrights, among them Tom Cone, Margaret Hollingsworth, John Lazarus, Sheldon Rosen and Tom Walmsley. NPC productions of this era which were later remounted elsewhere included Cone's *Herringbone* (1975), *Sqrieux-de-Dieu* (1975) by Betty Lambert, *British Properties* (1977) by Richard Ouzounian, and Walmsley's *Something Red* (1978).

In the late 1970s, the NPC's national reputation benefited from a growing relationship with the Stratford Festival through Stratford's then literary manager, Urjo Kareda. In fact, an NPC innovation which Kareda noted—that of playwrights workshopping a play with each other rather than with actors and a director—is now an element of his own play development program at Tarragon Theatre. In 1978 Kareda brought Hawthorn to Stratford to direct Tom Cone's *Stargazing*. Cone's adaptation of *A Servant of Two Masters*, another product of the NPC workshopping process, later appeared at Stratford's Avon Theatre. Sheldon Rosen's *Ned and Jack*, first produced by the NPC in 1976, played Stratford's Third Stage in 1978 and the Avon Theatre in 1979.

For most of its first decade, the New Play Centre worked out of an unheated cold-water loft on West 4th Avenue, with no performing space of its own. In 1979 it was able finally to establish a home base in the Waterfront Theatre. There the NPC's policy of play development combined with a full-scale production brought many more plays to national attention, including John and Joa Lazarus's *Dreaming and Duelling* (1980), Charles Tidler's *Straight Ahead* (1981) and *Blind Dancers* (1979), Betty Lambert's *Jennie's Story* (1981) and *Under the Skin* (1985), Margaret Hollingsworth's *War Baby* (1984), Ian Weir's *The Idler* (1987), and three plays by Ted Galay, *After Baba's Funeral* (1979), *Sweet and Sour Pickles* (1980), and *Tsymbaly* (1985), later an enormous hit for the Manitoba Theatre Centre. Another play to achieve national success was developed by the NPC but only produced elsewhere. Sherman Snukal's *Talking Dirty* went through at least six drafts in NPC workshops, over three years, before it finally opened in 1981 at the Arts Club. It ran there for over 1000 performances and later won a Chalmers Award in Toronto.

In 1989 Pam Hawthorn left the New Play Centre for similar responsibilities with Telefilm Canada, reading and evaluating new screenplays. She was succeeded by Paul Mears, a graduate of the University of Victoria's theatre program, who had worked as Hawthorn's assistant for five years. Mears has proven himself a capable director of new plays, with highly praised productions such as *The Idler* (a Jessie Award-winner for best new play in 1987) and this season's *Harbour House.*

While justifiably proud of the New Play Centre's successes, Mears is also acutely conscious of its problems, none more so than "the tension between the obligation to develop new writers and revenue demands of producing plays." Even more than Pam Hawthorn, Mears is insistent that the NPC remain a producing company. "I think it's really important, if you're going to develop, that you produce. No playwright wants to develop plays just for the sake of development." But a problem emerges at the bottom line. Play development by its very nature incurs costs for which there is no corresponding revenue. Funding bodies, recognizing the NPC's special status as a play development centre, accept that its proportion of earned revenue will be unusually low: fifty to sixty percent of an operating budget of about $425,000 in 1989–90. But even these numbers demand a substantial box office return. And, as Mears says, "producing a commercially viable and fiscally responsible season of world premieres is almost a contradiction in terms."

For one thing, commercial viability demands strong production values. Director Jane Heyman, a longtime associate of the NPC, agrees with the need to put more money into production. She argues that chronic under-funding is one of the reasons that NPC historically has shown little concern for formal experimentation. It is true that minimal design budgets and inadequate rehearsal time almost necessitate choosing plays relatively simple to stage. But upgrading production financing would mean having to drain funds from play development.

Whereas most companies develop new work for their own production purposes, the New Play Centre, says Mears, "is playwright-driven rather than production-needs-driven." Theoretically this should result in an equitable distribution of resources among the writers currently involved in play development, and something like equal opportunity for production. But a glance at the NPC's recent history suggests that this may not be the case. The dozen shows fully staged since 1987 have featured mostly established playwrights: David King (with two), Dennis Foon, Steve Petch, Bryan Wade, Tom Cone and novice dramatist but veteran fiction writer W.P. Kinsella. After the success of *The Idler,* Ian Weir's first play, the NPC also produced his next two. Apart from Weir, only Alex Brown (*The Wolf Within*) and Gordon Armstrong (*Mona Lisa Toodle-oo*) could be considered new writers.

Do the "revenue demands of producing new plays" then mean pressure to stage writers with a previous track record and some kind of name? Probably not. It seems doubtful that a Bryan Wade or Steve Petch play would attract much of an audience on the basis of playwright recognition. And in any case the NPC has always had an unstated policy of supporting its stable with a continuing commitment to produce their plays. Cone, Rosen, Angel, Hollingsworth, Lazarus and Lambert have all had four or more NPC productions.

But have fiscal demands resulted in a tendency to favour accessible comic writers like David King and Ian Weir for production? Mears replies that their shows have been balanced this season by Tom Cone's sexually explicit and highly controversial *Love at Last Sight,* hardly a safe commercial choice, and the Springrites Festival of four one-acts by previously unproduced writers.

If the Springrites plays are added to the dozen full-length productions since 1987, a glaring statistic emerges: only one of the last sixteen NPC shows was written by a woman (Maureen Robinson's *Nitebooth*). Mears says that the number of woman writers produced by the NPC has historically been proportional to the number of scripts submitted by women—less than 15%. He strongly denies any gender bias in the selection process. The fact that six of seven plays produced this season were written by men is no more intentional, he insists, than the fact that the production team for Springrites—two directors, three designers and the composer—was 100% female.

Jane Heyman, director of two of the Springrites, also co-founded Vancouver's Women in View performance arts festival. She expresses some frustrations with the NPC's hesitancy to give special attention to women writers. Apart from three plays produced in 1975 under the rubric "Mis en Scene," and five "Women's Short Takes" ten years later (performed only at midnight, Heyman notes dryly), the NPC has not attempted much affirmative action.

> Whenever the New Play Centre solicited plays from women we were inundated. But the usual attitude was, "we'll treat all plays as equal." Most of us were trained in a masculine model of what a good play is. We need re-education so women's plays can be seen as worthy of being done in their own right rather than being compared unfavourably to male models in the way early seventies Canadian plays were compared unfavourably to British and American models.

When asked about possible affirmative action, Paul Mears points to some bad publicity garnered by Vancouver's Firehall Theatre in trying to recruit a multicultural acting company: "Whites Need Not Apply!" screamed the local tabloid's headlines. But Heyman points out that in the mid-seventies some people reacted similarly to the NPC's doing only *Canadian* playwrights. "I always use the New Play Centre as a positive model when I'm accused of reverse sexism. In the same way we had to nurture Canadian writers, we have to nurture women writers. Cone and Rosen and Lazarus and Foon—they were given a chance to write dreck and then go on to do the good stuff."

That could be the New Play Centre's motto as it enters the 1990s: "Let them write dreck, and then go on to do the good stuff." For two decades the NPC has continually passed the two acid tests of a script development program: its plays have received second productions elsewhere, and its authors have gone on to write more, and better, stage-worthy plays. As one of the few professional theatre companies in Canada where opportunities for local artists and the right to fail are both built into its mandate, the NPC remains a model for moving locally created arts from the margins to the mainstream. The trick will be to find ways of balancing high-quality production with the risky, unglamorous business of grooming unknown writers.

(1990)

Table Stakes: Gambling with New Play Development
by Kathleen Flaherty

When I work as the dramaturge in a workshop, I like to sit away from the table where everyone else sits. I feel more capable of objectivity there, less susceptible to the moment-by-moment heat and energy of the process. I am less likely to join in the inevitable spiralling brainstorm that erupts over a line, a scene, and an image in the play. After all, as anyone who knows me will attest, it's hard to stop me once I get started. And if I leap into the maelstrom, how can I do my job as structural analyst and "friend of the playwright"? Away from the table, there is room for the implied images to develop in the air. The play is not trapped on the page. And by forcing myself to avoid participation in discussions and to *listen*, I inadvertently catch a lot of subtext. As a student of science, I know that even this physical arrangement is part of the process. The actors may feel that I am judging them, or that they need to perform for me. That changes what happens in the workshop.

Winter 1987. A farmhouse outside Picton, Ontario

Stephen Bush, Michael Riordon, and I are gathered at Michael's home to do early dramaturgical work on Michael's play *A Jungle Out There*. This draft is the result of a workshop with actors earlier in the year, May I think, at which I was not present. There are plans for another workshop before Michael is to produce the final rehearsal draft. There is snow on the ground; the upstairs rooms of the farmhouse are unheated but the sleeping bags are cozy; there is an outdoor privy with a miraculous toilet seat that doesn't cool off. The firewood is plentiful, Michael is a good cook, and I almost don't mind going outside to assuage my nicotine cravings. Stephen, Michael, and I work well together, we are all focused and our objectives for this three-day session are specific and attainable. The pressure to produce is distant—we don't have to solve problems, only point to areas of difficulty, make conjectures, fantasize a little. Michael clearly has "ownership" of the play and, although he likes to please people, he is an experienced writer with strong opinions. Stephen and I are careful to remind him occasionally that he can interpret any overbearing behaviour as excessive passion or, in my case, the need for a cigarette. *Jungle* is not a linear or naturalistic play. It has three "worlds," all more or less fantastical, inhabited by characters who have metaphoric relationships with characters in other worlds. This session is to help Michael identify through-lines of action in his complex script and to focus his objectives for the next rewrite. Stephen invited me as dramaturge to provide an outside eye and to mitigate any agenda he may have as producing director. What excites me (and scares me) is that there is no model, honed from centuries of critical dramaturgy, for this structure of play. We have only our instincts and experience to guide us. We know for sure it's time to leave Michael when we start suggesting how and what he "should" be doing in his rewriting. Statements like "I don't think Danny would say that" betray a yen for psychological realism that has little place in the style of play Michael is writing. They also indicate that we are getting ahead of ourselves, trying to accomplish something that can wait for detailed work with actors. But this is great—no immediate pressure, no outside distractions, and admiration and affection for the play and each other, a "history" with the play. The only things we lack are a common critical framework and a common theatrical language. It's an extended conversation, of course, with some hasty felt-marker charts as visual aids.

Summer 1991. Toronto

It's David Demchuk's *Mattachine* for the Toronto Fringe. It's in the heat of a sweltering humidity better suited to rehearsing Tennessee Williams (or better still, dreaming on the beach). It happens in various rehearsal halls including one with no furniture of any kind, a second with no light or electrical outlets, a third that is too small and too hot but clean, and a fourth which is part of the living quarters of a group of tolerant people. What the spaces have in common is a rental fee of $6 per hour or less. We work evenings and weekends because people have other jobs, it's a co-op, and everyone shares the box office. The play is complex, not naturalistic, attempting something no one can quite articulate. What we know is it isn't ready to rehearse and we have an opening in four weeks. The framing device of the piece is six actors who have come together to rehearse a play created from fragments and photographs left among the effects of a dead friend/love/teacher. This objective is not serving to keep the fictional group together and the collective is cracking, splintering, and in terrible danger of collapse. It should be no surprise that our little collection of neuroses, blind passion, drive, suspicion, talent, hidden agendas, ego, fear, love, generosity, intelligence, hormones, prejudice, and experience will go through the same kinds of crisis in miniature that the characters endure. What we are searching for as we develop alliances and nurture feelings of betrayal is something or someone to trust—a guarantee that this blueprint for a production will lead us to the goal of a comprehensible piece of theatre. We are looking for authority, either in the text itself or in a leader, to help us make that leap of faith that every creative act implies. We even have a group therapy session, which creates its own difficulties but relieves the tension for long enough to get some work done. So, part of the rehearsal process for *Mattachine* is actually a workshop from hell. It has all the worst aspects of a workshop: an imminent production deadline, no consensus about the structure of the process, serious communication breakdowns, especially concerning the objective (a piece of theatre to open in four weeks or David's definitive vision of the play?) and two people out of a dozen who have followed the play from its earliest drafts. Great potential for ugliness here. In the end, it is the audience that tells us that all the seams show but that we have made some kind of connection, communicated at least part of our message. That is as it should be. Only time can erase the damage we have done to each other and the work in getting there.

Neither of the above is a "standard" workshop process. I use them to underline my belief that process affects product, that structure creates process, and that the concept of product itself in the context of a new play workshop can be problematic.

Think what we were doing with *Mattachine*—trying to script the collective process using the tools of more conventional forms—and ask yourself what kind of miracles happen in theatre every day.

Fall 1990. Playwrights' Workshop Montréal

An organization devoted solely to new play workshops hires actors, director (Michael Devine) and dramaturge (me) to work on Kwame Dawes's newest play, *Passages*. Set in Jamaica, *Passages* is a surrealistic evocation of the torment of a woman whose abusive father has just died. (Well, on one level that's what it's about.) Kwame arrives in Montreal with a draft of the play that none of us has read. He and Michael and I meet to determine the goal of the workshop and its schedule. In the first two days, the actors read the play aloud and react to it. Kwame and I meet overnight to discuss the results, Kwame has two days to rewrite, and the actors read the new draft and work through the fifth day. Then it is read for an audience who are invited to comment. It is to PWM's credit that Kwame Dawes is recognized as a writer of lyricism, power, and theatricality. It is to the credit of Michael Devine and the actors that the reading is as clear as it is considering that the play takes place on three levels of reality and that some actors play as many as three characters. It is to Kwame's credit that he rewrites quickly and he knows what he needs to get out of a workshop. But two crucial things are wrong with this workshop: none of the actors is of Jamaican ancestry, so the cadence of the language and the cultural context are only hinted at; and the framework of *Passages* and most of its bridges are created by ritual and music (drums), which are missing. Without these, the structure and flow of the play cannot be addressed. The format of this workshop, including the public reading, was predetermined by PWM in accordance with its own existing structures and without consultation with Kwame, Michael, or me. That's how new play workshops are usually conducted—without reference to the specific requirements of the script being developed or to the strengths and weaknesses of the particular artists who are part of the process.

These days there are a lot of books floating around that either directly or indirectly address issues about the relationship between science and art. There is no question that the concepts of quantum physics and relativity have created a revolution in the ways we think about the impact of the observer on the observed and the subjective nature of observation. Both of these issues have significant relevance to our concept of the nature of theatre. And if the experiments are to be believed, the scientific method itself creates bias in the proofs of theories: if you hypothesize that light comes in the form of waves and you devise a method to test that hypothesis, you find that light is a wave; if you hypothesize that light is particles and you devise a test for *that*, sure enough, light proves to be particles.

In the fifty or sixty new play workshops I've been involved in, no matter how "beneficial," "positive," "gentle," "productive," or "thrilling," I've gradually learned that the way we do workshops affects the plays we end up with. And these processes have very little to do with the nature of the plays themselves. Let's not jump up and down in horror here, but for those who are weary with a sameness or lack of excitement, let us remind ourselves that, mostly, we get the plays we deserve or inadvertently design. How does this happen? We want to avoid reinventing the wheel and to save valuable time. Efficiency and cost effectiveness seem funny terms in which to talk about art, don't they? Most people would cite financial constraints as the major limiting factor in new play development. The standardization of process means we don't have to expend the time and energy to question our philosophical and aesthetic biases before getting down to business. Neither do we have to search for different people to work with or different ways to reach different audiences. We don't have to invent new vocabularies to work together or to communicate with those audiences. So, in the interests of efficient use of the valuable resources of time and labour, most theatre companies have standardized their workshop processes. Most of these are remarkably similar and few of them include consideration of the needs of the play in question.

So, how do we put together a workshop? Someone may suggest that the playwright write down in one sentence the dramatic action of the play. The workshop facilitators may agree upon and state the objectives of the workshop. There are some conventional wisdoms which may be agreed upon or may simply be assumed about how to avoid sensory overload or bogging down in pointless conflict. Many of these concern the role of each participant, a kind of division of labour: the director deals with the actors; the actors interact with the playwright in formal, scheduled sessions; the dramaturge is concerned largely with the structure and flow of the play; the actors are concerned with the development of character and getting from one moment to another in the script. A decision is made and announced concerning whether or not there will be a final "public" reading and if it will involve a formal audience feedback session or not. We get down to work. We sit around a table and read the play. I try to get the playwright to stop following the text as the actors read. There is a period of discussion/information sharing. The play is read again. The actors leave the director, dramaturge, and playwright to decide what to focus on, how deeply to investigate scenes, characters, whatever. When the actors return, maybe scenes are put on their feet, maybe rewrites are read, maybe a specific sequence of scenes is addressed. Maybe the reading is "directed" for public presentation. What I have described takes about three days.

The process is determined to maximize resources of time, space, and personnel. The available resources are determined not by artistic needs but by available funding. And the available funding is determined more and more by a corporate model of theatre production in which a play must pay its own way in a market-driven economy. To do this, it must be an identifiable product, easily marketed, relatively cheap to produce, capable of infinite reproduction (or a one-off with considerable prestige, and commensurate price tag). A play, a piece of theatre, must become a commodity that fits the limited profile of a product that can compete in the overcrowded marketplace of consumables. Theatre forced into the position of competing for consumer dollars (including grants) have responded in obvious ways: smaller casts, shorter rehearsal time, simpler productions or fewer productions, less challenging or complex subjects, easily recognized and understood forms. In order to assure ourselves of an income, theatres have adopted subscription seasons and corporate sponsorships, and in order to sustain these funding sources we have adopted the appropriate attitudes and artistic policies. This art-as-product attitude is responsible for a number of unexamined biases and for standardized processes in the new play workshop. Systemic bias. It makes sense that if you have the mould for a 1991 Subaru car door and the material to make this door and the people who know how to pour the material into the mould and recover it from the mould, you are very likely to end up with a 1991 Subaru car door. The only variable might be the colour. Allocation of resources to a new play workshop has the same effect. It's not simply a question of the number of plays developed, but the style, content, and form of these plays.

Personnel. Who is involved in the workshop? Rarely is there a designer, let alone a composer or choreographer. Considering the importance of visual and aural metaphor and their expression through setting, properties, costumes, lighting, sound, and movement to the theatre, it is remarkable how few designers are involved in the play-development process. Maybe we can imagine the eventual effects of these elements, but I have yet to see a storyboard in a new play workshop. This determination of personnel affects both the plays chosen and their eventual development. We don't tend to work on plays with strong visual demands because we don't have time or personnel to approximate the effect. *Tesla*, a very theatrical spectacle by David Fraser, for instance, has been considered by several theatres for workshop. It excites people, even in reading. But it has never been attempted because it requires a new approach. Such an approach, including a lighting designer and an electrician, was once proposed by Peter Hinton but never came to fruition. Who knows if it would have worked or not? *Sand*, a play by Colleen Wagner, was developed by Factory Theatre as part of Brave New Works. The surreal/imagistic quality of this work could barely be addressed in the workshop and the audience for the staged reading largely regarded the play as a failure. I believe the format misrepresented the play.

It goes deeper than that. Our corporate approach to theatre has led us to concepts of professionalism that determine that no one works on a project (except the playwright) who isn't being paid for it. And our roles in this work are also decided by professional agreements and job definitions. This is not, by the way, an argument against unions or support for the all too common artist-as-subsidizer-of-the-art. But let's face it, if you get hired to do a workshop, your investment in the work is dictated by your own sense of professionalism and your personal agenda, not by the work. It is not even necessary to care about the work except in the abstract. And what are some of our agendas? Actors want to be cast in the actual production; directors want a play appropriate for next year's season and a contract to direct it; dramaturges want to enhance their professional credentials so they continue to work; playwrights want their plays produced. This group of professional experts with a professional, not necessarily visceral, connection with the material, the text, are given one day to one week to get said text (which most have read a maximum of three times) one step further from page to stage. It is this minefield of conflicting needs and desires that has given rise to some of the standard workshop protocols.

I've been assuming a set text as the focus of the workshop. I've done that because this kind of set up is only prepared to deal with a set text. The script is something solid, a material object, something clearly a product. The script as object is more important in this setting than the piece of theatre for which it is the blueprint. It is tangible. Funding for new play development may be contingent on having a product, if not a production then a public reading. Certainly a new draft.

People get a measure of satisfaction from a process with a product, so a decision for a public reading is emotionally desirable. It also makes a lot of sense in an art form which depends on an audience to be complete. Still, something qualitatively different happens to actors and directors during the time they are focused on the reading; they actually move into a kind of rehearsal mode. Regardless of how magical the results of this performance segment of the workshop, it is accomplished at the expense of other activity. More alarming, to have or not to have a public component to the workshop is not a choice for many organizations. They perceive it as a requirement either to satisfy funding sources or to pay for part of the research and development.

Who contributes to/owns the text and what is the relationship of text and performance? Clearly, in a situation where only one of the collaborators in a workshop has an in-depth knowledge of the text which is the focus of the workshop, this person's judgment concerning what constitutes the text is central. At the same time, the playwright is generally the least likely to be "of the theatre." S/he is surrounded by people with knowledge of the practices of theatrical performance expressed through what may appear to be a formidable esoteric vocabulary. And what exactly constitutes text anyway? Many workshops designate "props" or other sensory material as elements of a play in *production*, not as text. If the workshop is intended to assist the playwright in realizing the play, perhaps it needs to address the physical element equally with the verbal. The way things are, playwrights are encouraged, either actively or by default, to leave these elements to the production, if it ever happens. Or they depend on the opinions of people who rely on the magic criterion for any decision—whether or not the moment, series of moments, the play, will "work." These powerful acts of imagination are fed by experience. They are also influenced by personal taste and socio-political beliefs as well as conventions and critical biases. This applies, of course, to the words themselves. It requires a strong playwright or a vigilant director to resist the desires of an actor to make a connection right now that would normally happen in the second week of rehearsal. Sometimes I'm afraid that we run roughshod over subtext and subtlety when we don't get it right away. And it's hard to remember that actors are making choices when they read—and sometimes they're making the wrong ones. In a Theatre New Brunswick workshop of *The Horton Syndrome* by Bill Gaston, Paula Wing approached her character one way the first reading and another way the second. If she hadn't had the instincts and skill to experiment, or if she had assumed that the character just didn't work, a cleverly written character portrait would have seemed like an underwritten cliché. It's Bill's first stage play—what are the chances that he would have stuck to his original instincts? If the play doesn't work on the level of the naked word, then it is unlikely to be workshopped in the first place; if it is workshopped, the non-verbal elements will be left to the imagination or read as stage directions. What does this do to the rhythm? The humour? The meaning? We support the belief that a script, an actor, and one light in an empty space is all that theatre is and all it needs to be. Maybe.

To leave the input of designers out of the process of play development reinforces the primacy of the word in a definition of what constitutes text. To develop a script with the aid of actors trained primarily in naturalistic theatre, with its demands for cause-and-effect motivation and "real" conversation, increases the likelihood that the resulting script will respond to the needs. To develop a script with the assistance of a professional dramaturge increases the potential for that script to conform to whatever critical bias that expert has but probably doesn't state (since there are an extraordinary number of theoreticians who will proudly argue that there is only one successful play structure: inciting action, rising action, complication, climax, denouement). To develop new plays under the auspices of a producing company and its strict needs is to limit the initial selection of plays and bias the results accordingly.

In case anyone forgets, I'm talking about theatre practices by people with the best intentions in the world, people who work astonishing hours in gruelling conditions, generally underpaid, scrambling for the tiniest amount of security or a bulwark against a growing deficit. Artistic directors are looking for plays to put into our theatres which will keep the theatres solvent for another season. They do new play development in these interests. Who is going to develop a play which promises to be difficult to cast? Or, if someone does, what do you imagine some of the advice for rewrites will be? Because it demands five senior actors to perform a dense, poetic script, Robyn Marie Butt's *Ghost House Blues* has never been produced. Who is going to develop a play by an unknown writer which is intellectually complex when they will have two and a half weeks to rehearse it? Who is going to develop a technically difficult play when their theatre is understaffed and under-equipped and they have four days to install the production? Who is going to develop a play which is difficult to describe in an ad? How many plays will a theatre develop that is doesn't hope to produce? And if it wants to produce a play, how big a stake does the theatre have in the results of that play's development process?

And what about the biases of the market economy and the subscription season that work their way into workshops? Every artistic director believes s/he knows what the audience will accept or wants to see. These beliefs filter down the organization. The result can be as simple as a suggestion to eliminate all but the most necessary "language." I was guilty of this in a workshop of Marie-Lynn Hammond's *White Weddings*. Luckily for us, her creative solution actually added to the richness of the play. More insidious is the unspoken controversy about the purpose of theatrical characters—that they are supposed somehow to serve as role models in our social system. Women are not supposed to appear as victims. No member of a visible minority, or character of identified ethnic origin, can be evil, nasty, or weak. Politically correct language is encouraged from all characters regardless of point of view or social position. Truly, we can all benefit from a close examination of the iconographic images we unconsciously project and the social realities they support, but let's really look at them, not just change them because "the audience won't like it." And we don't just create theatre to please an audience. We create theatre for critics to say wonderful things about so we can market it. And we know these critics, their biases, and their power pretty well. We create theatre that we *believe* will please the audience we *believe* we have. No one is to be distressed, displeased, challenged, or, God forbid, angered by what they see in our theatres or they will not renew their subscriptions. If we think that these worries don't affect the theatre professional's input in a workshop, then we don't understand what's going on.

So what does this mean? That workshops are of no value? Certainly I have participated in many successful workshops, successful as creative energetic processes, as sources of inspiration and impetus for writers, even resulting in producible plays. But when we create theatre we do not do it in a vacuum. Every circumstance, every choice, affects the results. During the workshop of *Passages*, Kwame Dawes discovered that his practice of editing on the word processor allowed him to rework material without re-reading the whole. I doubt that Kwame appreciated losing his entire play in a computer void, but the result was a closer-written draft with solid transitions and probably a hard-copy edit added to Kwame's future process.

And I'm not suggesting that "objectivity" or "neutral development" is desirable even if we could achieve it. What would the creative process be without passionate bias? But can we not monitor those biases which actually represent a system ensuring its own survival? (Read some cybernetic research—systems perpetuate themselves.) If we don't ask ourselves the questions about the influence of systematic biases on our work, we will only perpetuate them unwittingly. Can we change the systems? Do we want to? Do we have the will to be truly creative and approach each project individually? Or do we believe that people who create exciting theatre are intrinsically more imaginative than we are?

So, what can I do about it? I can insist on a design for each workshop of which I am a part. I can let everyone know (in short form) my biases, in the hope that others will share theirs and we will question all of them. Maybe I can go back to sitting at the table occasionally. Maybe I can remove the table. Maybe we can go outside and play.

(1992)

"Coming Together" in Lift Off! '93: Intercultural Theatre in Toronto and Canadian Multiculturalism [1]
by Mayte Gómez

One of the most remarkable developments in Toronto theatre in the 1990s has been the steady growth and proliferation of work produced by artists of diverse cultural backgrounds. As a result, provincial and local service organizations, funding agencies at all levels of government and even long-established producing companies are experiencing a shift in the way they conceive their support to artists and in the way they operate. It is no longer a matter of course to agree on what is "Canadian" or what is "professional," let alone how "art" or "theatre" should be defined. As the definitions of these terms are challenged, the city's 25-year-old alternate theatre community is being confronted by a younger generation of artists who, far from finding their strength in the search for sameness or in the euphoria of nationalism, unite in the celebration of diversity, searching for meaning in the disrupted narratives of migration and/or exile.

Activities which would have been considered anomalies ten years ago have now become commonplace. Arts councils have created special advisory committees to report on cultural and racial equity and there have been a myriad of public meetings to discuss these issues; service organizations like the Toronto Theatre Alliance (TTA) and Theatre Ontario now have a permanent cross-cultural coordinator in order to provide support to artists from all communities and to initiate new projects; Breaking Ground, a conference for theatre artists of diverse cultures organized by Theatre Ontario in 1992, is successfully establishing itself as an annual event; the TTA and Equity Showcase co-produce The Loon Café at the Equity Studios, a showcase of cross-cultural talent; well-established theatre companies in Toronto are also adapting to the new reality by revising their mandates to include support to artists of diverse cultures.

In their struggle for equality, these artists have touched the heart of the question: the Canadian federal policy of Multiculturalism has not served to ensure equality of access to funding for all professional [2] artists. Despite this policy, artists who work with non-European forms have been victims of the nationalist discourse on which Canadian cultural institutions have been founded, a discourse which inevitably sees Canada exclusively as Anglo-Saxon (or French) [3] and has instituted European-centred concepts of culture, professionalism, and art. Official support for the work of artists from cultures other than British or French has been historically relegated to funding of community art, widely considered to be *amateur,* by the Department of Multiculturalism (now called the Department of Heritage).

It is in the context of the Canadian federal policy of Multiculturalism that I want to look at an important intercultural event which took place in Toronto in the spring of 1993, a festival of play-development workshops produced by Cahoots Theatre Projects, and called "Lift Off! '93." In order to place Lift Off! in a social context, I begin my discussion arguing that the Canadian federal policy of Multiculturalism has served to promulgate a state ideology which, far from defending cultural pluralism, has instituted assimilation of all cultures (acculturation) into a norm. As an artistic event involving different ethnic and cultural groups, and produced in a society ruled by an ideology of acculturation, Lift Off! '93 provided a critique of that ideology while at the same time acting in complicity with it. For I would like to argue that while the content of many of the plays presented subverted to a large extent the ideology of acculturation, the form of dramaturgical development chosen in the workshops served to reproduce it and embrace it, a contradiction which was also present in most of the festival's conditions of production. Above all, it was the euphoria of "coming together" at this festival which allowed for the unconscious reproduction of ideology, the same euphoria which might have been Lift Off!'s most important contribution to theatre in Canada.

* * *

In the mid-1960s Prime Minister Lester Pearson fought against the threat of Quebecois alienation and possible separation by creating the Royal Commission on Bilingualism and Biculturalism [4] with a mandate to "examine how the public institutions should be modified, instrumentally and symbolically, to reflect better the bilingual and bicultural character of the country, while recognizing the contribution of others groups" (Breton 35). In 1967 the Commission published Book 1 of the *Report of the Royal Commission on Bilingualism and Biculturalism,* [5] which defined Canada as a "bicultural" and "bilingual" country, the home of two cultures—British and French—each of them with its respective language. Groups which were neither British nor French were discussed in Book 4 of the *Report* under the general title of *The Cultural Contribution of the Other Ethnic Groups.*

It was no accident that the *Report* chose to speak of the British and French as "cultures" and of the other groups as "ethnic." Modern social science has defined culture as "a way of life that a group of people develops in order to adapt to a set of external and pre-existing conditions" (Li 8). The *Report* also defined culture as "a way of being, thinking and feeling [...] a driving force animating a significant group of individuals united by a common tongue, and sharing the same customs, habits, and experiences" (1: xxxi). In these definitions, culture is an active concept, because it refers to a social system, to a way of life which can be chosen. Culture has a social referent and a social impact: it creates customs, norms, institutions, and, especially, forms of government. In other words, culture is a notion which denotes *material practice.*

On the other hand, modern social scientists have defined an ethnic group as "bound together by common ties of race, nationality, or culture, living together in an alien civilization but remaining culturally distinct" (Ware 607). An "ethnic group" is therefore, a social construct, for it does not refer to blood ties but to a relative social and political position which can be constructed. Thus, the terms "culture" and "ethnic group" seem to be charged with certain social value. A "culture" seems to be a majority group which imposes its material practice onto others. "Ethnic groups" seem to be the minorities which must practice the culture of the majority, their own cultural practice being symbolic in the context of the society at large.

This view by modern social science of ethnic groups has taken hold in Canada at a very grassroots level—in the language and thoughts of ordinary Canadians—but it has also been officially instituted by the *Report*. As a result, when the British and the French are called "cultures" they are recognized as having a social impact, as being the creators and safeguards of the material practice of this country. Offering the excuse that "there are many reasons, the first moral, against considering ethnic difference… as a basic principle for shaping society" (1: xx111), the *Report* argued for the *inclusion of all ethnic groups* into the *two official cultures* in a process of *integration*, for "the good of the society… and the country as a whole" (4: 5).

In 1971, a federal policy of Multiculturalism presented an apparently new vision of Canada: a country with two official languages but no official culture. This new vision, together with the use of terms such as "cultural pluralism" and "cultural freedom" seemed to depart from what the *Report* had proposed, for in coining the term "Multiculturalism" Prime Minister Trudeau was apparently raising the "ethnic groups" to the category of "cultures." The change was mainly nominal, however, for Multiculturalism included no discussion of how these cultures would have an impact on Canadian society. The new policy in no way meant that Canada was to accept different cultural systems, but simply that it was important to preserve "as much of ethnic cultures as (was) compatible with Canadian customs" (ECC 32). In this light, the apparently ground-breaking notion of "cultural freedom" simply meant freedom to honour one's ethnic origins, while "cultural pluralism" was reduced to an official recognition of "the many different ethnic origins" of the Canadian population, regulating "equality of opportunity for all *within the existing political system*" (Hawkins 11; emphasis added).

Throughout this essay I will refer to the acculturation instituted by the *Report* and the policy of Multiculturalism as the ideology of Multiculturalism, understanding ideology as the act of "*legitimating* the power of a dominant social group or class" (Eagleton 5), and I will argue that the presence of this ideology is the main "condition of production" as Althusser would call it, of intercultural artistic practice, just as it is of any other aspect of life in Canada. This is the ideology which was both subverted and reproduced in Cahoots Theatre Projects' Life Off! '93. [6]

* * *

Cahoots was founded in 1985 by Beverly Yhap, with an artistic mandate to develop and produce new Canadian work by theatre artists of diverse cultures, in order to reflect "the personal face of difference in (an) increasingly complex and multiracial society" (Cahoots, 1993/94, n. pag.). Some of Cahoots' major initiatives during its first years of operation were: "The Phoenix Cabaret," a collection of plays which had been banned in China, directed by Peter Hinton at the Factory Studio Café in 1988; the playwrights' conference Write About Now! in 1990; and the production of Daniel David Moses's *Big Buck City* at the Tarragon Theatre during the 1991–1992 season.

In the winter of 1992 Cahoots began a new phase under the leadership of two new co-artistic directors, Jean Yoon and Lynda Hill, [7] as well as a newly-formed advisory committee and a revitalized board of directors. The revised mandate of the company, as outlined in its mission statement, included a commitment to

> developing and presenting new Canadian work that recognizes the pluralities of Canadian society, and seeks the participation of artists of diverse cultures as writers and collaborators to create work that represents the full range and diversity of the Canadian experience. Within this framework, Cahoots Theatre Projects attempts to pursue work that is intercultural and interdisciplinary, that bridges traditions, cultural and artistic, and challenges them. (Hill)

An essential component of this new artistic phase, Lift Off! was conceived as a six-week festival of workshops in which seven new scripts would be developed. Among them were several from South Asian, First Nations, and Korean playwrights. *The Shaman of Waz* by Lorre Jensen, *Noran Bang: The Yellow Room* by M.J. Kang, *Seven Year Cycle* by Sonia Dhillon, *No Man's Land* by Rahul Varma, *Belle* by Florence Gibson, *The Moon and Dead Indians* by Daniel David Moses, and *Canadian Monsoon* by Sheila James were all at different stages of development: while some were collections of loose scenes, others were quite sophisticated and complete first drafts. The dramaturge/directors invited for the occasion were Lynda Hill, Marion de Vries, Sally Han, Sandi Ross, and Colin Taylor. In association with The Canadian Stage Company, Cahoots presented a weekend of public readings from Lift Off! at the Rehearsal Hall of the Berkeley St. Theatre during the first days of May. A Sunday afternoon public forum with all the playwrights and dramaturges involved in the workshops also took place that weekend. In November of 1993 Cahoots presented a workshop production of three scripts—*Canadian Monsoon, The Moon and Dead Indians,* and *Noran Bang: The Yellow Room*—under the generic name of "3D: Three Daring New Works by Playwrights of Diverse Cultures," in co-production with Theatre Passe Muraille as part of its Backspace Series.[8]

A few weeks after the workshop of Lorre Jensen's *The Shaman of Waz* ended, the entire team of actors, dramaturge, playwright, and musician got together once more in order to tape a rehearsal for the public reading. Judging by the mood and the spirit in the rehearsal space at that time, it was obvious that the workshop had been extremely successful, for everyone seemed to be quite happy not only to see one another again but also to have the opportunity to work once more as a group. Dramaturge Lynda Hill invited the actors to join her in a circle in order for them to welcome one another to the new session. She asked each of them to share his/her feelings with the rest of the group by saying one word, which all of them would then repeat ad infinitum while exchanging places with others in the circle. The actors responded to this request enthusiastically with words such as "ethos," "thrilled," "cool," "relieved," and "elated." One of the actors greeted the others with a magic word: "together!"

As I watched the group play the game, my thoughts remained fixed on that word. "Together" is the title of the official magazine from the old Multiculturalism and Citizenship Canada, a publication dedicated to convince new citizens that Canada is not a racist country. "Together" is the underlying romantic philosophy of the Multiculturalism advertisements which show the "happy" pictures of the Canadian "mosaic." "Together" can be a symbol for the ideology of Multiculturalism, a "nice," "tolerant," and romantic word which has only served to mask the reality of accultur-ation with the happy faces of Canada's many races. At Lift Off! '93 to come "together" was a source of power and liberation for many communities but it was also danger-ously similar to the masking of acculturation, although this time it was done quite unconsciously by people who thought they were liberating themselves from it.

It was in the content of the plays in progress submitted for the workshops that Lift Off!'s ideological subversion was more obvious, as many of them dwelled on the different ways in which acculturation takes place in Canada and searched for ways to counteract it.

Sonia Dhillon's *Seven Year Cycle* deals with the friendship between Jennifer and Mara (an English Canadian and a South Asian Canadian) and the lack of under-standing between them, or rather Jennifer's lack of commitment to "understand" Mara. Jennifer fails to appreciate Mara's desire to remain in touch with her own cul-tural background, her need to do political work, or her search for communication with people of colour. As their friendship becomes stalled and ends in rupture, Jennifer personifies the English Canadian who wants to "understand" the "other," wanting to know more about Mara's language or her place of origin, only for those to remain symbolic. "I am your friend not because of where you come from, but because of who you are,"[9] says Jennifer, oblivious to the fact that "who" Mara "is" is necessarily framed by where she comes from. Without her cultural background as part of her identity, Mara is "reduced" to being simply a "human being," one who presumably must be judged solely by the virtues of her soul. Jennifer is effectively re-stating an essentialist humanist vision in which the notion of the "universality" all humans are said to share often serves to ignore difference and legitimate the existence of a norm.

Foregrounding this issue as the major theme of the play served to not only explore what it means for people of different cultural backgrounds to make the effort to "understand," but it also served to affirm quite strongly that such "understanding" must be redefined. Indeed, to "understand" must go beyond the mere symbolism of "knowing" (what language one speaks, where one was born) or "respecting." Instead it should mean that the culture which occupies the position of power must actively step back while the "other" culture claims its own space, its own role as protagonist in its story, its own struggles and contradictions, its own searches, in a final attempt to erase its "otherness" and be equal.

The protagonists of M.J. Kang's *Noran Bang: The Yellow Room* are a Korean couple who immigrate to Canada with their two daughters. The couple represents two extreme situations: while the father seems to have accepted acculturation quite happily, Omma (the mother) rejects Canadian culture completely. The father aims to be like his "Canadian" co-workers, willingly assuming their patterns of behaviour and cultural codes. Omma only thinks of returning home to attend to her own mother, who is dying. Between these two extremes is their elder daughter, Gyung-June, occupying an unstable border in which she refuses to commit to either extreme. She is neither acculturated into a norm nor forced to go back to Korea in order to find happiness. For her, the cultural border is a place where both cultures, Korean and Canadian, are in continuous struggle but where she can also find the co-existence of the two, as they affect each other, allowing neither one of them to take over nor to remain static. On this border there is no symbolic ethnic background, but two live cultures which must come to terms with each other. The final message of the play, however, does not seem to have faith in this border, for the family eventually breaks up: Omma and Gyung-June go back to Korea while the father and the younger daughter remain in Canada.

While the content of many plays in Lift Off! [10] dealt directly with the acculturation suffered by many cultural communities in Canada, this did not seem to be an issue for the festival itself.

The politics of identity among such a cultural mixture were resolved by Cahoots quite easily, for, as might be expected to happen in a play-development workshop, the company constructed the playwrights as the focus of the workshops, which were "dedicated to celebrating their voice and their vision" (Cahoots, "Lift Off! '93," n. pag.) As a result, the dramaturges' role was defined as the selfless activity of "serving the playwright's vision" or allowing the playwright's cultural milieu to "flourish" in the text. Dramaturges were not offered a prescriptive model to achieve those goals. Instead, each individual was given responsibility for her [11] workshop and was encouraged to design her own model of work. Although presumably they were selected not only because of their talents but because of their different cultures and races, as it is clearly outlined in Cahoots' mandate regarding the work of collaborators, dramaturges were not given any indications as to whether or not their model should be culturally specific, the only unofficial agreement being that their role was to be "curious" about the playwright's culture and incorporate that knowledge into the work.

This mandate turned out to be an irony and a troubled space. In the first place, it is quite naive to assume that a dramaturge can selflessly "serve" a playwright without incorporating her own vision, whether she considers that vision her own as an individual or as culturally specific. Second, it is rather ironic that in a workshop with artists of so many cultures and produced by a company with an intercultural mandate, integration among cultures was not encouraged. As a result of this unacknowledged irony, it is not surprising that all dramaturges pursued quite a conventional dramaturgical model based on character development and play structure, traditional pillars of play construction as we know it in the West. Although this dramaturgical model was executed with different levels of ability, talent, and originality, it differed little from one workshop to another or from the one which could have been used by any other theatre company in Toronto, with an intercultural mandate or not.

Once all dramaturges were using similar strategies in order to achieve similar goals—improvisations to develop characters psychologically or to imagine scenes yet unwritten, discussions around the essence of a scene or a character in order to give new ideas to the playwright, editing of text to improve writing style and find the proper order of scenes—once, that is, all dramaturges were operating from a common norm, the playwrights' vision was no longer served. For in this way all texts underwent similar processes of development which, far from allowing the playwrights' cultural milieu to "flourish," buries them in a form to which they did not belong. For the most part, the workshops did not rely on artistic forms which might be considered South Asian, or First Nations, for example, to help develop the plays. In some cases, music and dance were used as additions to the scenes, but, they were simply ornaments or links between scenes rather than a tool for the development of the work.

Eventually, this structurally homogenous position from which all dramaturges worked betrayed their intentions. For, I would argue, the use of a theatrical form familiar to the West, and in this specific case to Canada, in order to work with plays written by a group of playwrights whose range of cultural identities goes from North American First Nations to South Asian, can only be read as a microcosm of a society in which members of these cultural groups are also integrated into a normative cultural practice, a society in which they lose their specificity and their difference remains purely symbolic.

Yet, it might be argued, these plays were given workshops which served to develop their texts during an early stage. Formal concerns need only be brought up at the time of full production. The way text is developed, however, is bound to mark the play's future development, and it is likely that the playwright will continue working within the framework in which her work is already evolving. More importantly, it is not clear to me why we should assume that the research of formal elements (beyond their role as ornamental) would not serve to develop the text, or, for that matter, why the text alone had to be the focus of the work just because the plays were drafts in progress. Could not the form have been considered an integral part of the play and, therefore, something which had to be fully explored as well, even at that early stage? Whether or not Lift Off!'s dramaturges and producers thought form was only relevant at the time of full production and whether or not these plays will end up being produced with a greater emphasis on form, the point is they were all developed under a theatrical vision in which form does not affect content. I cannot believe that South Asian, Korean, and First Nations theatres do not have a meaningful and challenging answer to that vision. Since the philosophy of the workshops and the dramaturgical exercises used in them did not differ much from those which could have been used in workshops led by English Canadians choosing to work in a conservative Western style, it becomes difficult to see in which way Lift Off! "bridge(d) traditions, cultural and artistic, and challenge(d) them".

At the forum held as part of the Lift Off! public readings, Sally Han remarked that all dramaturges seemed to have chosen an "English Canadian" model of work. Although other dramaturges might have also been aware of this contradiction at an individual level, it never seemed to be an issue of concern during group discussions or during actual work in the workshops.[12] I think it would be fair to say, then, that in the collective, acculturation into a theatrical form took place unconsciously. Even so, however, I think it would also be appropriate to say that the diversity of cultures was, in this sense, quite symbolic.

To illustrate how a stronger emphasis on form could have also helped the play develop, I would like to compare the workshops, public readings, and later workshop productions of Sheila James's *Canadian Monsoon*, directed by Lynda Hill, and of M.J. Kang's *Noran Bang: The Yellow Room*, directed by Marion de Vries.

Hill and de Vries are both white Canadians of European descent and they both chose dramaturgical models which heavily relied on psychological development of characters and play structure. However, while Hill seemed to focus only on text, de Vries focused as well on some formal elements, including a stylized and symbolic blocking used to search for the meaning of the play as the dramaturge, playwright, and actors saw it—the cultural border—and which began to give the play its specific form. Watching this form develop, M.J. Kang realized the nature of the scenes she had written (some were "dreams" and some "reality"), and understood better the frames of time and space she wanted to convey, all of which were built into the story. The workshop of *Canadian Monsoon*, on the other hand, focused much more on working with the text, developing existing scenes, creating and then developing others as well as correcting the lack of development of certain characters, as reflected in their text.

When *Canadian Monsoon* was read in public, the playwright received the only standing ovation of the entire event. A powerful cast and a more developed text, aided by some rehearsal, resulted in a good performance at the public reading. *Noran Bang*, however, did quite poorly, despite the fact that the reading was accompanied by live music. Stripped of its powerful symbolic blocking, which gave meaning to the text and which had been the focus to develop it, the actors' lines seemed rather lifeless.

Six months later both plays were given workshop productions at Theatre Passe Muraille's Backspace as part of "3D." When slides of South Asian images as well as South Asian music and dance were added to the text of *Canadian Monsoon*, the strength of the text seemed to disappear; form and text appeared disjointed, as if occasionally stylized blocking and the use of South Asian movement/dance could not hide the fact that the text had not been developed for them. It seemed more as if a realist text had been put onto some elements of South Asian form. In my opinion, the result was incongruous, and I do not believe this incongruity was the director's conscious intention. Rather, I believe it resulted from the interaction of a text and a form which had little to do with each other. Meanwhile, the workshop production of *Noran Bang* appeared more developed and advanced. I believe this was because the further development of symbolic blocking and the more sophisticated use of Korean music and movement was quite harmonious with a non-realist text which had already been developed by and for these forms.

Noran Bang, however, was an exception in Lift Off! For the most part, as formal elements were of little concern during the workshops, acculturation into an incongruous artistic form was pervasive. Content and form were seen as separate categories, and in that separation they contributed to create the festival's greatest contradiction: while it was pursuing an intercultural exchange, it ended up reproducing acculturation. This contradiction and the eventual betrayal of intentions was also a dialectical force in Lift Off!'s material condition of production. The festival of workshops and the public readings were a triumph for activists in cultural policy. In Lift Off! as a collective event, dozens of artists from several cultures assumed without apology the roles of protagonists as creators and organizers. As a group, they owned the means of production which made their work possible. They gained access to public funding, chose to work on specific scripts which were of interest to them, were able to have their work developed by actors from the same cultural groups, had a public reading, in which they were (and very importantly too, were perceived as being) the sole protagonists, and had an opportunity to voice the issues and struggles they believed are important in Canada. The workshops, first of their kind, became an event in the Toronto theatre community. The readings were well attended and well covered by the press, and in them the spirit was certainly one of empowerment for the community, both on and off stage. In this way, artists of diverse cultures reclaimed their voices as full protagonists in the theatre community and in society at large, occupying a place which was hardly "symbolic." By standing together and strong, they refused to simply be "melted" into a homogenized theatre community.

But the irony is always latent in any activity whose mandate is to empower those who might be considered "other" by a "norm," for such a mandate re-established the dichotomy norm-other and it furthers the separation. After all, Lift Off! isolated all participants as "other ethnic groups" in order to work "together" as "others," in a separate place from the "mainstream" cultures (and by that I mean both the Charter cultural groups and the mainstream artistic community). However, such irony might be impossible to escape. And the best Cahoots can do is to hope that it will "work itself out of a job," as its artistic directors and board members often say. The best, that is, might simply be to continue the fight so that there will be a time when theatre artists of diverse cultures will produce their work in equality of conditions with other artists in Toronto.

In Lift Off! '93 space was also an important material condition with ideological contradictions. The workshops took place next to the Cahoots office, in a space specially rented for the occasion, a place near the nurturer, a place where everyone was family, indeed a protected space. The public readings, however, were held in the Rehearsal Hall of the Canadian Stage Company, a significant change of context. The Canadian Stage Company might be regarded by many as the epitome of the Toronto English Canadian theatre establishment. Most often this is because of hegemonic connotations in the use of the word "Canadian" by a company founded and operating in Toronto, but in this case it is also because of the connotation of "Canadian" as "Anglo-Saxon." The presence in this space of Cahoots and its audience, a group in which the majority are not Anglo-Saxon Canadians, might be considered an act of defiance against the system from within. For the first time, "Canadian" Stage was to have playwrights of distinct cultural backgrounds in its space. However, the challenge was minimized by the simple fact that the audience would have gone to a different space—The Theatre Centre, for example, or even the workshop space rented by Cahoots—for it was clearly an audience made up of friends, colleagues, and sympathizers, a very faithful group. The work was not presented to the general audience of the Canadian Stage Company, which would normally consist of other people who might never go to Cahoots' own space.

Furthermore, the Rehearsal Hall of Canadian Stage became a symbol of inequality for these artists and the audience, as they were all relegated to a smaller space—one for "rehearsal," not even for full "production"—within a "Canadian" theatre, a space certainly separate and rather unequal. "Today the rehearsal hall, tomorrow the mainstage" was the statement made by the co-artistic directors as they introduced the readings, quite aware perhaps of the position they were occupying. With this statement, they unconsciously sent two contradictory messages to the audience: one of strength, for Cahoots will one day be powerful enough, and cultural diversity so widely accepted that they will be able to be produced on the Canadian Stage main stage like any other company; and another message of despair, for to get there Cahoots must first "grow up."

If Lift Off!'s most efficient strategy to resist acculturation was the power of coming "together," its most important shortcoming was to pretend to create that togetherness in isolation, without dealing at the same time with the "real" social and political milieu in which it was taking place. The "reality" in Canadian society is that we are affected by a policy of Multiculturalism which has strong ideological implications. To clear the way in order to create something else, we must first counteract the power of that ideology. Anything else is an illusion of freedom.

Freedom, however, could be less illusory. But to fully understand how it might be so is going to be a long and arduous task for all artists involved in diverse cultural communities. During the workshops and the public readings, participants in Lift Off!, and even members of the audience, seemed to build an unofficial but powerful discourse of universality, which seemed to suggest that despite cultural differences, everybody could relate to most of the plays, presumably meaning everybody could "understand" them. This, I believe, must be challenged on two grounds. In the first place, the desire to search for universality seemed to prevent participants in Lift Off! from dealing with the politics of representation in the workshops. Perhaps the clearest example was the way in which the workshop of *Belle* was constructed. Florence Gibson, a white woman, wrote a play about the struggle of a black woman suffering the double lot of her race and gender in the historical context of the suffragist movement. Throughout the festival, great efforts were made not to make an issue out of the fact that a white woman was writing a play about the lot of a black one. Of course, the presence of a black dramaturge and two black actors (as well as of Lynda Hill, Cahoots' artistic director, playing the only white character) might have been read as the first sign of the acceptance of the script. During the public forum, Sandi Ross, the dramaturge of the workshop, passionately argued that she did not see anything wrong with a white woman writing the story of two black people, or with herself, as a black director, supporting that, because—she said—the workshops "(were) not about power." In informal conversations during the festival, Florence Gibson was always zealously over-protected, leaving no room for anybody to judge her. More importantly, when one of the black actors in the cast began to feel uncomfortable about having a white woman writing the story, her discomfort was dealt with outside of the workshop and, as far as I could tell, it never became a collective issue to be reckoned with.

If the same situation had taken place in a company like Nightwood Theatre, for instance, a company where the issue of race and the politics of representation have been quite alive in recent years, it is likely that it would have been an issue with which to contend. In Cahoots, however, there was no space to discuss the politics of representation or the construction of "otherness," for the unspoken agreement among all seemed to be that all stories were "universal," and therefore anybody could write about anybody else.

The desire for universality must also be challenged on other grounds. In a social, cultural, and political reality of acculturation, it is quite dangerous to emphasize what different cultures have in common, what is "universal" to all of them, in order to search for empowerment. After all, the critique of liberal humanism should have already taught us that discourses of universality can easily turn into political strategies for powerful groups to perpetuate their power. In Toronto, to look for the universal characteristics of all cultures means to bring out of them what they share by virtue of being acculturated into the Anglo-Saxon dominant culture.

To focus on difference instead would not mean an inability to create strategic alliances when needed. It would not mean to encourage the maintenance of traditional cultural codes which might need to evolve. To encourage difference in a multicultural [13] society and multicultural theatre community would mean to encourage interaction among cultures which are always in constant movement and which are affecting one another in a very specific geographic, political, and historical context. To search for the universal takes us to the normative, to the static and unchangeable. To search for difference creates movement, interaction.

Otherwise, Canadian intercultural artistic practice might not be very different from what at the international level is known as "intercultural performance," as practiced by well-known directors such as Peter Brook, Eugenio Barba, or Richard Schechner. This kind of performance selects performative signs and performance styles from diverse cultures with the aim of selecting what is universal to all of them. In the process, the specificity and distinctiveness of a given culture might disappear for the benefit of what is "universal" from the point of view of a European or North American director. [14] The discourses of Canadian Multiculturalism and of the Canadian state in general have already bombarded us with enough romantic rhetoric about the "universal" values of Canadians, that is, about what makes us all the same. It is time, I think, to focus on what makes us different, not to separate us or to isolate us from one another, but to bring to the fore new cultural codes and practices so that they might challenge Canadian culture as we know it.

Perhaps we can take to an extreme what Barbara Godard has called the "aesthetics of difference," for it is not only a matter of different cultures and marginalized races enjoying a greater recognition. It is also a matter of making sure that in the theatre community this difference is truly "aesthetic," that is, of making sure it manifests itself in the form in which new scripts are developed. And it is also a matter of transferring the "aesthetics of difference" to the audience, so that the production of difference will challenge individuals and collectives to expand the ways in which they produce meaning and receive the production of art.

Freedom would also be less illusory if we could acknowledge the complicity of our artistic practice in the reproduction of ideology, for self-consciousness, as I would argue with Arif Dirlik, is the "point of departure for all critical understanding and, by implication, for all radical activity," for otherwise we "remain imprisoned... in the cultural unconscious" (395).

To be self-conscious means to produce in a mode of self-reflexivity. As Linda Hutcheon has argued, self-reflexivity serves to "de-naturalize some of the dominant features of our way of life; to point out that those entities that we unthinkingly experience as 'natural'... are in fact 'cultural,' made by us, not given to us." In a self-reflexive mode, one presents oneself as an ideological subject, one in dialogue with the dominant discourse, even if still determined by it, able to enter that discourse, exploring its cracks, its contradictions, so that one can counteract its power, creating "a field of contesting knowledges rather than [a] monolithic, totalitarian imposition of the Law" (Godard 195). Intercultural self-reflexive theatre might thus serve to underline the fact that all cultural forms of representation are grounded in ideology and that they cannot "avoid involvement with social and political relations and apparatuses" (Hutcheon 3).

At the individual level, artists might find personal ways to incorporate a self-reflexive mode into their work. At the collective level, intercultural theatre companies like Cahoots can defy reproduction of the ideology of Multiculturalism by interrogating its own practices, especially play-development workshops. As part of this interrogation, questions regarding intercultural relationships and homogenization, politics of identity and representation must be fore-grounded as important issues by which the artistic interaction of different cultures is irremediably framed.

Self-reflexivity is a process not only for artists but also for audiences. As Susan Bennett has argued, "Theatre audiences bring to any performance a horizon of cultural and ideological expectations," but those expectations should not be seen as "fixed," for they are "always tested by [...] the [...] production" (107) and therefore "open to renegotiation" (114). If multicultural audiences are exposed to theatrical forms which not all individuals might have the ability to decode, the existing interpretative processes might be "open to renegotiation." In this case, the audience of this intercultural event would also differ from that of an international intercultural performance. While in intercultural performance people are presented with cultural codes which are *out of context*, that is, which will have no effect in their own cultural milieu, in a Canadian intercultural event, *a context has to be created* for the interaction of cultural codes, that is, they must be used to produce real change in society. For the point is, precisely, not to *transcend* the difficulty in decoding the cultural codes, as practitioners of intercultural performance would have it, but to accept it until it produces a change both in the theatre and in society at large.

However we choose to approach this question, our illusion of freedom must be faced. Otherwise, is intercultural theatre not a naive attempt to assert that we are not framed at all by the ideologies of the society in which we live, that we can just get "together" and forget about relations of power because "our" work is not about that, because "our" work is about coming "together" instead of allowing the "norm" to separate us further from one another? The most crucial answer to this question is that ignoring the existence of ideology is, ultimately, the most powerful contribution to its reproduction.

As Terry Eagleton has argued, "[t]he study of ideology is among other things an inquiry into the ways in which people may come to invest in their own unhappiness" (xiii). It is true that, as individual artists and members of this society, many people are caught in the web of ideology in the form of quite a powerful (and often painful) incongruity between their political beliefs and their most "natural" thoughts and actions with which they unconsciously reproduce ideology. In discussions around issues of political and cultural activism, as well as in everyday life, many theatre artists and cultural activists have come to acknowledge the ingrained racism, sexism, and homophobia which their own actions perpetuate.

I think it would be fair to say that many of the individuals involved in Lift Off! '93 have experienced this incongruity at a personal level, as artists and/or activists. Yet it was remarkable how the apparent power of the collective, the power of being "together," erased all possibilities for that contradiction to emerge. Coming "together" became a way to survive, to become empowered, to create a new form in which ideological subtleties were no longer an issue, in which all participants could be free to be themselves and to be "different" from one another, as if the small rehearsal space—and even the Rehearsal Hall at Canadian Stage—could be a temporary haven, freed from outside influences and finally able to institute a perfect model of work, so "perfect" that possible confrontation was overridden by the feeling of empowerment. If the scripts dared to foreground ideological contradictions it was because they dealt with society. The workshops themselves, however, seemed to function as self-referential entities, which—unlike society—were not subject to scrutiny.

Without that self-scrutiny, Lift Off! '93 was free to act out what might be everybody's dream: a community of theatre artists of diverse cultures getting together in the most natural and innocent way, just going about their work without having to think twice about the political or ideological implications of what they were doing. Until that dream becomes a reality, however, the act of envisioning it alone will only make it impossible to accomplish, unless we also deal with the reality in which we live, for as we ignore the ideology around us we become more immersed in it.

As the ideology of Multiculturalism is confronted and our acts of coming "together" become less a danger of acculturation and more a simple political strategy, our notion of Multiculturalism might give way to the vision for which Lift Off! planted a seed: a theatre community and a society in which all cultures are practiced in equal terms, artistically and otherwise. The challenge is already here, as a new vision struggling to break free, a vision for a country which truly believes in social justice as well as in cultural and artistic freedom.

(1994)

Works Cited

Althusser, Louis. "Ideology and Ideological State Apparatuses (Notes Toward an Investigation)." *For Marx.* Trans. Ben Brewster. London: Allen Lane, 1969. 127–87.

Breton, Raymond, Jeffrey G. Reitz and Victor F. Valentine. *Cultural Boundaries and the Cohesion of Canada.* Montreal: Institute for Research on Public Policy/L'Institut de recherches politiques, 1980.

Cahoots Theatre Projects. *1993/94 Season: Dynamic New Work By Theatre Artists of Diverse Cultures.* Toronto, 1993.

Canada. Royal Commission on Bilingualism and Biculturalism. *General Introduction: the Official Languages.* Book 1 of *Report of the Royal Commission on Bilingualism and Biculturalism.* Ottawa: Queen's Printer, 1967.

————. *The Cultural Contribution of the Other Ethnic Groups.* Book 4 of *Report of the Royal Commission on Bilingualism and Biculturalism.* Ottawa: Queen's Printer, 1970.

Dhillon, Sonia. *Seven Year Cycle.* Unpublished ms.

Dirlik, Artif. "Culturalism as Hegemonic Ideology and Liberating Practice." *The Nature and Context of Minority Discourse.* Ed. Abdul R. JanMohamed and David Lloyd. New York: Oxford UP, 1990. 394–431.

Eagleton, Terry. *Ideology: An Introduction.* London: Verso, 1991.

Economic Council of Canada (ECC). *New Faces in the Crowd: Economic and Social Impacts of Immigration.* Ottawa: ECC, 1991.

Gibson, Florence. *Belle.* Unpublished ms. [Editor's note: since published, Toronto: Playwrights Canada, 2000.]

Godard, Barbara. "The Politics of Representation: Some Native Canadian Women Writers." *Canadian Literature* 124/125 (1990): 183–225.

Gómez, Mayte. "Shifting Borders: A Project of Interculturalism in Canadian Theatre." MA Thesis. U of Guelph, 1993.

Hawkins, Freda. "Canadian Multiculturalism: The Policy Explained." *Canadian Mosaic: Essays on Multiculturalism.* Ed. A.J. Fry and C. Forceville. Canada Cahiers no. 3. Amsterdam: Free UP, 1988. 9–24.

Hill, Lynda. Telephone Interview. 8 August 1993.

Hutcheon, Linda. *The Politics of Postmodernism.* London: Routledge, 1989.

Kang, M.J. *Noran Bang: The Yellow Room.* Unpublished ms. [Editor's note: since published, Toronto: Playwrights Canada, 2000.]

James, Sheila. *Canadian Monsoon.* Unpublished ms.

Li, Peter S. "Race and Ethnicity." *Race and Ethnic Relations in Canada.* Ed. Peter S. Li. Toronto: Oxford UP, 1990. 3–17.

Marranca, Bonnie and Gautam Dasgupta, eds. *Interculturalism and Performance.* New York: PAJ Publications, 1991.

Moses, Daniel David. *The Moon and Dead Indians.* Unpublished ms. [Editor's note: since published in *Staging Coyote's Dream*, Vol. II, Toronto: Playwrights Canada, 2009.]

Varma, Rahul. *No Man's Land.* Unpublished ms.

Ware, C. "Ethnic communities." *Encyclopaedia of the Social Sciences.* Vol. 5. New York: Macmillan, 1931. 607–13.

[1] This paper is a revised version of a chapter from "Shifting Borders: A Project of Interculturalism in Canadian Theatre," a Master's thesis submitted to the Drama Department of Drama at the University of Guelph in August 1993. I am indebted to Professor Ric Knowles, my thesis advisor, for his invaluable help and support in the process of writing that thesis.

[2] By "professional" I mean an artist who is recognized as such by his/her peers, who has some kind of training in the field (formal or not) and who would pursue his/her art on a full-time basis if he/she were able to do so. However, this definition has not been accepted by the arts councils until quite recently.

[3] The two "Charter" cultures in Canada, recognized by the Constitution, are the British and the French. In the context of this essay, I deal with an artistic event taking place in Toronto, in which the "Charter" culture is British, and therefore will refer to Anglo-Saxon culture as the norm, on the understanding that I am referring to Toronto and not to Canada as a whole.

[4] Canada's Royal Commission on Bilingualism and Biculturalism will be subsequently referred to as the Commission.

[5] Subsequently referred to as the *Report.*

[6] A more detailed discussion of the ideology of Multiculturalism and of the implications of the division into "cultures" and "ethnic groups" is offered in the first chapters of my Master's thesis, "Shifting Borders: A Project of Interculturalism in Canadian Theatre." As I begin now to discuss Cahoots Theatre Projects' Lift Off! '93, I must also thank Lynda Hill and Jean Yoon, artistic directors of the company in 1993, for kindly allowing me to be present as an observer during the six weeks of Lift Off!. I would like to take this opportunity to thank the playwrights, dramaturges, and actors involved in the workshops for their generosity and support. I was a silent observer of most workshops in Lift Off!, as well as the moderator for the public forum held as part of the public readings, to which I will refer in the rest of the essay. As a member of Cahoots' Artistic Advisory Committee, as well as a member at large and friend of the company while I lived in Toronto, and as a working theatre artist who is neither of British nor French origin, I have always had a personal interest in Cahoots' work, and this paper reflects that interest. In gratitude to the artists who allowed me to watch their work, I want to emphasize that the ideological analysis which follows is not meant to judge individual intentions or desires. Rather, it is meant to reveal the ways in which we are all ideological subjects. Thus, I do not attempt to judge anyone's work in particular, but to point out what our work implies. In the rest of this essay I sometimes refer to Lift Off! participants as "they" but for the most part I use an inclusive "we" in the discussion, as I wish to include myself and my work in it.

[7] In the spring of 1994, both Jean Yoon and Lynda Hill resigned as artistic directors, and Dillara Ally, a former apprentice producer for the company, became acting artistic director.

[8] In support of 3D, Theatre Passe Muraille also organized "The 3D Multimedia Festival," with lobby displays, a visual art/book exhibit and a late-night cabaret

which featured the work of South Asian, First Nations, and Korean artists in Toronto.

[9]   For this essay I have used the unpublished manuscripts of all of Lift Off!'s plays, of which I have several versions, written as the workshops developed. Therefore, I am unable to offer consistent page numbers.

[10]   I am constrained by reasons of space and I am not able to discuss the content of other plays. Rahul Varma's *No Man's Land* also dealt with acculturation in Canadian society, as well as with the particular struggle of the Indian people. The two First Nations plays were quite different from the others: *The Shaman of Waz* was a symbolic tale of spiritual search, and *The Moon and Dead Indians* was the story of two white men in the American far West and their construction of "Indians." *Belle* is discussed later in this paper. For more information see "Shifting Borders."

[11]   Since most participants in Lift Off!, dramaturges and playwrights alike, were women, I use the feminine form to refer to all of them.

[12]   I was invited by Cahoots' artistic directors to attend all workshop sessions with the actors. However, I had no access to meetings between dramaturges and playwrights, for those were organized privately. Only in a particular case, in which the dramaturge was a very close friend, did I attend a work meeting between her and the playwright. As a result, I cannot account for conversations which took place outside the rehearsal space, or even for those which took place during sessions I could not attend. Neither can I account for private conversations between the artistic directors or between either one of them and playwrights or dramaturges. When I say that a particular issue seemed to be of no concern in the workshops, I am obviously referring to the sessions to which I had access. I assume this clarification in future statements.

[13]   In this case I use the word "multicultural" with a small "m," for I am not using it to refer to the federal policy, but simply as an adjective to indicate the presence of many different cultures.

[14]   For a detailed discussion of intercultural performance, see the introduction to my "Shifting Borders," and for a comparison between this kind of performance and what I suggest could be a model of interculturalism for Canada, see chapter three of the same work. For controversial discussions on intercultural performance and cultural imperialism see Marranca and Dasgupta.

Opting In: Theory, Practice and the Workshop as Alternative "Process"
by Beth Herst

The space between two stools is, proverbially, an undesirable location, the place you fall to, if you're not careful, through lack of commitment, or agility, or both. It can, however, also be a rather interesting vantage point from which to consider the implications of bridges. As a practicing playwright who teaches what could loosely be called feminist theory, I have become increasingly aware of a tension between the two activities, a widening gap between these particular stools that threatens to turn into a chasm. As a result, I've found myself thinking about bridges a great deal, and still more about the spaces they traverse.

Conflict between theory and practice, teaching and doing, is hardly an unfamiliar dilemma. In my case, however, it is not my personal practice that poses the problem. As a writer I have no difficulty integrating my theoretical interests (representation, performance, feminist poststructuralist theory generally) with my imaginative concerns. The two are inseparable, and mutually informing. The difficulty comes, rather, after the writing, in that other half of a playwright's creative enterprise, namely, the collaborative business of turning text into performance. It comes, in other words, in the encounter with the institutionalized structures and practices governing the production of scripts in the so-called mainstream of not-for-profit theatre in this country.

The Mainstream and "The Process"

Teaching, and studying, feminist theories of theatre and drama, I am continually reminding myself and others that modes of production are both constitutive and "political." It is one of the first principles of my discipline: the way theatre is made has a determinant effect on the kind of theatre that results, and that way is never ideologically neutral. We cannot separate the "how" from the "what," the means by which theatrical meaning is, literally, produced and that meaning itself. Writing plays, however, and seeking both the widest possible audience and the greatest possible material support for them, I am confronted with a mode of production, a "process," predicated on precisely those forms and assumptions my theoretical commitments most impel me to challenge. The dilemma is not merely academic. Increasingly, for me, artistic and intellectual imperatives—and the two cannot be separated—battle professional self-interest, with the battleground the dominant mode of theatrical production, the very means of making theatre itself.

What is this problematic process? Simply, the institutional and creative apparatus for developing, rehearsing and mounting text-based productions common to most not-for-profit theatres in Canada. I am not claiming absolute uniformity. Clearly, the mechanism can, and does, vary in its operations from theatre to theatre and project to project. The assumptions shaping it, however, do not. And it is these normative assumptions which are the issue. For they ground a production process that is both linear and teleological, progressing through a series of developmental stages (the read-through, blocking, scene and character work, first run-through, "tech," previews) to the final goal: a coherent, unified performance text in the service of a master interpretation, or concept, or vision. Ostensibly collaborative in its involvement of writer, performers, designers, and technicians, it is a process that still presumes a fixed hierarchy of interpretive authority. To use the current jargon, it is, almost invariably, director-led.

In other words, "the process" is predicated on a particular understanding not just of the theatrical enterprise, but of interpretation and meaning themselves, an understanding so fully naturalized as to have become, effectively, transparent. As theatre practitioners working within "the process," we do not question or even articulate its premises, and yet this understanding informs virtually every aspect of our collaborative practice. For "the process" meaning is a stable, and unproblematic, phenomenon, the more or less self-evident destination to which interpretation naturally tends. It is not discursively produced or constructed so much as discovered, a latent content to be revealed and, again unproblematically, realized and communicated. And it is the director who effects this discovery, whose eye sees, and masters, a meaning conceived as both innate and transcendent. It is this conception of meaning and the interpretative act that gives it form, this epistemology, which "the process" not only relies on but reproduces. And it is here that the problem lies.

The point is not that "the process" does not work. On the contrary, it is very successful at producing the plays it takes as its implicit norm: character-based, narrative-driven, "realistic" dramas, emphasizing spoken text and illusionistic effects, plays informed by "the process's" own ideology of meaning and mastery. What is more, it continues to produce them within ever more stringent financial constraints. So successful is "the process," in fact, and so severe the constraints it presently faces, it can seem self-defeating for anyone committed to the idea of an indigenous Canadian theatre to challenge its monopoly, or question the ideological premises underlying it. Yet, as a feminist playwright, a "theoretical" playwright seeking to practice what she teaches, it is precisely those unspoken assumptions concerning authority and interpretation, meaning and power, "reality" and representation, and the dramatic conventions they ground, that I struggle to expose and interrogate in my work.

At a time when the very principle of public funding for the arts is under attack, I realize that such questioning may appear academic in a double sense, a myopic failure to recognize that there soon may be nothing left to interrogate. I regard it rather as an act of faith. For I believe that if a justification for the continued existence of not-for-profit theatre must be found—and nothing less now seems to be required—it lies in theatre's unique ability to function as a literal arena for intellectual debate, a public forum unlike any other. That being so, it is surely more essential now than ever to take the making of theatre seriously, to subject its forms and mechanisms of production to scrutiny, to be self-conscious, "theoretical." To do less is to participate in the devaluation of subsidized, not-for-profit theatre we are currently witnessing. To do less, in fact, is to treat that theatre as its critics do, that is, as nothing more than a discounted commodity in the free market of leisure and entertainment industries, a luxury item we can no longer afford.

"Out," "In," and the Space Between

To return, then, to the dilemma "the process" poses. The problem is not simply, or even primarily, one of access, the refusal of the mainstream to make room for the marginal subject matter and interests my work engages. Theatrical forms and themes labelled, vaguely, as "deconstructionist," or "post-structuralist," or even "feminist" are currently fashionable enough to find a (limited) place on mainstream stages. The issue is less inclusion than its costs, the question being whether oppositional texts can ever be realized within modes of production determined by the very structures those texts seek to challenge. How much of the original oppositional intent is lost when, for example, a play explicitly concerned with issues of power and access to interpretive authority is subjected to a production process predicated on the hermeneutic omnipotence of a single individual? How far can the destabilization of unitary, transcendent "meaning" be taken within a process which assumes the vision, or concept, as both its premise and goal? Can there be any potential for resistance when the questions themselves are seen as impractical, "theoretical," or simply irrelevant? Or is the resistance always already recuperated, co-opted by "the process" that ostensibly serves to give it form? (The issue has an interesting parallel in the current debate on "realism" as a theatrical form and its compatibility with a feminist artistic project.)

Although the questions have a particular relevance for my own current work-in-progress, the predicament they point to is hardly mine alone. Nor is one solution, at least, far to seek. Numbers of oppositional or "alternative" playwrights have resolved the issue of co-optation by simply rejecting both "the process" and the institutional framework associated with it. And this may be the only intellectually, and politically, defensible response. Anything else can seem uncomfortably close to deconstructing the hand that feeds you. What is more, it would appear to betray a considerable naïveté regarding the ideological work done by cultural forms, and norms, in general. For the function of a norm is, precisely, either to exclude or co-opt. Inclusion is always, necessarily, also recuperation. Dissent, to the extent that it is ever in fact possible, can only take form outside. Once inside it has ceased to represent dissent.

Yet we should be clear about what is being given up when a playwright chooses to opt out. And we should perhaps question too just how free that choice really is. Established theatres provide an infrastructure whose benefits no playwright can afford to underestimate. Chief among these are a venue with extensive, and expensive, technical facilities, resources and support which significantly extend the writer's own creative options; a (relatively) stable funding base providing at least temporarily a living wage and the ability to work on a project full-time, something many "fringe" writers simply cannot do; professional publicity and promotion and a dedicated budget for it, as well as a recognized profile among theatregoers, critics, and advertisers; and, often, a pre-sold subscriber audience considerably broader than the one drawn to independent, "alternative" productions.

These are factors which materially affect the playwright's abilities to create and communicate, determining both what he or she will be able to put on stage, and who will see it. And that is the reason I've found myself questioning whether it might not be possible to discover within "the process" itself a model of production compatible with my artistic, and political, project. It is why I question, too, whether opting out might not prove at least as problematic as opting in. Real as the danger of recuperation and neutralization is, I do wonder if there is not an equal recuperation being effected when I voluntarily marginalize myself and my creative enterprise, assuming the place the dominant discourse assigns us on "the fringe." I question just how alternative "alternative theatre" really can be when it increasingly appears to function as an institutional supplement rather than a challenge, a conduit for energies that might otherwise generate significant change from within. (It is from within, after all, that subversion must, by definition, take place.) Arguably, opting out, by reaffirming an increasingly institutionalized division between "mainstream" and "alternative" modes of theatre production, merely serves to entrench the hegemony an "alternative" practice claims to challenge.

Not all "fringe" productions make such claims, of course. And it may even be the case that "alternative" production outside the mainstream offers less rather than more opportunity for reconfiguring "the process." Most "alternative" productions rely heavily for funding on project-specific government grants, significant private sponsorship for such ventures being virtually non-existent. Granting juries, however, tend to assume "the process" as a professional no less than an artistic norm, an index of viability, and to award funds accordingly. Ironically, then, it may only be mainstream theatres, theatres whose institutional status serves as a guarantee of professional legitimacy, who can afford to challenge the practice they themselves enshrine.

Of course, it's always possible that this is nothing more than an elaborate rationalization for my own reluctance to forego the material as well as artistic advantages that the mainstream system of theatrical production can provide, even at the price of an inevitable recuperation. And yet "the process" has already generated an alternative model which, at least potentially, challenges some of the most fundamental assumptions on which it rests, those very assumptions, in fact, which are now so problematic. It is a model which, if adopted, could make the business of making theatre within the mainstream less structurally inimical to "alternative" creative projects like mine. I refer to that rather amorphous institution known as "the workshop," which has become in recent years an almost inevitable stage in the development of new scripts.

The "Workshop" as Potential Alternative

As any playwright can tell you, "workshop" is an elastic term, denoting anything from a single closed-door reading and discussion session to a weeks-long undertaking involving staging and production elements and even public performance. It is to this more elaborate form that I refer, though the underlying principle remains the same: collaborative exploration and interaction as the basis of an interrogation of meaning and its theatrical production. In my experience, and I have participated in a number of very different forms, the most successful workshops—the most productive, the most stimulating artistically, the most revelatory—were precisely those that challenged most directly "the process" and its linear orthodoxies. They redefined the power structures that conventionally govern rehearsal and production, democratizing interpretive authority and displacing the hierarchical orderings "the process" continually re-inscribes. Actors and playwright communicated directly rather than through the director alone; designers participated in discussions of staging and interpretation; technicians moved from the shop to the rehearsal hall; territorial prerogatives, and their accompanying restrictions, were abandoned.

It is here that the strength of the workshop model, and its importance for writers like me, lie, in this ability to redefine creative authority, to transform interpretation from an individual to a collective act. Potentially, at least, the workshop can make "meaning" a problem rather than a premise, a plural and unstable construction to be investigated rather than a fixed and manifest "truth" to be discovered. It can create a space for multiplicity, encouraging, even demanding, a self-consciousness about theatrical mediation and its effects that "the process," by definition, can scarcely allow. And, arguably, by doing this, the workshop proves truer to the unique nature of the theatrical enterprise, with its complex interaction of systems of meaning production, than the linear and unitary "process" it is currently employed to serve.

This is not to suggest that all workshops function in this way. Many are simply "the process" in condensed form, equally determined by the vision or concept they are designed to realize, and reproducing the familiar interpretive hierarchy to do so. Nor is it to claim that what we are calling the workshop model, if adopted in production, would necessarily result in a performance event any less committed to a single, univocal and exclusive "meaning," or less determined by the ideological formulations on which such "meaning" rests. Given the extent to which mainstream theatre has institutionalized the notion of the shaping interpretive vision, it would require much more than lip service to a principle of collaboration to effect such a change. It would require, in fact, that the workshop model be seen as a viable production alternative and not merely a useful adjunct.

For the most part, however, it is the latter view that prevails. Typically, the workshop functions as a preliminary phase of the larger production process, a developmental phase to be completed, and left behind. It is considered undeniably valuable, even, increasingly, essential. Most new scripts that proceed to full production now undergo some form of "workshopping." There is, in fact, a very real danger of a workshop ghetto developing within mainstream theatre as financial pressures make new work ever more risky to produce, a production limbo in which new scripts languish without much hope of redemption. For, ultimately, the workshop is seen as necessarily separate from—even opposed to—the real business of production. Indeed, the arguments against using the workshop as a model for the production process are generally considered to be not only self-evident but conclusive. Not surprisingly, on closer inspection, those arguments can be seen to assume the same ideological premises as "the process" whose necessity they are invoked to prove.

And what are some of these conclusive objections? The collaborative nature of the workshop model, it is claimed, is fundamentally unsuited to the creation of a coherent, consistent, unified performance text. The conclusion is debatable, and is, in any event, precisely the point. If such a text is no longer seen as the only possible or desirable goal, the objection becomes moot. The workshop approach is time-consuming and inefficient—all that questioning and experimentation and debate—and therefore incompatible with the rigours of a "three weeks to rehearse, one week to tech" production schedule. Just how much more time-consuming a workshop-type production process would be, and whether impossibly so, is also open to debate. And is this time frame, in any event, the only possible production configuration? Could other production schedules not be devised that would allow for the different demands of a different process? Current institutional frameworks such as standard contract regulations and programming practices make the present logistical arrangements appear to be inevitable, but that is only an indication that these too have a normative function to be exposed and challenged. Actors, designers, and technicians, it is asserted, both want and need a director-led process. They want a clearly designated—and limited—role within a familiar and stable rehearsal hierarchy. It provides them with the security they need to experiment and create. But this is to assume the very point at issue. We have been conditioned to accept "the process" and its creative hierarchy as the only possible—and practical—production structure. Any variation from it appears threatening, anarchic, impracticable. That it does so is an indication of the norm's persuasive powers, its ability to naturalize itself, not a proof of its necessity.

The point I would make, finally, is not that the only solution to my dilemma is the abolition of existing roles and functions within the production process, whether of actor, designer, technician, writer, or director. It is rather to raise the possibility of redefining their relations to each other, and to the process of "interpretation" and production generally. The model for such redefinition already exists within "the process" itself. That the adoption of this model would involve a significant loss of traditional creative autonomy for some (playwright no less than director) is indisputable. That it would necessitate the exposure and reformulation of some of the most fundamental ideological premises determining how theatre is currently made is no less so. Indeed, that is what makes the workshop so attractive a model. At its best, it foregrounds the construction of theatrical meaning, assuming plurality as its premise, and its form. The potential gains from such a rethinking seem clear: a truly collaborative theatrical enterprise, both multiple and polyvalent, a "process" that continually redefines itself, proliferating meanings rather than foreclosing them. The gain would be a theatre truly capable of questioning rather than simply, and inevitably, reaffirming, one that questions itself no less than—and as an integral part of—the culture it engages. And that, theoretically at least, would surely be a theatre worth opting into.

(1995)

Genre Contention at the New Play Centre
by James Hoffman

In his introduction to *Twenty Years at Play*, an anthology of plays from the New Play Centre in Vancouver, editor Jerry Wasserman begins with the statement that the Centre is "relatively invisible," that it "has been one of the best-kept theatrical secrets in Canada." This seems a surprising remark in a book intended to celebrate the success of a play development organization now well into its third decade, many of whose plays, according to this same introduction, have had notable productions and have won numerous awards, and many of whose playwrights, such as Margaret Hollingsworth and Sharon Pollock, have achieved critical recognition. Indeed, its stable of playwrights, which also includes Tom Cone, Sheldon Rosen, Leonard Angel, John Lazarus, and Betty Lambert, is well-known, and there have been impressive box office hits—notably Sherman Snukal's early 1980s comedy, *Talking Dirty*, which ran for over one thousand performances at the Arts Club Theatre. Approximately one hundred and fifty plays have been developed and then fully staged by the Centre: these include one-acts, an early success being Cone's *Herringbone* (1975), lately developed into a full-blown musical which played at Playwrights Horizons in New York; full-lengths such as Lazarus's *Dreaming and Duelling* (1980), which has enjoyed numerous stagings across Canada; musicals, notably Ted Galay's *Tsymbaly* (1985), a hit of the 1986 Manitoba Theatre Centre season; and occasional experimental pieces such as Angel's *Six of One: A Playscript in Progress* (1985), a play about a multicultural group of dancers in which the actors frequently exchange roles.

Yet it is invisible; it has, as Wasserman put it, "managed to get through its first two decades without having been the subject of even a single article in a national publication" (7). How can we critically discuss the New Play Centre? It seems to be a special problem, existing in a privileged theatrical space beyond criticism or representation other than progress-narratives and other developmental constructs.[1] In my research for this article I examined founding documents,[2] reports and promotional materials, and I interviewed most of the managing directors as well as several prominent playwright "graduates" of the Centre. Generally I found a predominant "we were just doing theatre" type of self-construction. According to these sources, there were twenty-four years of fairly neutral activity at the Centre, not unlike that of amateur theatre. Nowhere does there appear a strong set of beliefs or manifesto; Douglas Bankson, one of the co-founders, stated that the Centre's role was to be a humble one, simply to encourage the writing of local plays in order to, as he expressed it, "serve those theatres that were active in Vancouver at that time." Beyond this, somewhat surprising in the charged theatrical world of the late 1960s and early 1970s, the period of *Hair*, *Che!*, and *Paradise Now*, as well as Vancouver's own controversial *Captives of the Faceless Drummer*,[3] there has been a distinct refusal to commit to notions of self-image or vision. Rather than overt theory, ideology or even a continuity with history, there was emphasis on practicality and practice—Pamela Hawthorn, its major director, telling me: "We had no theoretical base... we were a bunch of practical theatre people." Repeatedly, in my interviews with Centre directors, I found that while Hawthorn emphasized the Centre's intense commitment to what she called "the art form," that is to the promotion of Canadian plays on Canadian stages, the strongest self-expressed tendency at the Centre was towards a lack of fixity, to a kind of shapeless multiplicity, to being many things to many people.

I wish to consider the New Play Centre as a site where largely unspoken genre dynamics seriously compromised understandings of purpose and operation and at the same time created significant potential for metatheatrical activity—that is, activity with the potential for functioning as a different order of theatre itself. Why a genre study? Given the uncertain suppressed character of this institution, we need a criticism committed to bringing some sense of typological clarity—the traditional task of genre study. It seems appropriate, given the Centre's uncertainty, to make some attempt at description and classification, especially at locating its position vis-à-vis theatrical types. Has it functioned, for example, as a traditional genre of theatre—perhaps in disguise? How many genres have been in operation at the Centre? Was one dominant?

At the same time we need a criticism capable of responding to transparency and the blurring of boundaries at the Centre, where, clearly, there has been an unsettling dynamic of re- and de-categorizing. This too is the domain of genre, especially as understood by postmodern theorists who, alert to the destabilizing effects of marginalized voices on established generic norms (for example, feminists have questioned generic tradition as male-dominated), see genre as essentially an historical and political construct. As a result there is particular interest in genre formation and change, as well as in the altered and altering relationships between genres. Thus genre is valued not for its normalizing, essentializing typologies, but as a kind of model for process and change.

Ralph Cohen, among others (Chambers, Bauman), sees genre as "perfectly compatible with multiple discourses, with narratives of discontinuity, with transgressed boundaries" (241)—all of which seem in operation at the Centre. And the work of Michail Bakhtin, although designed for the study of the novel, seems useful. I am thinking specifically of his description of complete versus incomplete genres, the identification of generic canons, the behaviour of genres vis-à-vis other genres, and consideration of structural characteristics as outlined in *The Dialogic Imagination*. His methodology, since it deals with emerging genre and with genre in process and in relation to other genres, seems applicable to the situation at the Centre.

What are the major genres at the Centre? The most obvious one is playwriting. This theatrical genre, certainly one with ancient roots, has attracted the most attention in the Centre's various descriptions and activities, indeed has mostly determined its raison d'être. In fact, most of the Centre's activities in the formative early period, under Bankson's direction,[4] were devoted to script development—almost to the exclusion of other theatrical practices. The development process, however, was borrowed at least in part from another institution.

The tone and much of the Centre's style was set in the early years: playwrights, mainly from amateur theatre groups, were encouraged to submit scripts. These were read and returned with critical commentary, and here the development ended for the great majority of writers. A small number of plays was selected for workshopping, and then several were modestly performed at first in rehearsed public readings at the Vancouver Art Gallery in the summer of 1971. The whole process was a replication of the amateur drama festival, such as the Dominion Drama Festival, with its system of competition, selection, adjudication and awards. Indeed, the Centre's origins are found in a group who called themselves the "lunch bunch," who met regularly to discuss theatre. Two of them, Sheila Neville, a University of British Columbia (UBC) librarian, and Douglas Bankson, professor of creative writing at UBC, became co-founders of the Centre, while another, Anne Cameron, became an invaluable secretary in the young organization. All were involved with the DDF in the ongoing project of encouraging Canadian scripts in the festival. Thus the Centre achieved what the DDF could not: the institutionalizing of playwriting.

This particular focus on playwriting led to the establishment of another genre: the play development centre itself, a new, largely post–World War II phenomenon (Anderson) still very much in formation and therefore an undetermined genre of theatre. Is it, for example, primarily a writing or primarily a producing theatrical institution? [5] If it is essentially a place of writing, then it may be a metagenre of theatre, that is, it could have potential for transforming the theatre itself, for utilizing theatre to transform writing, or perhaps for influencing the wider regional culture itself. For example there was the possibility that the Centre may have been asserting or reclaiming writing in its post-colonial setting. At times, as in a 1980 New Play Centre report, this seems to be the case, as there is commitment to process, to "the emergence of a strong meaningful culture... [and to] the needs of individuals and the community." Two of the words chosen for its name, "New" and "Centre," suggest the reclamation of identity from an imperial centre, the granting of status to a (formerly) peripheral language; while "new play" seems to announce a challenge to imperial writing, an assertion of a writing that is in formation and potentially at least recuperative. This recalls the post-colonial strategy of questioning generic assumptions, and is perhaps best shown in the harsh street situations of Tom Walmsley's plays, in the portrayal of Ukrainian immigrant life in the plays of Ted Galay, or in the depiction of a contemporary local figure as in Eric Nicol's *Ma*—all works developed at the Centre.

However, there is also indication that writing was merely sub-generic, a minor genre of theatre. When I asked key figures such as Bankson and Hawthorn whether they might have been operating a centre not so much to develop playwriting as to teach the elements of theatre to writers, there was significant agreement. Even the Centre's singular commitment to local plays was problematically not elaborated. Was it understood as referring to imperial canon-making or canon-breaking—to the standard American or British play in a Canadian setting or to some kind of post-colonial variant? As we'll see, evidence suggests an uncertain middle ground between the two. Meanwhile, how successfully did the Centre achieve its initial aim of "serving" the Vancouver theatre? A retrospective article (1990) admits that "Vancouver playwrights have not by and large been a dominant force in Vancouver's own theatres" (Johnston 25). The reason for this has much to do with a pervasive conflict that limited the Centre's notion of playwright and play.

Indeed, within the Centre there are two major theatrical genres in an unstable relationship: playwriting and directing. Playwriting, the creation of the dramatic script, is continually represented as the primary activity of the Centre, the preference for new plays and one-act plays being a significant departure from the norms of other professional theatre groups. The other activity, directing, is largely unspoken, the silent partner; in fact, from the very beginning the Centre has been a haven for directors. Most of the managing directors of the Centre, the most notable and influential being Pamela Hawthorn, have been stage directors and not playwrights. Of the original Board of Advisors, none were established playwrights. In the first two years, in 1970 and 1971, all plays submitted for critiquing were read by Bankson, himself both a director and writer, as well as by a theatre director. Thus the major impetus for play development at the Centre has been from the director.

There has in effect been an ongoing dialectic between these two major genres. The choice of name, New *Play* Centre, seems to indicate a privileging of playwriting. Even during the first two years, however, when the major activity was a script critiquing service, there were workshops, in effect a form of directing; indeed the first constitution speaks of the Centre's "objects" as being "(a) to promote a play-reading program which leads to (b) workshop productions...." Bankson, in a letter to the Canada Council, in 1971, stated: "The aim of the Centre is to aid and encourage the writing and production of plays...." This dialectic has existed throughout the Centre's existence and although questioned, it has never been fundamentally altered. We can question some of the assumptions behind it.

It was implicit, for example, that the Canadian playwright existed in a subservient relation to imperial norms. This was due in large part to the Centre's unspoken relationship with the Dominion Drama Festival, which folded in the early 1970s just as the Centre was founded, and where the non-existence of the Canadian playwright was assumed. A key document, written by Bankson in 1969, when he was a governor of the DDF, entitled, "Some Observations and Proposals addressed to the D.D.F. Committee Studying the Original Play in Canada," stresses the need for Canadian playwrights to be "*made equal partners with the Director, Actor, Designer, and Technician*" (underlined in original). It is important to note that while there were acting and directing workshops and frequent difficulties in finding good adjudicators at the DDF, only playwriting was seriously problematized. Denis Salter has noted the DDF's "failure to realize the Bessborough ideal of a national repertoire of producible plays" (13). Thus the attitude that directing is closed and complete while playwriting is unformed was taken from the DDF to the New Play Centre.

This is interesting, considering that directing as practiced at the Centre was only invented in Europe in the late nineteenth century, and to this day remains an imprecise, developing genre, with a wide range of practices. If we use Bakhtin's concept of an incomplete genre, one that is still developing, such as he has discussed in relation to the novel (3–40), then directing is in the state of evolving while playwriting—its object in our case being to construct a form more or less as practiced for centuries—could be viewed as a complete, somewhat ossified genre. As Bakhtin notes, a developing genre, will, in its interaction with other genres, dominate, infecting them with that same sense of becoming (7).

This is what I think occurred at the New Play Centre: playwriting, in its interaction with directing, was destabilized and characterized as an incipient art. This can be seen as differing from regular theatrical practice where there are normative assumptions regarding the writers, director, designer, and actor who are understood to work in collaborative harmony, in what are perceived to be stable and complementary generic practices.

How has the production of playscripts at the Centre been affected by this? For one thing, there has not been a strong concept of the playwright or the play, both of which are constructed in terms of reduction and concealment. The relationship between director and playwright is expressed as a hierarchical one, that of a master and apprentice. Early publicity talks, of the "prospective playwright," never the prospective director, who will be assisted by the Centre. The emphasis on new plays, while it might seem to promise a re-examination or reconstitution of playwriting, in fact conceals a preference for traditional modes, ones amenable mainly to the needs of the director. A letter written by Bankson, July 20, 1971, to David Gardner, Theatre Arts Officer of the Canada Council, notes the "aim of the Centre is to aid and encourage the writing" of plays. The first instruction, in a document, "Guidelines for Readers of Scripts for the New Play Centre," written by Bankson, asks the reader to "approach the script from the point of view of a Director (note upper case) who is considering it for production." A few sentences later, the guidelines state that "the correction of weaknesses is obviously your most important function." Overt here is the notion of the playwright as a dependent, perhaps even resisting, participant in the theatrical process, as well as unstated assumptions about the nature of the play.

Another result has been a dominance of realistic scripts and a particular interest in the one-act play. Hawthorn admitted that a major unresolved artistic issue was that the Centre's work was "too realistic [...] (that) the best work available was realistic." Margaret Hollingsworth said that she disagreed with Hawthorn's insistence that "plays should be realistic, (and) have a through-line [...] I fought her on that." Thus it was axiomatic, despite Hawthorn's statement that there were "no guidelines" in recognizing a "good script," that certain kinds of play creation, such as that of collective or experimental works, were inappropriate at the Centre, and therefore the work of certain writers, such as Atom Egoyan, now a notable Canadian filmmaker, were rejected. Then, according to Hawthorn, writers who used language well were especially favoured; Tom Cone similarly talked about the importance of an "original voice." How language became realistic was at least partly due to the Centre's routine model of workshopping, in which a group of actors read and then commented freely on a new script. This practice concerned playwright Ian Weir, who said that it tended both to diffuse the script and to intimidate the playwright. And Tom Cone was cautioned: "Workshops can ruin a playwright [...] we can't overrun the writer" (Waddel 44). At the same time, we might add, most actors and directors, now acting as dramaturge, are trained in the methods of psychological realism.

This preference is in line with the Centre's expressed desire to be practical and non-ideological, since realistic plays are often perceived to be a neutral, scientific genre, and since the Centre's purpose was to serve the mainstream theatre. We know of course that some critics have seen the realistic play as ideologically closed and conservative (Knowles). In any case, the Centre believed that other groups, such as

Tahmahnous Theatre, founded almost at the same moment as the New Play Centre, would serve the alternate theatre.

Then, particularly in the early years, it was felt that the writing of one-act plays was the best means of developing playwrights. This can be seen as an admission that the traditional form of the full-length play was problematic for the Centre, although what the one-act offered in its place was never articulated. The choice of the one-act is, however, in itself indicative of a submerged ideology. Gail Finney, in discussing modern attempts to elevate the one-act play, has noted the form's deterministic aspects, especially in tragedy, where "characters [...] are without free will, incapable of altering their conditions" (453). Of the five plays published by the Centre in *West Coast Plays* (1975), many display the "human victimization" observed by Finney. Thus this alternate form, the one-acter, proposed by the Centre as a pedagogical tool, instead set in place a limiting, even repressive structure. One could question, for example, the inability of characters "altering their conditions," indeed engaging with regional issues in this volume. Malcolm Page has observed the lack of nationalist assertion, noting that there is in fact "very little British Columbia content" (95) in *West Coast Plays*, a comment he similarly makes in reviewing *Twenty Years On: A New Play Centre Anthology* (82). Thus we have to question just what the New Play Centre was proposing in the construction of its dramatic canon.

How then can we view the operations of genre at the New Play Centre? Perhaps the key question is to what extent the Centre's generic strategies can be seen as the assertion of cultural difference, arguably the greatest artistic need in the post-colonial milieu of Vancouver. What challenges were there, for example, to the characteristic of genre usually associated with colonial structures? In particular, can we see alteration of the canon or evidence of the appropriation of the playtext; that is, was there significant liberation of playwriting from the authority of an imposed colonial system? While some aspects of the Centre do point positively in this direction, there was, as noted, an alienation of vision, and therefore of generic questioning, that suggests the effects of cultural denigration common in colonial cultures.

This preliminary analysis suggests that the New Play Centre has accomplished two things. First, by refusing to represent itself as a traditional form of theatre, it has fostered notions of generic transformation and appropriation, and therefore opened the way for marginal or subversive forms, perhaps best shown in the dramatic work of Tom Walmsley, Leonard Angel, or Tom Cone. By maintaining a self-determined, somewhat open approach to play development, the Centre has subverted traditional methods of accessibility of the theatre by privileging the work of the playwright and opening the way to revised dramatic creation. Thus were denaturalized some of the features of colonial theatrical practice—such as existed at the DDF. This argues for a constitution of the New Play Centre as a kind of metagenre, somewhat beyond the norms of theatrical practice and available to a wide variety of post-colonial revising and reappropriation strategies.

However, in practice there was compromise, as in its insistence on the primacy of the director and on the diffusive workshop model. Thus were qualified many of its own, and therefore its culture's, redefinitions of genre, the result being a kind of self-proclaimed non-genre: "We were just doing theatre." At the same time as it worked to liberate writing from an inherited/imposed colonial system, it quietly imposed its own essentializing notions, as in its privileging of language and realistic structure. Thus what seemed to be a site of metatheatre, a site for revising the place of dramatic discourse in the grip of coloniality, became instead an elusive entity fluctuating uncertainly between metagenre and non-genre.

(1995)

Works Cited

Anderson, Douglas. "The Dream Machine: Thirty Years of New Play Development in America." *The Drama Review* 119 (Fall 1988): 55–84.

Ashcroft, Bill, Gareth Griffiths and Helen Tiffin. *The Empire Writes Back: Theory and Practice in Post-Colonial Literatures.* New York: Routledge, 1989.

Bakhtin, Michail. *The Dialogic Imagination.* Ed. M. Holquist. Trans. C. Emerson. Austin: U of Texas P, 1981.

Bankson, Douglas. Personal interview. 2 July 1993.

Bauman, Richard. "Genre." *Folklore, Cultural Performance, and Popular Entertainments.* Ed. Richard Bauman. Toronto: Oxford UP, 1992. 53–59.

Brissenden, Connie, ed. *West Coast Plays.* Vancouver: New Play Centre-Fineglow, 1975.

Chambers, Ross. *"Describing genre." Paragraph* 16.3 (Nov. 1993): 293–306.

Cohen, Ralph. "Do Postmodern Genres Exist?" *Genre XX* (Fall–Winter 1987): 241–58.

Cone, Tom. Personal interview. 2 July 1993.

Finney, Gail. "Theatre of Impotence: The One-Act Tragedy at the Turn of the Century." *Modern Drama* 28.3 (September 1985): 451–61.

Gilbert, Reid. "Introduction," "A Production Journal," and "Interview." *The Capilano Review* 35 (1985): 4–73. This issue also contains the script of Leonard Angel's *Six of One: A Playscript in Progress.*

Hawthorn, Pam. Personal interview. 2 July 1993.

Hollingsworth, Margaret. Personal interview. 25 August 1993.

Johnston, Denis and Jerry Wasserman. "The New Play Centre: Twenty Years On." *Canadian Theatre Review* 63 (Summer 1990): 25–28.

Knelman, Martin. "Hothouse Mama," *Saturday Night* (April 1981): 99–100.

Knowles, Richard Paul. "Voices (off): Deconstructing the Modern English-Canadian Dramatic Canon." *Canadian Canons: Essays in Literary Value.* Ed. Robert Lecker. Toronto: University of Toronto P, 1991. 91–111.

Page, Malcolm. "Fourteen Propositions About Theatre in British Columbia." *Journal of Canadian Studies* 25.3 (Fall 1990): 90–104.

Salter, Denis. "Declarations of (In)Dependence." *Canadian Theatre Review* 62 (Spring 1990): 11–18.

Selody, Kim. Personal interview. 5 June 1993.

Waddel, Steve. "Canada's Big Apples for Playwrights." *Performing Arts in Canada* (Spring 1981): 41–44.

Wasserman, Jerry, ed. *Twenty Years at Play: A New Play Centre Anthology*. Vancouver: Talonbooks, 1990.

Weir, Ian. Personal interview. 7 August 1993.

Zimmering, Suzann, ed. *The Catalogue: B.C. Playwrights*. Vancouver, Athletica Press, 1977.

---

[1]   See Knelman; Waddel; Johnston and Wasserman.

[2]   The earliest founding document seems to be a New Play Centre constitution, dated May 5, 1971. The same year, in a July 20 letter to David Gardner, Theatre Arts Officer of the Canada Council, Douglas Bankson applied for funds and briefly describes the Centre's accomplishments in its first year. Then, in August, for writers using its service, Bankson wrote a two-page document providing a general description of the Centre and its operations. These documents are located in the Vancouver City Archives.

[3]   In late 1970, the Playhouse Board suddenly decided not to stage George Ryga's new play *Captives of the Faceless Drummer*, which is based on the FLQ crisis in Quebec that caused the country so much anguish at the time. The play had been commissioned by the Company and was scheduled to play early in 1971. Ryga and his supporters made the affair public, and much controversy ensued.

[4]   Bankson was director of the Centre from its founding in 1970 until 1972, when Pamela Hawthorn became managing director, a position she held until 1989. She was replaced by Paul Mears, who had worked for five years under Hawthorn. Kim Selody, the current director, assumed the position in late 1991.

[5]   The debate over whether the Centre was a playwriting or a producing agency exploded with some rancour in the early 1990s, and led to the formation of an alternate group, the Betty Lambert Society, organized entirely by playwrights solely to support playwrights. The group's first *Newsletter* (September 1992) declared: "(the New Play Centre) is primarily a theatre company, not a service organization." Recently, in August 1995, the New Play Centre and the Betty Lambert Society merged to form a single entity: Playwrights Theatre Centre.

Writing for a Playwright's Theatre:
Urjo Kareda on Dramaturgy at Tarragon
by Deborah Cottreau

In the 1970s, Tarragon Theatre emerged with a mandate to develop new Canadian plays, and to give the best possible production to the scripts chosen to premiere there. Since his appointment as artistic director in 1982, Urjo Kareda has devoutly upheld Tarragon's goals by reading every script submitted to the theatre, personally developing those with potential. Deborah Cottreau spoke to Urjo Kareda last winter (1996) and asked him to reflect on his role as dramaturge/artistic director.

COTTREAU: *My first question for you is in three parts. How would you define your various functions at the Tarragon, first of all as artistic director, then as literary manager, and finally as dramaturge?*

KAREDA: I can't really take them individually because for me they're all the same thing, given the peculiar nature of my artistic directorship. I'm sort of the dramaturge as artistic director. One of the most important things for dramaturges in any theatre structure to have is the ability to have access to the artistic director's ear. If a dramaturge has a script or a writer that he believes in, he can persuade the artistic director this is something that should be programmed. I've eliminated that leap. If I'm persuaded by a script, I don't have to persuade anyone else to do it. I think this has everything to do with the nature of what the Tarragon is, which is a playwright's theatre. Nothing happens here until a script or a writer walks through the door. As artistic director, I'm the one who wants to know who's out there, who's writing what, and what the writing is like. I read everything that's submitted because I want to know the community. I guess that's the literary manager's job, reading scripts.

Then as a dramaturge, I work with writers either personally one-on-one, or through things like the Playwrights Unit, or by phone, or by mail or by acting out long-term relationships to develop scripts. It takes, on an average, two years to make a play from an idea to something you put into rehearsal. As artistic director, I program the ones I really think make most sense to put together in a season—which involves making an educated guess. Things are not necessarily finished and on your desk by the time you program the season. It's a part of what your expertise is—who will go the distance, what will make an interesting combination of plays. You want to do an interesting span of work in a season, to give your audience enough variety and diversity. And to show, in fact, the diversity of new work so that the audience can enter a new world every time they come and see a play. But I can't, myself, draw the line among those three functions. They're welded into one.

You're very fortunate because you can wear various hats at the same time.

That's how I'm different from Bill (Glassco). Because I hardly ever direct, I'm freer to have a much wider range of taste, and to be more excited by diverse kinds of work.

Then I can make a marriage with the individual directors, with the individual play-wrights to affect the work. For me, variety is extraordinarily important. The variety of genres as well.

Being artistic director, making script selection part of season planning, working dramaturgically with the plays that are submitted, how do you incorporate the concerns of the Literary Manager and find new trends, or even call those trends by a specific name?

That's the wrong way around to look at it because, really, the trends have to show you where they're going. Being artistic director is very much a reactive job in a playwright's theatre, because you have to put together our seasons based on what the writers of your time, your city, your community are interested in writing about. If you read enough work and talk to enough writers, the trends bubble to the surface. What you have to do is monitor it and shape it so that, when you put together a season, it makes a statement about that particular year in our time.

Let me rephrase the question. How do you put your thumb on the local pulse?

That comes from the writers you work with directly. Here, in the Playwrights Unit, we work with six or seven writers over a year. What's also important is that local and Canadian are two separate things. There are a lot of important regions beyond the local just short of the international, which we also have to deal with. Somehow, they shape themselves into some sort of pattern. Sometimes you have to wait a year for a play to make just the perfect statement in a particular season, because it just isn't ready.

You talk about Tarragon as being a playwright's theatre. So, how do you select the playwrights? I know that's a very old and tired question, but I think a lot of people would be interested in finding out if there is a formula.

People used to. Often when you talk about young writers they think, "Oh, I'd really like to write a Tarragon play," as though I could define it, then they would go out and write it. Perhaps twenty years ago that was truer when the writing community was younger and a large number of them were writing autobiographically at the beginning. You had a lot of "family" plays and "leaving home" plays, all those things which come naturally. We have had several generations of writers since then. Now, the community has been exposed to much more theatre and many different kinds of theatre. What I look for is a writer with a very distinctive, individual voice. That you can identify within twenty pages as you're reading it. It may not be a voice that's found itself yet, but you know that it's there. My taste is for a voice that is muscular, that leaves a lot of air, that asks more questions than it answers, that is interested in various kinds of form, that has a nose for the theatrical, that knows about the theatre, about what the theatre's strength and power can be. With someone like Guillermo Verdecchia, his *Fronteras Americanas* is a "leaving home" play. But if you think of the distance between it and the David French works, it shows the kind of range the

Canadian theatre has developed. And with Guillermo, as with David, we are simply held by the mesmerism of the individual voice.

This is not the first time you've mentioned Fronteras Americanas. *I think this particular play strikes very resounding notes with you. What specifically attracted you to this piece and why did you think it was an important venture for the Tarragon to do?*

The story is one I'm very personally attached to: the story of the immigrant in Canadian society, the temptation of assimilation; the huge ambivalence about what you were and what you are; your relationship to your own heritage; the whole hyphenated existence. Changing your name to become accommodated in the way that Guillermo did, allowing yourself to be called "Willy" in grade school so people would talk to you. It exactly mirrored my experience when I came to this country—what you had to accept to be welcomed. I felt that we hadn't exactly heard that on stage in this country in such a vivid way. Guillermo is shrewd in his theatrical instincts. Such a wonderful mind. It seemed to me an exhilarating piece to put out because although it appears, at first, to be a piece about Latin Americans and the American continent, it isn't, in fact, it's a piece with a much wider resonance. Lots of people responded to it in a very, very deep way. It moved me and excited me in a way that I always want theatre to do.

Two things I particularly appreciate in your last comment are the ideas of finding a new voice with deep resonances, and of appreciating theatrical instinct. There's an element of text and there's also an element of staging which are inherent in the script.

That's the bonus if you find it in a young writer. The sense of the dynamics of the stage, the sense of a balance between the text and the visual. The exhilaration of performance. The kind of giddiness. The joy of performance. Lots and lots of young writers have absolutely no idea of what designers do, or what they can do, or, indeed, what actors do or can do. So, plays are both under-conceived visually and overwritten dramatically, because young writers don't understand the resonances that their collaborators will eventually add. This is the thing you try to move them toward. Guillermo's piece was conceived half visually because it involved, as his previous pieces had, slides and captions. It included things like disguise, impersonation. And two personas. It already had a lively cast of characters, even though it was a solo show. And, it was conceived with the stage, rather than the page, in mind. What was always important for Guillermo was to have that intimate eyeball-to-eyeball contact with the audience—the danger that involved, the intimacy that involved. Both of them were incorporated into the very persuasion of the play. It is a dialogue with an audience. It really is confrontational. That is, again, part of its excitement. That is where elements of performance are. More and more actors are becoming playwrights. Their theatrical ability, their built-in sense of how theatre works, is ahead of their writing ability. You wait for the two to catch up to one another. But, I do think that the instinct for the chemistry of performance is more present in the texts I see now than what it was fifteen years ago.

When I look back on the late sixties and early seventies, there seemed to be a pattern of nation building there, whether recognized as such or not, simply because voices unfamiliar to us spoke directly to us from other regions in Canada. We shared the experiences of people we didn't necessarily know, and were drawn into their landscapes by the plays we read. They became a part of the Canadian fabric. They told us more about who we are. Do you think this historical use of the dramaturge as "nation builder" in Canadian theatre has come and gone?

I suppose it is an ongoing process, rather than one that's come and gone. In the last couple of years, there's been an urgent sense among theatres to find and to present alternate voices, or voices which speak of our social diversity, more than we've done in the past decade. That, probably, is a very conscious, political, artistic drive, one that we're all struggling with.

How do you struggle with that here at the Tarragon?

To try and find those voices. To persuade those voices that theatre is the medium they want to pursue. To try to cultivate those voices. One runs a new play theatre partly for audiences, partly to develop the work itself, but also to encourage potential writers. People can walk in off the street and start something, even without a strong self-definition of the writer-for-the-theatre. Theatre provides a context in which that kind of growth can be encouraged. You can't artificially create, suddenly, a whole new generation of alternate voices. You have to do it one by one—and work hard. It's just getting people to the stage where they can accept the fact that they are writers. That is the big challenge. I'm working with M.J. Kang who's writing *Blessings*, a play about being a Korean Canadian. *Blessings* will open our season next year. I find her work appealing in two ways: a) she's a very imaginative and a very hard-working, disciplined writer; b) she has shown me that world from the inside which, to me, is extremely attractive—in the same way that Guillermo showed me the inside of the Latino world in our society.

Do you think there's a functioning definition of the word "dramaturge" within a Canadian context? Or are you changing approaches with each writer?

It is very much one-on-one. It's very character driven. Lots of people have talent. But what will make a career is character. You have to suss out, through your working with people, whether they have the discipline, the maturity, and the life experience to go that distance. The danger of dramaturgy, of course, is sometimes the work will never be better unless the life can be fixed. You're not there to try and fix the life.

What important ideas give structure to and inform your personal dramaturgical practice here at the Tarragon? What would be the kind of ideas shaping the structures that you're working with?

I'm obviously interested in writers who have distinctive ownership of language, something that is theirs and theirs alone. I'm obviously looking for characters that I would like to spend two hours with, not that I have to like them, who are compelling or engaging for me. I like open narrative structures. I like plays that are thematically open, that don't close themselves off too early. You have to write for a very long time, almost wildly, as Judith Thompson says, before you start to tidy it up. It's dangerous, writers who need to edit themselves too early. If it's too tight too early, there are lots of things that you are denying yourself. Most things still begin with text. That's what begins the dramaturge's dialogue with the writer in most cases. Since we are a playwright's theatre, we probably still are more script driver than not. More literary than not, before literary became such a dirty word.

What is the role of structure in your process? How does it affect your process? When you're reading a play, how do you respond to the structure? How critical is that element for you?

I'm going to have to use another old-fashioned unpopular word, and that's plot. Does the text have a plot that releases the play's meanings, themes, and characters? Does it have a narrative that will engage us in the issues of the play? It's not enough just to have issues, it's not enough just to have characters. Somehow, storytelling has to be in there. Often that's very difficult to achieve. You can have very gifted writers who create a character, who create dialogue, with wonderful ideas, but it's difficult for them to find the story that contains all those elements. To see how the pieces can be added together, how all the elements can be attached, one to another, to create a structure which releases meaning. It opens things up for debate rather than closes them down. This leaves the audience with something to do.

One of my anxieties is dealing with plays that attempt to give the audience the whole experience in the text, leaving not enough for the audience to do, to question, and to respond to. Airless. I think I'm probably much more friendly toward plays with gaping, interesting holes, rather than nice, neat constructions. I do think the plot element is extremely important and very difficult to talk about with writers. They say, "Oh, I didn't know we were doing that anymore." There must be a different word, now, that would be more acceptable than plot. I think story—the storytelling impulse is not as prevalent as I would like it to be.

How do we get an audience, who are accustomed to exploring a certain kind of theatre, to reconfigure themselves as they're watching something in process to a completely different approach—or is it the approach itself?

Well, I think it's the approach itself. Also, I have to trust the intelligence of our audience. We give our subscribers lots of information about what they can expect to see before they come so it isn't a complete surprise. I spend a lot of time writing newsletters. The diversity of the programming is what's important to them. They don't want to come and see the same kind of play over and over and over again. That's one of the challenges of putting together a season, to give them perhaps a realistic play, and a poetic play, and a piece of performance art, and something as strange as *Sessions*, which is its own genre. But I think the quality of the production and the conviction of each production will persuade them. So that they might come out saying, "That really isn't something I like. But I have to say they did it awfully well."

(1996)

Dramaturgy for Radical Theatre
by Sky Gilbert

The dramaturgy at Buddies in Bad Times Theatre has always been controversial. Basically because, as far back as 1983, I have boldly come out in favour of "opportunity without interference," and of festivals of small productions. As opposed to workshops and to readings. It has been assumed by the unenthusiastic that Buddies does not believe in (or in fact practice) any sort of dramaturgy or play development. People now seem to assume that we throw the doors open to a very eclectic bunch of new work and hope for the best. This is simply not true.

Let me start at the beginning and talk a little bit about what Buddies is:

> ...an artist-run, non-profit, queer theatre company committed to the development of radical new Canadian work. As a pro-sexual company, we celebrate difference, and challenge the professional theatre experience by reinventing boundaries between: artistic disciplines, performer and audience, gay and lesbian, queer and straight, male and female, good and bad.

By "artist-run" we mean that artists have a great deal of power at Buddies in programming work and in developing policy. At Buddies, the Artistic Director is on the board of directors, and the programming is done by myself and a staff of assistant and associate artists. Aren't all theatres artist-run? No, many are run by producers. To some, this distinction is a fine one. Why should we care whether artists or producers run a theatre company? Because by giving artists power, we assure that Buddies remains art-driven and not money-driven.

This brings us to "non-profit." Buddies is presently in the centre of a storm of controversy surrounding non-profit theatre. The mainstream newspaper critics, as well as the politicians in Toronto, have made it clear that American musical commercial theatre IS the *new* wave of Toronto theatre. *Tommy* and *Sunset Boulevard* define theatre for most of Toronto. In this climate there is constant skepticism around artists who require government funding to produce non-commercial, new, Canadian work. It's not that we don't like audiences; it's that our prime motivation is not to fill seats. Our aim is to discover and to encourage great and beautiful art. If people come and see it, we are happier still.

And finally, our theatre is one which breaks down boundaries. We are careful to indicate that "queer" simply means "pro-sexual." This is to make it clear that all pro-sexual people of any sexual persuasion will find Buddies' work provocative. But what about those boundaries?

Basically, at Buddies we don't think that art need have a moral purpose. One needn't come out improved or "redeemed." We are excited by theatre which involves the audience, which does not rely on traditional plot. Dance which seems to be theatre, and theatre which seems to be dance, also are of interest. This is the "radical" theatre you've heard us talk so much about. Now, no one is saying that non-narrative, cross-disciplinary, audience-involving, non-moralistic work is something new. It was done in the sixties. Hell, it was done in Paris by Alfred Jarry and theorized about in an insane asylum by Antonin Artaud! Nobody said our concept was new. But for a theatre town which embraces *Crazy For You* as a new and exciting production, our theatre is intensely radical.

I've just noticed that I've defined the work in terms of "negatives," what our theatre is NOT. So, perhaps if I talk about our dramaturgy in detail, you will discover a little more about what our theatre actually IS.

Traditional dramaturgy assumes that the playwright comes to the dramaturge to learn how to make his (or her) play better. The dramaturge, using a very specific idea of what theatre is, will analyze the play. If the play fits well into this model, it is a good play. The model used in traditional dramaturgy suggests that plays contain four elements: plot, character, dialogue, and theme. Traditionally, the dramaturge will analyze the play to make sure it contains equal and balanced contributions from these elements. Then, the dramaturge will say to the playwright, "The theme is not clear." Or the dramaturge will say, "The characters are not fully developed." The results of this kind of dramaturgy are painfully evident. I have seen many a play in many a Canadian theatre which pauses to extemporize on its "theme," or which boasts an obviously extraneous monologue in which an actor fills out the missing details of his character. Proponents of traditional dramaturgy will insist that this is simply bad dramaturgy (the fault not in its being "traditional"). I will reiterate that it is this insistence on certain fixed elements to define a play that shackles writers and damages creation.

At Buddies we feel that plays are made up of many elements, including plot, theme, character, dialogue, poetry, image, movement and music. A play can contain all of these elements, or only one of them. It can contain other elements as well. It will be theatre if it is live. It will be good theatre if any combination of the elements or any single element is produced with skill. In other words, a great play may contain only great poetry spoken onstage. Or it may contain only great images. Of course, if a play is to be made up of only one element, that one element had better be plenty powerful.

As an example of non-linear work which had its dramaturgical development through Buddies in Bad Times Theatre, let's look at Hillar Liitoja's DNA Theatre production of *Sick*. Typically, Hillar dramaturged the piece himself. As the writer/director/designer this was his style. *Sick* was produced at Buddies in 1992. The developmental process began in 1990 with *The Panel*, which was inspired by New York's Wooster Group's production *The Road to Immortality, Part Two LSD*. *Sick* was, as its title suggests, an unscripted panel in which people actually discussed AIDS. The panelists improvised on topics such as AIDS' cultural effects, its causes, its cures, and its relationship to gay politics. All the panelists were allowed to speak for a specified length of time on certain subjects, stopped by a bell. However, the production became controversial when, at specified moments in the piece, a short period of time was allotted for audience members to express their opinions. During the original Rhubarb! production, people literally cried and screamed and fought not to be cut off by the bell. The production was emotional and political: audience involvement at its best. Hillar was developing a production about AIDS, but he had to control the polemics, the diatribes, his own anger at governments and at heterosexist homophobia. A second production of *The Panel* the next year was longer and invited even more audience participation. This allowed Hillar to spend, as it were, his didacticism. The resulting *Sick* production at Buddies contained a brief section devoted to *The Panel*, but the rest of the production was a movement-oriented imagistic piece which explored the pain and anger around AIDS. This was hands-off development by Buddies, allowing a mature artist of genius to develop his work.

But Buddies is also capable of traditional, hands-on dramaturgy, if the artist so requires. Certainly in last year's Rhubarb! Festival the dramaturgy on certain pieces went no further than discussion in Buddies' Tallulah's Cabaret after the show. But in the case of *Faghag* by Anne Farquahar, Kirsten Johnson not only directed the piece but arranged and cut sections of the text with the writer because Anne desperately wanted this kind of in-depth editorial attention. She got it. The importance of dramaturgy connected to small productions is clear to me when working on RHUBARB! Work which is stylized or experimental often depends so much on heightened performance that no amount of discussion around a table can get to the heart of a piece.

This year we will be developing Moynan King's production of *Bathory* through workshops in the Buddies' Cabaret. The visual and highly theatrical elements will be developed during rehearsal. But the dialogue will be developed through small performances in the Cabaret, which will be open to post-show discussion.

This is just a taste of the style of dramaturgy which goes on at Buddies. It is completely responsive, not paternalistic. We try to help the playwrights do what they want with their work, help them refine their vision.

Buddies also has a history of encouraging writer/directors and director/creators. We are not afraid of the singularity of vision which comes from one source. At the same time, Buddies has been the home of countless collective creations. What do all these approaches have in common? Why, their diversity, the fact that Buddies doesn't insist that a playwright must only write a play, and that a director must only direct. The only thing we do often demand is that the actors simply act.

Unless it is a collective creation, we like to see the actors offering the best of their craft as performers. We do not encourage them to do dramaturgy. (Don't get me started, let's just say I don't have much faith in actors as dramaturges!)

Of course many theatres will claim that their dramaturgy is also not paternalistic, that Buddies is not the only theatre which has a responsive dramaturgy. Since I first talked about "opportunity without interference" in the early nineteen-eighties, I think that changes have been made. And I'm certainly not claiming to be responsible. I think that, as Canadian theatre has become less white, less straight, and less male, diverse cultures have brought different demands to dramaturgy. Because theatres have had to respond to non-linear feminism, or Persian dance/theatre, they also have become more responsive to all artists' particular needs. But I insist that too many theatres still define theatre according to a very narrow list of four elements; no matter how responsive they are, they often cannot respond to a play which arrives on their doorstep which has, for instance, no written text. At Buddies we can, and we will.

(1996)

Power in the Performers' Hands
by Lois Brown

In the past ten years, Resource Centre for the Arts (RCA) Theatre Company has pre-miered over fifty new plays. Among them, *Young Triffie's Been Made Away With* (1985), recently produced and toured by Ship's Company; *Catlover* (1990), also produced by Tarragon Theatre and by the Stephenville Festival; *Flux (1991),* also pro-duced by Eastern Front Company, Live Bait, and as part of the film *The Hall Trilogy;* *Possible Maps* (1991), also produced by Tarragon and published by Coach House Press; *Hanlon House* (1991), also produced for film as a part of *The Hall Trilogy; Time Before Thought* (1991), also produced by Great Canadian Theatre Company and by CBC Radio for national broadcast; *Urbanite* (1993); *Still Alive* (1994), co-produced with Factory Theatre; *The AlieNation of Lizzie Dyke* (1994) and *Murder at the Royal Café* (1995).[1]

> Resource Centre for the Arts (RCA) Theatre Company has been part of the development of important Newfoundland writers who have acquired national reputations. Artists include Andy Jones, Mary Walsh, Greg Thomey, Ray Guy, Cathy Jones, Janis Spence, Rick Mercer, Ed Riche, and Andrew Younghusband. The Theatre Company resides in the LSPU Hall, "home of the best original theatre produced in Newfoundland." (Peters xxxi)

At the inception of RCA in 1979, ideas generated by local artists echoed concerns of young theatre radicals who, during the 1968 student uprisings in Paris, called for a theatre that did not separate its artistic activities from the political and social context. RCA began as a "grand experiment" to bring together art and community; it was an "artist-run community-based organization." After four years of operation, RCA was plagued with a lack of funds and by accusations of exclusivity. While there was certainly a lack of capital, the charges of exclusivity could not be upheld. In fact, RCA had the most open programming policy conceivable. Its program was selected by a board of directors elected from the membership; proposals were solicited from both artists and the larger community. Its membership was open to any resident of Newfoundland and Labrador.

In the early seventies, the creation of original, indigenous theatre was a part of a cultural renaissance in Newfoundland. It was a time when CODCO thought to turn St. John's into the centre for comedy in North America. It was a time when Figgy Duff began to recover and to popularize many almost-forgotten Newfoundland folk songs, to create music based on our traditional music. It was a time when Chris Brookes, inspired by the Fogo Process, the use of film and video for community development, founded a theatre of political protest and social animation; The Mummers Troupe. The Mummers Troupe's first project was the recovery of *The Mummers Play*, a Newfoundland folk play which had not been performed in most of Newfoundland for about a hundred years.

At that time, there was a deep sense of loss. Only a quarter of a century earlier, Newfoundlanders had voted away their independence. There was a pressing need to deal with the oppression, the trivialization, and the homogenization of Newfoundland culture and society before it was too late. There was a sense of urgency to recover, to create, or to perish.

Before long, CODCO, The Mummers Troupe, Sheila's Brush, and others established a professional, indigenous theatre, a Newfoundland theatre. Built on over four hundred years of history, influenced by the collective creation movement, it was experimental, political, and comic.

To appreciate Newfoundland theatre requires an understanding of theatre as collective creations, of montage, of structures, that are episodic rather than narrative, of text that is sometimes improvised rather than set. Often, situations and characters are presented rather than represented; sometimes one actor plays many characters. Song, storytelling, and dance could be a structural part of the work. Newfoundland theatre is theatre created by the performers from their own experiences—the power is in the performers' hands. The result is reminiscent of traditional storytelling: the story, the telling, and, usually, the teller are inseparable. Ultimately, our indigenous theatre requires an understanding of theatre as performance.

It was in this setting that RCA Theatre Company was established by RCA, albeit with the same mandate and board of directors. RCA Theatre Company would help both artists and non-artists to create theatre. Its open programming, consisting of four productions a year, included issue-oriented collective creations of relevance to Newfoundlanders and Labradorians. The board decided the general artistic direction of a given season with the help of an Artistic *Animateur.*

The way RCA Theatre Company develops plays has been influenced by both its democratic policies and the emphasis it places on performance. In 1986, the Theatre Company instituted a second space program designed "to put money into […] ideas." Productions were granted by the parent body. The second space program also tried to provide writers and performers with "an immediate opportunity to get it seen now; to evaluate it in a performance context now."

As elsewhere in Canada, things have changed since the seventies. Collective creations have been replaced by collaborations, by performer-authored scripts, and by playwriting. The vision is more specific and complex. Despite this evolution, writing and performing continue to be closely connected. In eight of the ten plays listed at the beginning of this article, the author was either a performer in, or the director of, the show.

The sprit of RCA Theatre's play development process can be demonstrated by looking at three recently produced works. *Time Before Thought,* directed by Andy Jones, performed by Mercedes Barry and Agnes Walsh, written by all three, is an example of collaborative writing with a specific artistic vision in mind. Some of our strongest work has been what Peters calls "the author-acted show" (cf. *Stars*), such as Liz Pickard's *The AlieNation of Lizzie Dyke,* which Liz performed and Teri Snelgrove directed. Sometimes a writer is inspired, even challenged, by a performer to write something for him to perform, as was the case with Ed Riche's *Possible Maps.* Directed by Lois Brown, *Possible Maps* (although it was produced at the Tarragon without Charlie Tomlinson) was inextricably bound to Charlie's qualities as a performer.

Time Before Thought is the "new" Newfoundland theatre. It tells a distinctly Newfoundland story based on the experiences of Mercedes and Agnes, two childhood friends who are courted by American servicemen stationed in Placentia. They marry and leave Newfoundland to live in the States. Though they live great distances apart, their friendship sustains them through difficult marriages. Eventually their marriages, as well as their romance with America, end and they return home. A story of true love, friendship, and home is interlocked with a fairy tale and an imaginary story about Mercedes's and Agnes's love affair with Bob Dylan who, as it turns out, is a Newfoundlander. The play is a montage of film sequences, and dramatic scenes, as well as reflective and lyrical monologues.

During the creation process, each of the three writers independently wrote blocks of text: stories, imaginary scenes, poems, reflections, journal entries, screenplays. It was as if the parts would disclose their own order as the writers continued to work, almost like a sculptor sensing a form in marble. The structure that emerged is complicated: the filmed fairy tale mythologizes Agnes's and Mercedes's love affairs with American servicemen and creates a psychological context for the main story. Each story, each element of the work varies in style, so that not only the content but also the style contextualize the other elements. The writers, as Andy Jones puts it, worked "backwards toward the script."

Performance was what actually shaped this wonderful rich material that kept pouring out of the writers to the very end. When I came to rehearsals as a script consultant, the rehearsal performance was the script we discussed. Even the initial performances were a part of the work's development and helped to further disclose the script. I was told that on opening night Andy came into the dressing room at intermission and said to Mercedes and Agnes, "I've got a great idea for Act Two." Whether this story is true or not isn't the point. The point is that anyone who knows RCA Theatre Company's deep commitment to the process could believe it of almost any artist associated with us.

Performance was also an important part of the development of *The AlieNation of Lizzie Dyke*. It is a story about Lizzie Dyke's life from childhood to death, including a lesbian love affair with an extraterrestrial. Liz Pickard periodically performed parts of Lizzie Dyke before it premiered, calling her performances "From the Book of Lizzie Dyke." She also performed segments after the play was produced and used these performances to evaluate her work in order to revise it for publication.

The aesthetic of performance was of primary import to help create a structure for this work. For example, during the production of *Lizzie Dyke*, Teri Snelgrove and I persuaded Liz not to cut the song "Blue Skies." We argued not that it was essential to the story but that it was essential to the rhythm of Act Two. This proved to be true.

Many of the works like *Possible Maps* are as much literature as they are theatre, but the developmental process is still performance-oriented. *Possible Maps*, the story of a son's admiration for his father's visionary ideas and his fear of inheriting his father's madness, was written on a dare. Charlie Tomlinson challenged filmmaker Ed Riche to write a play. Charlie's contention was that Ed would find it much more difficult to write a play than a screenplay, because theatre is a superior art form. Since Ed had seen everything Charlie had ever done and knew Charlie's ability to give an idea emotional life, the text was written for Charlie to perform. The play was conceived as a particular performance by a particular performer. The play's development revolved around the notion that it would be performed live by Charlie, that *Possible Maps* would be a performance.

In summary, RCA Theatre Company supports a developmental process that has performance at its centre. This process does not defer to the primacy of literary text: the Company is not committed to the development of literature, but rather to the development of theatre as an art form. Despite this commitment, the more prevalent notions of drama as literature often compete with the notion of theatre as what is performed. The legacy of the play as literature is so pervasive that even young Newfoundland artists fall victim to it, writing scripts without any sense of their own Newfoundland theatrical context. But it is not just Newfoundland theatre practitioners, but dramaturges everywhere who have a responsibility to support the kind of processes that develop theatre—what is performed—first and foremost, and to elucidate them so they can gain legitimacy through practice.

(1996)

Works Cited

Lynde, Denyse, ed. *Voices from the Landwash*. Toronto: Playwrights Canada, 1997.
Peters, Helen, ed. *Star in the Sky Morning: Collective Plays of Newfoundland and Labrador.* St. John's: Killick, 1996.
Sherman, Jason, ed. *Solo.* Toronto: Coach House, 1994.

---

[1]   *Young Triffie's Been Made Away With, Flux, Hanlon House, The AlieNation of Lizzie Dyke* can be found in Lynde. *Possible Maps* can be found in Sherman. *Time Before Thought* can be found in Peters.

Dramaturgy: A Nightwood Conversation
Re-imagined by Diane Roberts

The following excerpts are taken from a two-hour conversation with Diane Roberts, Kate Lushington, Monique Mojica, and Dawn Obokata.

Diane: Shall we begin by introducing ourselves?

Monique: Monique Mojica.

Diane: And... what was your involvement with Nightwood?

Monique: Nightwood developed, supported, and co-produced my play *Princess Pocahontas and the Blue Spots*. I have done several stints as dramaturge ("drama-kewable") in Groundswell. Two other shows I was involved in were supported and developed at Nightwood.

Dawn: I'm Dawn Obokata. I'm an independent artist working in movement- and image-based theatre. My current project *Soulscapers I: The Wilderness Trilogy* has toured internationally. I've been on the Groundswell Selection Committee forever...

Diane: ...I did that too, didn't I?

Dawn: Yes, you did. I'm on Nightwood Theatre's Artistic Advisory now and, more recently, I have joined the board.

Kate: I'm Kate Lushington and I was Artistic Coordinator for two years and Artistic Director for nearly four at Nightwood Theatre. I also wrote a play with a group called "The Clichettes" which Nightwood produced and performed at Groundswell some years before I became involved in such a full-time capacity.

Monique: I did that too.

Kate: Yes. *Sea Cows*. I found an old program, which had a most extraordinary group of people in it. There was, I think, your *Sea Cows*, and Djanet Sears's *Africa Solo*, and my *Sex in a Box*, and, oh yes, Lillian Allen did *One Bedroom with Dignity*. This was all at Groundswell shortly before I took over.

Diane: I am Diane Roberts and (at the time of writing this article) I am Artistic Co-Director of Nightwood Theatre, along with Alisa Palmer. Leslie Lester is our Producer. I've been involved with the company for five years.

Dawn: An impressive group of women.

Diane: How do we go about defining dramaturgy for ourselves?

Monique: I'm not sure what it is. My aunt Muriel (Miguel) says it sounds like dermatology. I always thought that people said dramaturgical, but I found out recently that the word is "dramatalurgical."

Dawn: Really, that sounds like metallurgical!

Monique: That's right, it's like metallurgical. It's alchemy.

Diane: So, what is it that we actually do?

Monique: Well, I don't know. I don't know that I really know what it is, even though I have had that title. When Djanet Sears worked with me as dramaturge for *Princess Pocahontas and the Blue Spots* she always said, "I'm here to make sure that what you want to say gets out." That makes a lot of sense to me. The way I go at it probably has nothing to do with definitions, structures, or straight lines. When I think of what dramaturgy is, I think it's like being on a wave—you're on a current, and you try to do everything you can to keep that current going. You're grabbing thoughts that come from other levels and trying to connect them. When there is a vital germ, an essential vitalness to something a writer or a performer is trying to discover, or uncover, a dramaturge helps the creator to identify it and form it.

Diane: I agree with you. It can be an overwhelming process. Sometimes I wonder if my tendency to veer away from any one way of working is a feminist or woman's approach, or if this is just a "me" approach.

Monique: I've certainly encountered many other women actors and directors who are very linear in terms of their thought, and very academic in terms of their process for creating theatre.

Kate: I redefine it as an alternative to what came before, as opposed to something specifically feminist.

Monique: For me, it's stuff like finding out from Mark Haslam that they're trying to get Saartjie Baartman's bones back from the museums. I phone Djanet and tell her because I know it would help her with the piece she is working on now.

Diane: You look at a piece and are touched by the piece. So, your senses are open. Just having your senses open to the piece allows information to come in from different sources.

Dawn: Yes.

Diane: …and because you've got that distance, you can filter it and feed it to the playwright.

Dawn: Like a receptor. It seems that, often, in the creative process, it's difficult for a director and a writer to see everything. So, it's good to have another body in that creative stream.

Kate: There is a real danger of changing its function from a nurturing one to an impositional one. That's why I think that dramaturgy, in its best sense at Nightwood (when it works), has tried deliberately to create a different kind of approach than, say, the dramaturgy that has developed through some of the other new Canadian theatres.

Diane: Can you describe that difference?

Kate: The word "midwife" comes to mind. The role of a midwife is to support the woman who is in control of her own birthing process. The role of midwife is not to have her own baby through the other woman as a channel.

Dawn: But do you think the dramaturge as midwife is in service to the writer, or to the project, or to the process?

Kate: Well, a midwife does not serve the baby but serves the woman, because the idea is that the woman will best know how to serve her own baby.

Monique: At the same time, the woman doesn't do anything to endanger the baby.

Kate: No.

Monique: And there is intervention if needed.

Kate: Yes. The other thing I loved was that you mentioned alchemy. I think there is a specific craft to dramaturgy, to dramaturgical skills. Skills and knowledge.

Monique: What are they? What about them?

Kate: In order to develop the language of theatre, you have to understand there are elements of language that are not textual. The language of gesture and of the power differences between people.

Dawn: It sounds like an understanding of the dynamics of performance is essential.

Kate: Exactly.

Diane: We should talk about the history of dramaturgy at Nightwood.

Kate: Nightwood started with a group of women (Cynthia Grant, Kim Renders, Mary Vingoe, Maureen White) who defined their work in opposition to some of the collective creations that were being made in those days—a historical storytelling style, very much dependent on men. Founding members created works that were more imagistic, following less a single narrative or a chronological narrative structure. Nonetheless, they were a collective.

Diane: I wonder how they dealt with the role of the dramaturge?

Monique: As part of the collective process. They all had to be able to do it before something got scripted, even if it was still being scripted when it went on (as often collective works are).

Diane: What do you think, Dawn, in terms of the process you're a part of?

Dawn: Nightwood offers a kind of centre, both with the space and with the incredible resource of people—something Kate often pushed with Ground Talk. Even if you can't be one of the few that goes through the whole process, you will have access to people who will take an afternoon, or a couple of hours, to sit down and talk about your work or read it through.

Diane: The current Groundswell committee reads as much as it possibly can and really considers each play. The members have gut reactions, spend time, and take care discussing the plays so that writers can get feedback in any form. More and more, we have to be inventive in our approach to play development.

Kate: What is exciting about the Nightwood process is that there is an openness to surprise, to things that could not be predicted. For foolhardy reasons, or whatever, we leave ourselves open to longer-term projects. We don't have the funding for them, so I suppose that everyone, to some extent, subsidizes this process.

Diane: Nightwood's approach is not product-driven. It's not driven by saying, "Okay, Dilara Ally, you've got this feminist approach for a Classical Indian play. Great—on the stage with you tomorrow." Dilara experienced a long developmental process that opened her up, that allowed her to stretch the boundaries of her ideas in a significant way.

Kate: I often call it "trial by fire" dramaturgy, because even after it's over, it will still feel as though it's not really a long enough process.

Monique: It takes at least two years to develop something.

Kate: Right. I wanted to ask Diane about *Mango Chutney*, because you've now moved into production of the piece. It's going to go up in March, is it?

Diane: Yeah.

Kate: And you mentioned that Sally Han had been the dramaturge. How was she integrated into the developmental process?

Diane: Last spring Dilara and I decided to bring in another dramaturge, since our vision for the project was beginning to merge. I invited Sally to be an advocate for the writer. I also solicited feedback from Nightwood Theatre's Artistic Advisory. All of the dramaturgical feedback was (and continues to be) filtered through my and Dilara's joint vision of the project.

Kate: Right, which is really an important point because the dramaturge is not there to have a vision, but to serve the vision.

Diane: Absolutely.

Monique: To come back to the first question we started with, "What is dramaturgy?", it seems to me to be an ongoing thing. That's contradictory to the way theatre is usually done where dramaturges are there at the beginning of the process and not heard from again. When a production comes down, if you are passionate, and you are driven, and you have the need, then you keep working on it.

Kate: When is a piece finished?

Dawn: That's a whole other discussion.

(1996)

We would like to thank Carolyn Hay and Kevin McTavish.

The ATP Experience: Giving Good First Production in a Supportive Atmosphere
by Bob White

New play development at Alberta Theatre Projects (ATP) in Calgary is centred on playRites, our annual festival of new work. Four mainstage productions presented in rep, as well as a host of ancillary events (workshop readings, noon-hour "brief new works," competitions, cabarets, youth showcases, site-specific performance arts and more), crowd our calendar from mid-January through to the beginning of March. We bill playRites as "the Hottest Six Weeks in Winter" and, after ten years, it has become the signature event for the company.

The idea for the festival originated with ATP Producing Director D. Michael Dobbin. When engaged by the board in 1983, Dobbin was charged with returning ATP to one of the cornerstones of its original mandate: the development of new work. After experiencing John Jory's highly successful Humana Festival at the Actors Theatre of Louisville, Dobbin was convinced that a medium-sized regional theatre in a medium-sized city could produce a new play festival to launch Canadian plays into the national and international repertoire. While the showcasing aspect is still a major part of the festival's mandate, playRites, in my opinion, is really about exposing our own audience to new writing from across the country, about developing appreciation and support for the process of original creation. In a society almost addicted to the notion of "consuming product," a cultural event that attempts to create appreciation and understanding of process may, in fact, be the single most important thing we do.

Ironically, although the festival celebrates the process of creation and creativity, the play development team at ATP is really only interested in finding and working on plays that we are going to produce. If we had more money and more staff, perhaps we could engage in more "social service" dramaturgy—extensive community outreach, providing detailed responses to unsolicited manuscripts, encouraging writers through many drafts in the hope that "some day" they'll create something you might actually want to produce, and so on. However, our reality is that each and every year at the end of November a company of close to forty actors, directors, designers, technicians and support personnel will gather to start rehearsals on four plays. Our job in play development is to make sure they've got the four best possible scripts to work on.

At ATP, we like to call ourselves "second-tier" play developers. Material is developed in-house, but we find the majority of plays we produce at play development centres and other theatres. We like to find those plays that have had significant development elsewhere and then do what we think we do best: give a good first production. In essence, we go shopping and endeavour to find those scripts that can best be served by the kind of production and exposure playRites provides.

The real dramaturgy at ATP, then, occurs during the run-up-to and rehearsal of the play. We don't hold much store in traditional, literary-based dramaturgy. Once a play is selected, we try to provide the playwright with the director of his or her choice. It is at this point that a production dramaturge is assigned to the *production* of the play. A script becomes a play in the crucible of production, and we see the dramaturgical job as part of the production process. In this regard, then, the dramaturge is charged with being the show's "outside eye" and monitoring the development of the production as it relates to the original scheme developed by the playwright and director. At ATP, the production dramaturge isn't there to make a reluctant playwright make cuts, or make suggestions about the act-one curtain, or commiserate in the bar with the playwright about how badly the actors are mangling the beauty of the text. Although the production dramaturge might engage in any, or all, of those activities, we don't engage dramaturges to be the playwright's keeper. Their job is to assist in the delivery of the best possible production of the play and to serve as advocate for that great invisible presence in the rehearsal hall: the audience.

The preview schedule at playRites plays an important role in the dramaturgical process as well. Because of the repertory system we use, all four shows have three previews spaced over a two-week period prior to the openings. This means that there is actually time between previews to discuss and implement changes based on audience response. Since we are doing these shows for our audience, we, as producers, take the feedback provided by our audience quite seriously. The response almost always indicates where there might be confusion, boredom, and resistance, as well as sincere appreciation. By letting our audience directly help shape the production in this manner, we feel we are engaged in a "real world" situation, far removed from the abstract speculations of academic dramaturgy.

The "cold bath" which accompanies confronting a real audience during production makes play development at playRites most useful to the playwright. Public readings and workshops can provide a real service in the development of scripts. However, the audience present at these events is hardly representative of the audience at large. Comprised as it is of friends and relations of the artists, potential producers sitting in judgment, cynical theatre types, and those clearly demented members of the public who actually find under-rehearsed actors blowing through a script entertaining, the reading/workshop audience is a placebo at best. It might look like an audience, it might smell like an audience, but until someone has laid out the fifteen/twenty/thirty/forty bucks for their best girl and themselves for a Saturday night out, it ain't the real thing.

The most important feature of the play development process at ATP is the obvious one. We are actually producing the plays. The focus on production forces everyone involved to make real decisions. As [David] Mamet has observed, most of us in the theatre would rather spend our time avoiding getting down to the real work. We'll do just about anything to avoid actually committing ourselves. This is a swamp made to order for the kind of dramaturgy that loves to revel in possibilities and luxuriate in "what ifs?" This kind of dramaturgy makes everyone feel just great. Not a few so-called dramaturges have built their careers on their ability to entertain and stroke playwrights with wonderfully supportive observations and witty philosophical speculations. Unfortunately, it's all worth bupkis if, on opening night, the audience contracts communal bronchitis ten minutes into the show, making you realize nobody gives a fig for what's going on up there on the stage. Ultimately we feel that any development process that doesn't focus on production is incomplete. What are we doing this for, after all?

Most of the time, playRites has been able to deliver on our pledge to present a good first production of someone's script. We haven't held up our end a few times when we haven't brought the right people together, and we've been stiffed occasionally by writers who haven't had the experience or the heart to engage in the collaboration that theatre requires. And playRites has its limitations. Repertory casting means that the absolutely perfect cast for each play may not be possible. Further, the festival is a bit of a gilded ghetto. The plays are protected by the festival umbrella—harder knocks might lie ahead if the play has to stand alone as part of a regular season. However, playRites has premiered forty plays on the mainstage to date, and over half have gone on to further productions. Most of the writers enjoy their experience. We've developed an audience in Calgary that is keen and sophisticated in their appreciation of new work. A play could have a more uncomfortable birth.

(1996)

240 Cups of Play Development
by Peter Smith and Lise Ann Johnson

Last May [1995], the staff of Playwrights' Workshop Montréal set aside a day littered with the three "Cs" (coffee, contraband cigarettes, and croissants) in order to evaluate the work we had done during the 1994–95 theatrical season. We had started out the year as a brand new PWM team (comprised of Artistic Director Peter Smith, General Manager Rebecca Scott, Associate Director Lise Ann Johnson, and Associate Dramaturge Deena Azia), and had enthusiastically plunged into an eclectic season of workshops, translations, and artistic exchanges. In the spirit of evaluation, Peter popped the big question. "How do we get better at what we do?" It turned out to be a query with a philosophical heart. How, in general, do people discover, learn, and improve? Propelled by caffeine, nicotine, and sugar in equal and excessive amounts, we bandied about numerous theories, finally agreeing upon a few common notions. Foremost, we agreed that in order to get better at something, one had to avoid assuming there was only one way to do it. With this in mind, we looked back over the year. In September, we had devised a mission statement which stated the following:

> Playwrights' Workshop Montréal is a professional theatre centre dedicated to developing contemporary work and new writers for the Canadian stage. From dramaturgical consultation through to public readings, we offer a unique passage for each play, our belief being that each project defines its own needs.

The mission statement supported our idea that there was always more than one way to do something. So, we asked ourselves, "Do we follow through on our own mission statement?" Had we really approached each play on its own terms? Did we find an individualized means of developing each script? In other words, did each project define its own needs?

We discovered that although we had worked on a great variety of scripts (from Kent Stetson's *Sweet Magdalena* to Linda Gaboriau's translation of *Je vous ecris du Caire* by Normand Chaurette) and with many idiosyncratic artists (from Canadian playwright John Murrell to Mexican playwright Sabina Berman), we had used similar, sometimes identical means in developing each play.

Our methods of workshopping were extremely conventional, probably the same ones employed by other developmental theatres in this country. Following several ad hoc dramaturgical discussions, we would bring the writer together with actors, a director, and a dramaturge for a maximum of four days to "workshop" the script. Typically, the first couple of days would be comprised mainly of table work. The play would be read in its entirety several times and then examined scene by scene. The last couple of days were often spent in preparation for a public reading. The readings generally involved very little staging, physical exploration, or technical support (i.e., lights and sound). Following the reading, the dramaturge and director would meet with the writer to discuss both the workshop and the script. Occasionally, a writer would continue an informal relationship with the dramaturge into the next draft.

In planning our '95–'96 season, we decided to explore different ways of working with writers and different ways of developing a script. In particular, we wanted to extend the amount of time we could spend with writers, and we wanted to find more active and less literary means of workshopping. As a result, we came up with three new additions to our regular programming. First, we established a Writer's Unit, which will enable us to work with seven local writers over a period of eight months prior to rehearing their scripts for public readings in May '96. Second, we have initiated an artistic exchange with Theatre Columbus, a physical theatre company which often creates new work through improvisation. We hope to secure the means to co-develop the next draft of *Betrayal*, a play penned by Leah Cherniak and Martha Ross.

We have also initiated a new workshop format which we have entitled "the Extended Workshop." The Extended Workshop has been designed for theatrically innovative scripts which are between a first draft and a production-draft stage. As the name implies, the Extended Workshop extends both the timeline of the workshop and the resources available to the writer and the director. This format invites a writer to spend up to a month in residence at PWM, and allows the director to work with actors over a period of three weeks. In addition we've allowed for a designer [or designers] to create a skeletal set, lighting, costume, and sound design—with one element taking predominance over the others.

We completed our first Extended Workshop in November. Much was discovered. Sean Dixon was the first author to swim in the Extended waters, and so became our proverbial guinea pig. Sean's play, *The Cabinet Maker's Wedding*, was chosen with an eye on the amount it could benefit from theatrical, rather than table-based, exploration. The script, lyrical in style, is peppered with sequences which are image or movement based, and incorporates music and song into the action of the play. The workshop was directed by Lise Ann Johnson, and the cast was comprised of John Dunn-Hill, Jacqueline Blais, Gordon Masten, Peter Smith, and Jennifer Morehouse. Kairiin Bright, the Design Coordinator of Concordia University's Theatre Department, along with two design students, Tiffany Oschmann and Marie-Josée Perron, created a set, lighting, and costume design for the workshop. The set, essentially abstract and metaphorical in nature, was a series of curved, elongated wooden ribs which ran from the floor to the grid, and marked a painted, circular playing space. The ribs and the shape of the space evoked the hull of a ship, the inside of a musical instrument, and the rib from which Eve was created. Last, but not least, David Williams, a local composer and musician, created a live soundscape for the presentation with additional musical support from Jennifer Morehouse. The sound design incorporated no electronic sound, and relied mostly on string instruments such as the banjo, the mandolin, the harp, the dulcimer, and the violin.

Based on our experience with *The Cabinet Maker's Wedding*, the Extended Workshop process offers a number of advantages over a shorter, more conventional one. The short-term workshop is particularly valuable in allowing the writer to hear the broad strokes of their script: the general rhythm of each character's speech pattern, the overall structure and pace of the play, where to cut, where to elaborate, what is clear, what is obscure, and so on. However, it also comes with certain limitations, usually created by a lack of time, money, imagination, and resources. Generally, in a short-term workshop, the writer spends less than a week with the dramaturge and director; the writer has little or not time to make, incorporate, and test changes to the text; the actors and director do not get away from table work; the actor must make broad choices; the staging possibilities and theatricality of the play are not explored; design input is either nonexistent or theoretical; and the playwright hears the play read in front of an audience once.

In contrast, courtesy of the Extended Workshop format, Sean had time to rewrite, and time to test new material in front of more than one audience. During the initial week, Sean made minor changes to the first act and wrote a complete new draft of the second act. Throughout the second week, he made small cuts to the text that he felt was repetitive or overwritten. During the third week, having witnessed the first series of public readings, Sean rewrote the first act to expand the narrative role of a previously minor character substantially. We incorporated the changes into the presentation and tested the new material in front of an audience during the third reading. At Sean's request, we went back to the original version of the first act for the final public reading. Although some of the new material worked to his satisfaction, he felt that the weighty narrative of this new draft slowed the pace of the play and distanced the audience from the action. Rewriting is by no means a requisite part of the Extended Workshop. Each writer has an individual, idiosyncratic process, and many writers prefer to rewrite with great time and distance from any other creative influences. However, for a playwright who can rewrite quickly, the Extended Workshop offers a prime opportunity to test out new directions and new material.

In a four-day workshop, it is very easy to lose the spirit of discovery inherent in rehearsal. When restricted to discussion around a table, actors are placed in a position to judge the work as *dramaturges*, rather than to approach the text as *actors* seeking the actions and objectives of a character. Although discussion can and should be reined by an experienced director, actors disengage from their bodies in a four-day workshop, search for the broad strokes of the character, and often stop asking "actor questions." They focus, instead, on thematic and metaphorical concerns. The premise of their exploration is no longer the discovery of action, but too easily drafts toward "what needs to be changed in this script?"

We discovered that the Extended Workshop is a more "active" form of dramaturgy, that moving from the table onto our feet allowed actors to ask relevant, active questions: "What has just happened? What have I come from? What do I want in this moment/this scene/this play?" and, "What do I do to get what I want?" Ultimately, these are questions that service authors and enable them to distinguish between necessary ambiguity and the unnecessarily cryptic.

The other main advantage of the Extended Workshop process is that the interpreters of the script (the director, the actors, the composer, and the designers) can offer the playwright, in a limited way, their physical understanding of the world of the play. Although the Extended Workshop is by no means a workshop production, the playwright witnesses a skeletal version of blocking and design. This opens the writer up to theatrical possibilities they had not envisioned; it can also pinpoint conventions and transitions that are potentially awkward or repetitive. In the case of *The Cabinet Maker's Wedding*, Sean had written a series of transitions which included turning a store counter into a bed and back again. Although the transformation is potentially magical, we discovered that our version of the action quickly became a repetitive bit of stage business.

We also discovered a few weaknesses in our plan, which we will address before attempting another Extended Workshop in April with *Reading Hebron* by Jason Sherman. Under the mistaken belief that we could serve double duty, we did not hire an outside dramaturge to work with Sean during this workshop. Unfortunately, with the addition of so many technical elements, Lise Ann's focus was split between the actors and the designers. Peter's role as an actor in the workshop necessarily meant that his focus was too specific and subjective to act as the writer's "outside eye." In the future, we will ensure that both a director and a dramaturge are engaged for the Extended Workshop process. We are pleased that Brian Quirt will be working as a dramaturge with Jason Sherman on *Reading Hebron*.

We also plan to re-evaluate the extent to which we incorporate design elements into the process. During our first time out we were overly ambitious (over sixty lighting cues and a makeshift snow machine!). As a result, we lost valuable rehearsal time trying to incorporate far too much tech into the presentation. This was further complicated by the fact that the technical aspects had to be reworked whenever major changes to the script were incorporated. Next time out, we plan to scale back some of the design elements, and introduce one "10 out of 12" technical rehearsal during the final week.

CBC Radio recently broadcast an interview with American novelist and essayist Wendell Berry. He told a story about a potter he once knew. This man, as the story goes, had travelled to Japan to study with a master potter. During the first part of the apprenticeship, the man spent his time cleaning windows and toilets. After a while, the apprentice asked his mentor when he would begin to pot. He was assigned a slew of other menial tasks. A month or so passed, and the apprentice repeated his question. To his surprise, the master said, "You will make 250 cups today." The apprentice worked like a fiend, but, by the end of the day, had only managed to make 240 cups. The master took the cups and threw them away. "Perhaps you will make the 250 cups another day."

We're not sure what the point of this is. In fact, none of us can agree on either its general philosophical pertinence or its specific relevance to this article. However, most are certain that the story is relevant in some way: that the actual cups are not as important as the artist's ability to make them; that the process of discovery cannot be hurried; that failure is a necessary part of learning; that Japanese potters are not only insane, but wasteful, and so on. In the end, we've agreed to disagree. Just as there is more than one way to do something, there must be more than one way to interpret the world. In the spirit of "getting better at what we do," we will continue to revise the way we work and will continue to explore new avenues of development so that each project can define its own needs.

(1996)

Learning to Hate the Bingo Scenario
by DD Kugler

May 1998. Playwrights, directors, designers, actors, dramaturgs, administrators, even academics like me, gather at the Canadian Theatre Conference in Saskatoon. One breakout session on dramaturgy evolves into a lively discussion on the dramaturgy of artists such as designers and choreographers. The artists are articulate and passionate about their contribution, or potential contribution, to scripts. No one, however, mentions the playwright—until at the very end, an artistic director describes a particular developmental process in which, he says, "even the playwright might take part."

I find it surprising, and perhaps illuminating, that respected artists can discuss "play development" for an hour and a half and never feel the need to mention the playwright. When I speak, I note the absence of the playwright from the "dramaturgical discussion," and wonder aloud if we are shifting away from the primacy of the playwright in creating new plays? I am met with blank stares.

At the LMDA (Literary Managers and Dramaturgs of the Americas) Conference in New York (June 1998) I raise the question again, as I also do at the Theatre Centre Mini-Conference on the Architecture of Dramaturgy in Toronto (July 1998). No one returns the volley.

I may be alone, but I can't shrug off the question. Is the collaborative relationship between the playwright and other theatre artists subtly changing in the play development process?

Let's pause for some terminology.

Fumblings

I offer the following distinctions without any authority. They are not universally accepted, nor do they necessarily refer to the historical models you might expect. Don't get distracted by the terminology, stay with the ways of working. My distinctions are tentative, and very much a work-in-progress. I'm fumbling—trying to articulate nuance in a complex creative relationship.

Play creation is possible, of course, without the benefit of a playwright. But for the purposes of this article, I am speaking only of a play creation that includes in its process an artist (perhaps formerly) known as "the playwright." A playwright can write a script in artistic isolation as well, but this article assumes a development process.

I make a distinction in theatre between collaboration and collective creation. It's a question of ownership.

In *collective creation*, individual contributions constitute collective ownership. In this often improvisational and rehearsal-generated process, a multiplicity of "artist authors" (actor, designer, choreographer, composer, director, dramaturg, playwright, etc.) collectively create, and own, the "script." The writer often documents and assembles, on paper, the breadth of artistic contribution.

In *collaboration*, individual contributions do not constitute ownership. In this process, the artists collectively develop and interpret the playwright's script. Individual artists may well make significant contributions to dialogue, imagery, shape, and feel of the script, but the playwright remains the sole owner.

Either the playwright's script is the primary source, and the other artists collaborate in an essentially interpretative act (even if it results in changes to the script), or the artists are engaged in an act of collective creation. I don't think there's much middle ground. Both are legitimate means of play creation, and neither is superior, but the artistic roles are different. More important, neither process can be assumed. In fact it is essential from the outset to make sure everyone agrees about the process he or she is working in.

I also make a distinction in the collaborative process between script development and production development. *Script development* shapes the words on the page; it clarifies the author's script, the primary source. *Production development* shapes a three-dimensional stage performance; it is a broader collaborative process that initiates an interpretive transition from the author's page to the ensemble's stage. Of course, the distinction is somewhat arbitrary: script development generally implies certain production elements; production development, even rehearsal, almost always alters the script. Yet I think it's useful to locate a line between clarifying the script (a focus on the page), and interpreting the script (a focus on the stage).

With these provisional distinctions in mind, let's return to the discussion in Saskatoon. Which play creation process was the breakout group discussing, and what were the implied relationships?

On the surface it seemed as though they were talking about production development—a collaborative process of interpretation. But they weren't, because they were adamant about how their varied contributions could develop and shape the script itself, the words on the page. Fine. Then perhaps it was a dramaturgical discussion about script development—an attempt to clarify the author's voice. But it wasn't, given the complete absence of the playwright from the discussion. I think they were actually discussing collective creations, in which they were equal owners of the script and its development.

I'm not objecting to collective creation; that's not my point. Indeed, the degree and quality of artistic contribution in some contemporary play development may well be collective creation (as I've defined it) rather than production development. But if that's the case, let's acknowledge the shift from one process to the other, so that we can clarify the admittedly subtle relationship among the working artists.

If those relationships are not mutually understood, the consequences can be far-reaching. In fact, it's not a very large step from the ambiguous discussion in Saskatoon to the suits and countersuits in New York between dramaturg Lynn Thomson and the estate of Jonathan Larson.

Rent Fallout

I don't want to talk about *Rent* because understanding the artists' relationships during *Rent*'s development is complicated, even undermined, by the untimely death of

Jonathan Larson. The fact of the playwright's death is so exceptional that the specifics of *Rent* are neither useful not illuminating. But the *Rent* case is broadly relevant because it exposes implicit tensions among artists in the development process.

Witness the two-page "commentary," "An Author Is an Author Is an Author," that recently appeared in *American Theatre*, signed by thirty-five playwright members of New York's New Dramatists:

> We can—and feel we must—cite some general truths about a potentially dangerous trend: the sometimes subtle, sometimes overt appropriation of a playwright's claim to authorship... the proliferation of workshop and developmental programs... —well-intentioned as they are—may perpetuate the misguided notion that everyone involved in a play's long journey to the stage becomes, in some way, its author...
>
> As playwrights—now more than ever—we find it necessary to reassert the primacy of our place in the theatre.
>
> Obviously, theatre is a joint affair. It requires the participation of skilled artists to realize any play. And the challenges weathered by a text in the face of a demanding director and inquisitive cast are crucial to its completion. A play is, after all, the painstaking recipe for an ultimately three-dimensional "event."
>
> But realizing a play—the task undertaken by our collaborators in the theatre—is an essentially *interpretative* act. To stage a play, to edit a text or to act a role are distinct form *authoring* it; they are all acts of *rendition*...
>
> An excess of development can undermine the most ephemeral but distinctive tool a writer possesses: authorial voice [...] True authorial voice always predates the first rehearsal of a text. And it is—and will always be—an author's most distinguishing and valuable feature.
>
> Therein lies the true nature of authorship, and no other party can lay claim to it. (Wright 6–7)

There's not much I disagree with in this "commentary." The tone, however, is troubling because of its underlying assumption that collaborators in general, and dramaturgs in particular, want to own the script. The playwrights clearly feel defensive, under attack, and they have mounted a counteroffensive. In light of the vague artistic parameters of that discussion in Saskatoon, it's easy to see why. In a creative process with broad and significant artistic contribution, it is easy to shift unknowingly from the assumptions of script or production development into the assumptions of a collective creation process. And that shift fundamentally alters the playwright's relationship with fellow artists.

Any attempt to clarify the relationship between the playwright and other theatre artists must examine the assumptions around the issues of ownership, recognition, and compensation.

Ownership

I have tried to clarify the issue of ownership by making a distinction between collective creation (collective ownership) and collaboration (playwright ownership). As I have also noted, the line between the two processes; and therefore the issue of ownership, is getting less and less clear.

There are also degrees, or kinds of ownership. I have been talking exclusively about ownership of the script. The composer, like the playwright, creates and owns a document, a score. But there's also ownership of the more ephemeral artistic elements of a production. The actor, the designer, the choreographer, the director, for example, each make a personal creative (interpretive) investment in the script that results in a unique "product"—the performance, the design, the choreography, the direction— very much their own.

I'm not sure this constitutes legal ownership—court cases are already in progress that may determine this—but the ownership is clearly "felt." When I work as dramaturg/director on a new script, I know precisely when I shift from my role as dramaturg into my role as director. It has to do with ownership.

As *director*, I struggle to achieve a personal and unified interpretation that is consistent with the play. Despite broad artistic collaboration during the process, I feel a tangible possessiveness about that intangible "product"—the direction. I'm sure the actor, the designer, the choreographer feel a similar possessiveness. As the discussion of intellectual property rights heats up, more attention will be paid to these ephemeral areas of ownership, I'm sure.

Oddly enough, I have always felt that one of my strengths as *dramaturg* was that I had no claim to ownership of any "product." What could I possibly own? Not the script, that's the playwright's. I bring my aesthetic to the service of the process. Don't read that as martyred servitude. I am passionate in my aesthetic arguments because I do care. Although I have no real control, my opinions may have additional weight because they are untainted by issues of ownership. The actor, the designer, the director are legitimately concerned with the needs of their performance, their design, their direction, and so on. "My dramaturgy," whatever that is, is utterly invisible.

Recognition

Recognition is the public acknowledgement of those who have contributed to the development of the script. Simple enough. And yet, recognition is often neglected or incomplete. When few artists reap any significant financial reward, public acknowl-edgement for creative contribution becomes increasingly important.

At a session on intellectual property rights at the Association for Theatre in Higher Education (ATHE) Conference that took place in San Antonio, Texas, in August 1998, one producer complained about having to list twelve lines of acknowledgments in the program. Well... too bad! In a collaborative art form a wide range of artists and organizations make significant contributions to the work, and they should be recognized. I suspect the omissions are often oversights, but perhaps playwrights could be more conscientious. Perhaps acknowledgement needs discussion and contractual agreement from the outset of the working relationship.

Compensation

Compensation is remuneration, usually monetary, appropriate to the level of contribution. Most often non-playwright artists are either on salary with the producer or compensated in a fee-for-services contract that's negotiated with, and paid by, the producer. End of story.

Not so fast.

Compensation is complicated by a different kind of remuneration that's a percentage of the playwright's royalty. I admit, I have trouble separating this percentage-of-royalty compensation from ownership. But it's not about ownership—only the playwright's name is there under the title. It's about compensation, and here's how it works.

Many developmental theatres contract participation rights. The theatre company doesn't own the script, but they do expect a percentage of the playwright's royalty in compensation for their role in the development of the script. Similarly, while making no claim on ownership of the script, collaborative theatre artists could request a percentage of the playwright's royalty—participation rights—as compensation for their significant contribution to the play's development.

Obviously there's a range, among collaborators, in the quantity and quality of contribution. Which are significant—therefore worthy of compensation—and which are not? What is an appropriate level of compensation? Unfortunately, we can't assume that all parties will ultimately agree.

When I was artistic director at Northern Light Theatre, I never asked for participation rights—I found them inappropriate, given the low playwright's royalty at NLT and the fact that I received public funding to develop new work. Other developmental theatres, however—citing long-term commitment to the project and high financial risks—make a strong case for participation rights.

It's an honest, and deeply felt, philosophical disagreements. Must the playwright negotiate with each collaborator are likely. Must the playwright negotiate with each collaborator, contractually clarify first compensation and then the appropriate level thereof? Should this be the primary concern of the contemporary playwright?

In terms of remuneration, the playwright holds a unique position. Most theatre artists are paid for gigs—readings, workshops, and productions. The playwright, on the other hand, is compensated over the production life of the script. Perhaps, given the increasingly collaborative nature of play development, it is unfair that the playwright alone has access to these benefits. Perhaps significant collaborating artists deserve an appropriate long-term cut—in addition to their salary or their fee-for-services contract.

Participation rights may not, technically, constitute ownership, but they are clearly a portion of the playwright's potential livelihood. While most theatre artists cobble together a series of gigs each year, a playwright may work three or four years on a script and feel fortunate to get two productions in a decade. The playwright's income, even accrued over time, is miniscule if you consider the extended personal investment required.

When you start talking about participation rights in the face of the playwright's pathetic return on investment, it's hard not to recall cartoons of a carcass in the desert and buzzards circling above. Why this interest in having a piece of the playwright? How many ways can you profitably cut up zero? Ah, but then there's the "bingo scenario."

Bingo

The *bingo scenario* is that very rare case when a playwright's script becomes a monstrous commercial success (the regional circuit, Broadway, film, etc.).

I admit I've always hoped that, if a playwright fell into an obscene amount of money on a script that I dramaturged or directed, she or he would honour my contribution with a wee cut. It would be an additional acknowledgement—in money—because money happens to be the currency of the bingo scenario. Rumour has it that George Lucas went back, after *Star Wars'* success, and gave points to all his collaborators—even technicians. (What a mensch!)

But I've never contractually obligated the playwright to compensate me in that very unlikely scenario. I fear that it muddies the collaborative relationship by raising the spectre of ownership. And, given the remote likelihood of the bingo scenario, why bother?

Because of this very slim possibility, however, collaborating artists and developmental companies are increasingly contracting participation rights—claims on the playwright's potential revenue. I have serious concerns that a preoccupation with the bingo scenario lays the groundwork for an adversarial relationship that runs counter to collaboration.

Confession

In describing the new play development class at Brigham Young University, Robert Nelson concluded his presentation at the ATHE conference by calling for "an assumption of goodwill." Or, as George Walker put it: "Generosity. I think that's the most important thing in theatre" (qtd. in Corbeil 59).

I'm starry-eyed and naive beyond belief. I would like to see more generosity in new play creation. Let's bring an assumption of goodwill to the areas of potential tension. If it's about ownership—wanting to create collectively as co-authors—let's admit it to the playwrights, and work together to develop those structures. If it's about recognition for artistic collaboration in the development of the play, let's ask for acknowledgement. If it's about compensation, let's not allow a remote bingo scenario to dominate the foreground of our artistic discussions.

Let's create a contract that obligates the playwright to acknowledge the extent and degree of collaborative contribution, but restricts the issue of participatory compensation to a clause that exclusively covers the bingo scenario. Such a contract would allow artists to collaborate with a spirit of generosity. It would relegate the slim prospect of financial bonanzas to its appropriate place in the nether regions of the contract and the minds of the collaborators.

Big Picture

I feel oddly small, diminished by working through the nuances of playwright-artist relationships in the microclimates of new play development. So I'd like to leap out, way out, to the big picture. George Walker says,

> When I first talked to Ken Gass (artistic director of Factory Theatre), when I was made resident playwright when I was twenty-three years old, all I felt that I wanted to do, even then, was to make a body of work. And he said he would protect me so that I could do that—so that falling in and out of fashion or having hard times and easier times would never be the issue. He said, ["]You write, we'll protect you, and you'll do it. That's an investment in the writer. And once we're investing in you then we've an obligation to let you do the work.["] (qtd. in Corbeil 59–60)

Two decades ago, the young George Walker began an exceptionally generous relationship with Ken Gass and Factory Theatre. What theatre makes that kind of commitment now? Bob White's commitment to Eugene Stickland resulted in three premieres over fours years at Alberta Theatre Projects. At Necessary Angel, Richard Rose is in the middle of a three-year cycle of working with playwrights Colleen Murphy, Jason Sherman, and David Young. I'm sure there are others, but they feel like exceptions that prove the rule.

Given the Canada Council's funding criterion of "Canadian creation," we should ask ourselves what creation are we committing to—the play or the playwright. Obviously, they are not mutually exclusive. We all commit to the play in its development and production. But is the play the end, or is it part of a larger commitment to, and development of, the playwright? I'm not implying that one is good, or appropriate, and the other is not. Both are worthy. They are very different objectives, however, and imply different artistic relationships—perhaps even different futures—in the creation of Canadian theatre.

(1998)

Works Cited

Corbeil, Carole. "A Conversation with George Walker." *Brick* 58 (January 1998): 59–67.

Wright, Dove. "An Author Is an Author Is an Author." *American Theatre* 15.6 (July/ August 1998): 6–7.

The Nike Method
by Djanet Sears and Alison Sealy-Smith with Ric Knowles

Djanet Sears and Alison Sealy-Smith talked with Ric Knowles about process for two and a half hours in a wide-ranging conversation at the Tequila Bookworm on Queen Street West, Toronto, on 20 May 1998. The following is a severely edited version of that conversation, as transcribed by Christopher Tracy.

Djanet: Okay, we're talking about process, and the thing that always comes up is whether the process is more important than the product.

Alison: I'm sorry. It's all about product. You've got to be going somewhere; otherwise you might as well stay at home and play with yourself. *(laughter)*

Djanet: That's right. People always have a goal. They say, "We're exploring, this is about process," but they're aiming for a show. I think you have to be honest about that, and chart a course. It's like I've decided I'm going to the CN Tower. Now I can see the Tower, and I can walk straight towards it, and bump into a building. So I go, "Okay, that's what I'm aiming for, but what's the best route?" I plan a course. It's probably better for me to go across to Augusta and down this way.

Alison: But you might want to get to the CN Tower, and can probably do it by the best route, but what would happen if you turned north and came at it from the other side? You could find something really interesting. But unless you know where you're going, take a bus tour of the city.

Djanet: Absolutely. So let's start with the writing process. It's totally mysterious to me. You have a kernel of an idea that might not even end up in the play. A lot of it happens in your head. A lot of it is vomiting up something, and you're not sure where it's going to lead. But eventually you've got to shape it.

I like the element of exploring and chance. Writing a play, you're exploring an idea. It's only after a while of vomiting stuff up, you want to start shaping the vomit. You're digging up the clay and now you have to mould it into a bowl. So you start to knead the air out of it. You can make a bowl by rolling the clay into a snake, making a coil, and smoothing it out, or you can use a wheel. But the vomit is the essential element—in alchemy they call it the "lead"—the shit that turns into gold. When you start to shape, you use the more conscious part of the brain, so you're more aware of what's going on.

Alison: How do you do that? Do you work with a dramaturg?

Djanet: I've worked with two. Because I find you can *write* a play for a dramaturg. A dramaturg can say, "This play should do this, you should develop this scene," and take the story and make it work for them. So *I* feel dramaturgy involves service to the *writer.* It involves at some point holding your hand and helping you finish your vomiting, but at some point it also involves responding to the text. Now because *Harlem Duet* dealt with contentious issues around race, I wanted to be on the edge. I got two women, Diane Roberts, a Black director and dramaturg, and Kate Lushington, a white director and dramaturg. I'd have them respond to drafts with questions, and I'd take those home and sit with them. I found that helpful, because sometimes they didn't have a similar opinion, and it made me sure that I had to decide where I needed to go to make the edge razor sharp. It made it clear that not everybody was going to react the same way. I found it overwhelmingly opening and freeing.

And then there's workshopping. Once I'd finished my second draft of *Harlem Duet,* they gave me six days to workshop it, including one day as a performance day. That was five days for me as a writer. Usually workshops are a week long. The first day you do a reading, then you do another reading and then you do exercises. But I didn't need exercises. I just wanted to hear what I'd written. So I told Nightwood that I'd like to do one day a week for five weeks and do the reading in the sixth week. That way I'd have a week each time to make changes, and the following week see how the changes worked. I like workshops, but the way I ask people to comment in the initial stage is to just ask questions. Because early on, your ideas are fragile, you just want to hear the words, and use people for questions, to make you think. "Why does this character do this?" as opposed to "The way this character does that doesn't make sense." I get defensive. "It doesn't make sense to *you.*" And we get into an argument. But you have to use whatever process is good for you.

Directing is the same idea. Again, you start with the vomit. As a director, the first thing in analyzing the play that I set down is my gut impressions. The gut impressions have nothing to do really with analysis, or any of Aristotle's fundamental elements. They're colours, emotions, ideas, and I write them down, even if they don't make sense. One of my gut impressions for *Harlem* was, you know, deeply purple.

Alison: *(chuckles)* What does that mean?

Djanet: It means a passion, rich passion! It's not hot red, it's a deep purple. To help to make the deep purple come up would be one of my aims as a director. Part of the work is to find a way to articulate your gut impressions to the artistic team. I saw richness— one of the things I like about the commercial you're in, for Shopper's Drug Mart or whatever, is that they coloured you a kind of sepia brown and lit you well, and it's soft. My pet peeve about theatre and film is lighting black actors. It's ridiculous. We have brown skin, and if you light it with just white light, you get a green tinge. It's not warm. And we need more light, we're darker. It's simple. We need more light! It's not difficult, we just need more light! So, we're doing a black show?

Djanet, Alison and Ric: Put in more light. *(laughter)*

Djanet: So I wanted people to look rich. I wanted rich colours, but bright enough so that you can see their eyes, the characteristics of the face, the emotions. I wanted to find that passionate purple, which wasn't really the colour but the richness, and as many elements as possible had to have that.

Alison: As writer and director on *Harlem Duet,* when and how do you turn off the writer process? I'm trying to figure out the difference between literary dramaturgy, which is one kind of process, and production dramaturgy, which is another. What happens when the director says, "This is just getting too damn difficult, how do I get three different timelines onstage at the same time?" and the writer is going, "Well I'm, sorry, you're just going to have to figure it out, because my play happens in three different time periods." Do you have these conversations with yourself?

Djanet: Yes, I do. So I decided to not wear the hats at the same time for *Harlem Duet.* I said, "Okay, this is the script I'm going to direct, and it has three time periods." So when I first started design meetings, this was the structure. There must be a way not only to have three time periods but to go back and forth through them, not have a moving set, and not have huge changes in the eye. That was the demand I made on the designers. I was going to help by giving them the metaphors, the basic action of the story, and I wanted to tell the story visually from beginning to end, to tell another *layer* of the story: at the beginning the whole place is full, and at the end it's empty. That's the story. It's about loss.

One of the things I did, because I feel I'm not as visual as I could be, is spend a month looking at African-American art. Composition, colours, what struck me as good. Not asking why at first, but later, when I had to convey it to the designers. You have to do the homework. If I feel something is important, then we have to find a way, in collaboration, to accommodate it. If I don't find it important, then it must be cut. But with *Harlem Duet* I decided beforehand that using three time periods was very important. It gave depth that I wanted. It supported many layers of the play, of the language, and of the contradictions around race.

Alison: How does your process differ when you're directing a play you've written yourself compared to a Shakespeare play, a Noel Coward, whatever?

Djanet: It doesn't differ at all in a sense. Ideally you would know as much about the play. I would know more about a play I wrote, but as a *writer.* I don't find I know how to articulate it to a designer any better. I had to make a kind of academic study of *Harlem Duet* so that I could talk with the creative team. I wanted to be very clear about what I was aiming for, so that how we got there could still be open. I found I needed to articulate clearly the elements of the play, the action, the metaphors, the story. I know more about my own plays in my heart, but if I can't articulate them, it makes no difference.

I think I have a deeper understanding of my work because the writing is part of me, but sometimes I don't *know* how the voices come out. The weekend before the first workshop of *Harlem Duet,* I called the producer at Nightwood and said, "We need another actor, another character is coming out." And she said *(laughter),* thinking, "This is some strange writer shit going on," she said, "Well, you know, we can't pay for that actor." And I said, "That's fine, I'll pay," and I did. I paid for this man to read the part of Canada, the father. But I don't know why the character came, I just knew he had to be there and I don't know now how the play could have done without him. But if I hadn't had the extra cash, I'd have squeezed that character out.

Directing someone else's work, I know I should know it, and love it. That's why I don't think I could be a career director. I don't love everything. Theatre takes a powerful life force out of you. You have to love it. Because the amount of time will not be recuperated in monetary terms for what you give out. I turned down the last couple of plays someone gave me because I don't love them. And I know what it'd take to make them good, and I just can't do it. I'd rather put the energy into my writing.

What about acting? What did you feel about the acting process in *Harlem*? How does it relate to your process? How do you prefer to be directed?

Alison: At this stage *Harlem* was pretty much how I like the rehearsal process to be. I've been through a few, with the Company of Sirens, which were truly collaborative, which at some points felt like there was no head to them. There was something we had to get out because we got the gig. Some government agency hired us, or there was an issue to be addressed, and we sat around and came up with stuff, shaped it ourselves, and went on. I did that for a number of years, and realized I didn't like it much. But every actor has an individual process, and I'm still working out what mine is. I've always said it's the "Nike process."

Djanet: The Nike process?

Alison: "Just Do It!" *(laughter)* To hell with the angst! But if that's what you think then you have to be doing it in a secure, clearly delineated context. I don't want anybody to give me readings. I don't want somebody to get up and tilt my head a certain degree and put my hand in a certain position. But I need a clearly delineated thing. I feel that as an actor, I'm supposed to serve the text, and this particular director's version of the text. So what I need is somebody to say, "Look, this is how I see the play, and this is what I want to do with it. I'm not sure yet how we're going to get there, and there are going to be some problems along the way, but we're going to solve them together." And as an actor, that's wonderful. I'm free to do what I want within this context, trusting that the director knows enough about their vision to be able to say, "That was really interesting, Alison, and if somebody else directs it, try that choice with them. *(laughter)* But, you know, in this particular version of *Harlem Duet,* Billie is not a dribbling psychopath." *(laughter)*

That's where I've been comfortable for the last little while, but I'm conflicted. I'm moving towards wanting to get back to a more collaborative process. I think I'm tired of having the vision given to me at the top. There's part of me that wants to explore. I've been acting for seventeen years, and after a while you can start feeling you're out of the creative process. Especially if you do three seasons at Stratford, which has little or nothing to do with the creative power of theatre. There is a director's vision and a designer's vision and you move through it, trying to get through the verse as well as you can so they understand what you're saying, being true to your director's vision and trying to negotiate a sometimes very actor-unfriendly environment. And because of that, and because I've met some interesting people along the way, there's part of me that wants to have more input from the beginning.

I think the closest I will come will be pulling together a team of people—a designer, a writer, a director, and a couple of actors—who from the beginning create completely collaboratively. *Start* with the designer, don't bring the designer in later. Somebody has to come up with the nub of the idea, a premise, an issue, an image, a something that we're exploring, but I'd like it to be a much longer process, keeping the CN Tower very much in mind. It has to be about getting to the CN Tower, but let's *explore* how we get there and agree, the group of us all together, with no route mapped out. All we know is that the CN Tower is over there.

Djanet: I find that unnerving, and scary. Remember, years ago, when we worked on that piece with Pierre Tetrault, *Double Trouble.* I would work with the head writer and we were basically throwing the script together. The actors would improvise on certain ideas and I would take them home and extrapolate, and write scenes. I suppose if you have people who say, "I'm the head writer" or "I'm the director"—if the jobs are clearly delineated, and if there's a goal—I think you can do it.

Alison: The only element that was missing from that configuration was a designer—

Djanet: —a designer and more money.

Alison: What about the question Ric asked us to think about, what our *ideal* process would be. We've grown accustomed to doing things a certain way, and sometimes don't even question it. If we weren't under this pressure, what would my process be? Is it the Germans that work three years on a piece before performing it, and then it might change after that for the next two? So you dedicate five years of your life to one piece before you move on to the next? A part of me is repulsed by that idea. I don't know how much of that is just that we've been working in three-week stints for so long it reels your mind. There's a kind of high that you get from doing one show, leaving it, and the next thing you know you're in a room full of completely different people with a completely different style, and you're putting *that* show on and then you're home for a couple of weeks and you're back into *another* one. And you get… addicted to that kind of process, for the energy: something new, something new, something new.

Djanet: Right. That's right! Bam, bam, bam, bam.

Alison: But I have to weigh that against the number of times I've closed a play, woken up the next day and thought, "Oh THAT! SHIT! THAT's what she was trying to tell me! I want to do it again, because I understand now what Djanet was telling me from week one. I get it! I know how to do it!"

So, okay, so if we could change it, what would our process be?

Djanet: For me, it would first involve having enough money and time to sit at home and let my mind and my emotions grapple with what is curious or makes me angry or hurts me about this particular idea. And to listen to a voice that comes up, and think, "Who's this voice?" and maybe turn it into a character. And research. Finding more information. But the next phases might be different. I might have a longer workshop phase. I might do it for six months. Maybe one reading every two weeks. And I would elongate the rehearsal period. I don't know, have rehearsals maybe just a half day three days a week, or two full days a week for six months, because I think the creative process is mysteriously slow. And things pop up. The bubble. Bubble contradictions, tension, and then: "AHHHH!" And that's why an actor's an artist, because things pop up from underneath. I think for the actor to be more a part of that bubbling up… people could bring more of their lives to it, it would be more relaxed, and we could do it more slowly, more richly. It would be lovely to have time to discover that the answer we found was working, and to say, "Let's look at that again." That would be lovely.

What would you change?

Alison: Part of me would love to go away, to put a team together, actors, designers, directors, and be sent somewhere for six to eight months. Anyway, I want a year. I want to be funded for a year to work on one piece. I think five years is too long. After a while it becomes navel gazing, but a year. Maybe eight months to create and four months to run it. And I think we should all live together. I think everything else should be left behind, families, everything. We should be tossed together to do this creative thing. I mean we've got nine months just to create a baby, and yet we put out this creative piece in three weeks. I usually only give my full attention to the play I'm working on for the rehearsal period and the first week of the show. After that half my brain has moved on to the next gig. I'm probably auditioning during the day at this point, so half my energy is about getting my audition ready and hoping like hell I get the part because I've only got two more paycheques. And you don't realize how much energy that takes until you get a gig like Stratford. I wish every artist in Canada could have that feeling of knowing where your rent is coming from for nine straight months. It isn't until you've experienced it that you realize how much of your energy is focused on that other stuff… on money! On money!! On surviving.

I thought, okay, but to be able to have that, but be much more a part of the creative process. I had a hard time at Stratford because I just couldn't figure out why we were rehearsing so damn long. It's not like anyone's really feeding you to make beautiful dramatic, radical choices. So why are we dragging this out? The combination of having that kind of relaxed time just focused on my stuff, with a beautifully challenging creative process at the same time I think would be great. I want a year. I want a year with the right team.

Djanet: Wouldn't that be wonderful? But it sounds very intense. I don't know if I'd like it. I need to break away.

Alison: Yeah. That's what I was thinking when you said "more relaxed." I'd kind of like it to be...

Djanet: Really intense for a long period of time.

Alison: Really intense. For a longer period of time. Because the eight months is not all about getting the piece on. It's about feeding each other as artists. We don't do this, because of this concentration on getting the show up. I do think we have to concentrate on product, but being focused too *much* on product means we don't feed each other as artists. There's no time! Because there are things I'm good at, and there are things you're good at, but we've got this little bit of time and can't exchange. It's about feeding it all into the show. But a year's enough time that you could actually grow as an artist. It doesn't have *as much* to do with the product. We get to discuss and analyze what we're doing and how we do it.

Djanet: One of the things you touched on was working with a group of people. One of the ways *Harlem Duet* was very different from a lot of things I've worked on is that everybody who worked on it, whether they agreed with the ideas or not, loved the play. It set us off with an energy between us.

Alison: A part of that—I don't know how much of this you're going to want to use, because I don't know how controversial this is going to be. I don't know what I'm saying yet... but "Soulpeppa'"???

Djanet: What's it called?

Alison: Soulpepper. It's an all-white group. It's Albert Schultz, Diego Matamoros, a whole group of friends who came together to form this company. And my first instinctive reaction was, "Jesus Christ, it's 1998. Put together a theatre company that reflects the community that you're doing the theatre for. The province doesn't look like you anymore. This city doesn't look like you anymore. Stop. You have absolutely no right to public funds if that's what your theatre company looks like." On the other hand, what was wonderful about working on *Harlem Duet* is that we never get to have all black people in a room. It doesn't happen. And we weren't working on Shakespeare, we weren't saying to the world, "let's just see what happens when these words come out of black mouths instead of white ones."

Djanet: Right. We were actually looking at issues that we—

Alison: —that we feel! That matter to us. And sometimes we were articulating them for the very first time. Because it was a safe, secure environment, you weren't constantly monitoring yourself, as I did right now, thinking as soon as I bring up this black-white thing I'd better be careful about how this is going to come out in a piece in *CTR*. It's stuff you've got to be *veeerry* careful about, because not everybody under-stands where you're coming from. To be in an environment where you didn't have to do that, you assumed there were going to be certain things you could say that would resonate with people, even if they didn't completely agree with you!

I'm, I'm trying to work out in my head whether there is a black aesthetic to theatre.

Djanet: Yes. *There's* an interesting question.

Alison: Do we actually have different ways of doing things, different processes, because our life experiences are different? I don't know yet, because we've worked so long in one way, and you don't want to segregate yourself, to say, "Well, this has to be different cause it's a black thing." But it would be really interesting to explore whether there are ways of working that are not Eurocentric. Are there differences in directing an all-black group of people?

Djanet: Yes. Yes. Yes.

Alison: What are they? Do we have to use different processes?

Djanet: There are differences. But at the same time we've all been trained in a Eurocentric way, so it's part of us. When I was looking at how to approach *Harlem* as a director, the first question—"What kind of play is this? Is this a comedy, is this a tragedy?"—I came up with this phrase that this was a "*rhapsodic blues* tragedy." That phrase talks about my cultural ties, my history. So I think there are differences, in the same way you can say there are certain cultural foods from different black people, people of African descent around the world. There are different musics. There are different dances, different forms of visual art. There's a wonderful book called *The Blues Aesthetic and African Americans*, and Amiri Baraka wrote a book called *Blues People* that talks about how blues music can be deconstructed and applied to any art form. So you say, "What is the construct of blues?" You have call-and-response. You have fragmentation. You have polyrhythmic solos. You have a whole list of different parts of that idiom that you can apply to theatre. Syncopation. This is a polyrhythmic solo! This is a saxophone solo! An Ella Fitzgerald solo! In *Harlem Duet* I wanted a *tension* between European culture and African-American culture. I used blues music, but I asked Allen [Booth] to create blues music for a cello and a double bass. But double bass and cello says chamber music. So the blues creates that tension, it's beautiful and it has that drama implicit in it.

Are there processes that are for people of African descent? I don't know. Do you remember that day we did that exercise and Barbara [Barnes Hopkins] brought in the food? She brought in collard greens, sweet potatoes… Southern dishes. So we were in it physically! People brought things in, created things, we had pictures on the wall, we read things, we listened to things, we saw videos. I think getting it into our bodies is very helpful. And I know it's something that I want to continue to explore. But there are white directors doing the same thing.

Ric: What about something like improv? There's Theatresports, there's Keith Johnstone, but on the other hand there's jazz. Is European improv different? Is it possible to create a process where the improv used in rehearsal is African-American and, say, draws on jazz?

Djanet: I think there could be. I think we're still exploring. Only in the last thirty years have many of us decided, "Oh my gosh, we are African." I use black and African-American interchangeably, but really, black is not a country, it is not the colour of our skins in actual fact. When you say "someone of Asian descent" it denotes a place, it denotes a culture, a history, and I think that the word "African" denotes history and "African-American culture" denotes a history, and I think there is a way to look at jazz and relate it to a play, to a text, to a context. You can do that. I've got something here about the blues that might be helpful: "The Blues aesthetic is a true art in multiples of compositional elements based on a panorama of extra musical associations which provide much contemporary literary, theatre, dance and visual arts with the necessary elements for defining an approach to these various art forms as intrinsically Afro-American." This is a quote from Amri Baraka. And then I was listening to Wynton Marsalis deconstruct the blues. He said there's rhythm, tempo, syncopation, harmony, solos, fragmentation, repetition—inside and outside of the structure of the song—call-and-response, polyrythmic improvisation, the sliding and blurring of notes. All these elements can be transposed from music and applied to other art forms, layering them with a textual vitality and reinvesting themes and subject matter with a mythic, emotional, and cultural dimension. So, when you look at improvisation, if you're going to improvise on a text and develop it all together, I can see how you'd say, "Okay, this is the song, this is the beat, this is the rhythm, these are the chords." I feel there's something that's more interesting about that approach to theatre, too, if you include dance, if you include music, if you include a lot of the visual art forms. I think that there could be a process that could create a theatrical performance involving the basic components of jazz. And not only would you be creating something around the topic or the idea you started out with, but you would be exploring different formal elements too.

Alison: It's all new to me, and it's so weird, just at the time I'm starting to get into directing. I don't know.... It exemplifies what the tension is, though, of a working artist. Because you talk about this, and this is where you want to go—and it's a new feeling, so you're still exploring what this *need* is for new process, where it's coming from, and what we want to do with it—while at the same time I'm directing *Treasure Island* for Young People's Theatre [now Lorraine Kimsa Theatre for Young People]. Because that's what I have to do. And you *do* have to. There's a certain amount of skill you still need to amass, and this is the context you're going to be working in. So it's just part of the tension we have, working as black artists in this environment.

Djanet: Remember during the African-American Playwrights Conference, the question was asked whether as black playwrights or artists we should focus on black theatres or on changing white theatres? And the answer was "Both. Both!" Our children grow up in this world. I read *Treasure Island* when I was a kid, it's part of me, so to look at it is essential. But to also do the other is essential, and they're not mutually exclusive.

Alison: I think you're absolutely right. I mean, I'm glad I didn't stay out at Stratford, I didn't need another year there, but I'm forever grateful to Stratford. And spending the years of my life that I've spent dedicated to Shakespeare helped with *Harlem Duet*. How could it not? You got a much better actor to do *Harlem Duet* because of that. It's all got to feed. But there is something about the comfort level, and I think that comfort and trust in these processes are important, which is why the Soulpepper thing came out. Because although there's a part of me that really disagrees with the look of that company, there's another part of me, an artist part of me, that wants to be comfortable, to be able to trust. And I know I do that when I'm in a room where everybody looks like me! *(laughter)* Shared experience. So in the case of Soulpepper, who am I to say, "Well, no. Since theatre school you guys have been friends, and you want to pull a company together because you have similar experiences, similar tastes, there's stuff that you say that is going to resonate with people in the room, whether they agree or not… and you're comfortable." Who am I to say, "You're not supposed to have that kind of company?"

Ric: But it goes back to the question you asked earlier about going both ways. The experience at Stratford changed *Harlem Duet*. At what point does *Harlem Duet* change Stratford?

Djanet: Well, let's approach that question by asking how the play ended up at Canadian Stage. Before *Harlem Duet*, Canadian Stage had never produced a work by an author of (black) African descent. And the problem with Canadian Stage is that it's called Canadian Stage, so it represents Canada, and I'm thinking, "I'm Canadian, so it must represent me." But Canadian Stage knew this, and working with Candace Burley and Iris Turcott we developed the First African Playwrights Conference, which also involved YPT. What we were going to do was locate writers of African descent in Canada and gather them together. Because that's where the impetus for black work comes from. You can say to all the theatres, "Cast black people in these plays," but it's still work from the European perspective. After the keynote session all the writers read from their work, all forty-eight of them. And it went way into the evening. They didn't close the doors until four in the morning at Canadian Stage.

Alison: And out of that event *Harlem Duet* happened at Canadian Stage, Richardo Keens-Douglas is having his play *The Nutmeg Princess* produced on the mainstage at YPT—

Djanet: —and they're doing a new play by another black author at Canadian Stage next year, Andrew Moodie's *A Common Man's Guide to Loving Women*. So I think that, while it might seem having a conference at that space was a contradiction, what came of it seems to have ongoing possibilities. It'd be nice for the next African-American Playwrights Conference to bring in other theatres and create those relationships on a broad front. So something *can* happen.

(1998)

A Fringe Odyssey: 20th Annual Edmonton Fringe Theatre Festival, August 16–26, 2001
by Shelley Scott

2001 marked the 20th anniversary of the Edmonton Fringe Festival. The scope and success of the festival—involving 153 theatre companies and selling 85,000 tickets to indoor productions, with an overall attendance of 500,000—invites a closer look at the theatre being done there and its place within the larger context of Canadian theatre. The most obvious influence of the Edmonton Fringe is that it has inspired more than twenty-five other Fringes across North America (*Program* 6). I would argue that the Fringe circuit in Canada has great potential to play an important role in new play development. It is already, to some extent, a source for new Canadian plays, but this role could be enhanced if the Fringe were promoted as a viable, low-risk venue for exploratory productions of plays in some stage of dramaturgical development. It could also be a place to see lesser-known Canadian plays that have been published, but not remounted, bringing such plays to a much larger audience. In considering the example of the most recent Edmonton Fringe, however, there is one particular obstacle to this potential: the tendency of the local media to emphasize familiarity as the highest virtue. Valorization of familiarity as a sort of consumer guarantee tends to mitigate any process which could truly be called developmental.

One could certainly argue that the Fringe has evolved into a phenomenon of commerce and entertainment. The Edmonton media play a powerful role in perpetuating that ethos through their aggressive reviewing strategies and the nature of their coverage, which, while frequently amateurish, is nonetheless influential. The rhetoric of the Fringe organizers themselves, however, strongly implies a mandate to develop new work. According to the "Fringe Philosophy," the Fringe is "dedicated to the creation of theatre that challenges and celebrates the cultural fabric of our communities, with an emphasis on *emerging artists*" (*Program* 6).

According to the festival publicity package, 70% of the works presented are "world premieres," and over the past twenty years the festival has "*nurtured the creation* of more than 1,500 new plays." Some have been published and "new work presented at the festival is picked up to be presented all over North America. The Fringe remains the leading *laboratory* for and *showcase of new work* in Alberta" (*Program* 6). The emphases are mine, but it seems to me that phrases like "laboratory" and "showcase of new work" sound a lot like the kind of new play development being done across the country, from Alberta Theatre Projects' Platform Plays to Buddies in Bad Times' Rhubarb! Festival, and that the Fringe organizers see themselves as involved with this same kind of process. But is the Edmonton Fringe part of this network? Is it participating in the cultivation and development of new Canadian work as much as it could be?

There is no doubt that the Edmonton Fringe is a great resource for artists based in that city. One of the ways the Fringe generates new work is by offering the opportunity for Edmonton theatre artists, such as actors and designers, for example, to also try their hand at writing. Actor Adam Joe premiered his first play, *Chicken Man*, at the

2001 Fringe, motivated by the belief that "We need more Canadian playwrights.... It's sort of a mini-movement in the city, where there's more of a personal responsibility taken by younger artists… to create work and not just rely on employment from other sources" (Matwychuk 10). Actors such as Beth Graham and Daniela Vlaskalic, who are both graduates of the University of Alberta, were heralded in the press as emerging Edmonton-based playwrights, joining Fringe veterans in developing a career and a following. Possibly the most prolific of these veterans is David Belke, who started out as a designer and has been writing new plays for the Fringe for twelve years; he and Stewart Lemoine are probably the Fringe's biggest success stories. At the 2001 Fringe, Belke presented a new work (*Between Yourself and Me*) and, for the first time, a remount of an older work. *Blackpool and Parrish* "premiered to sold out houses at the 1993 Fringe," won the Sterling Award for Outstanding New Fringe Work that year, and has been produced across Canada and internationally (*Program* 6). Writers like David Belke credit the Fringe with allowing them to be playwrights by providing a showcase and an opportunity for development within a supportive community.

Stewart Lemoine, who has been writing and directing for his company, Teatro La Quindicina, since the first Edmonton Fringe in 1982, also had a remount in this year's Fringe: *Cocktails at Pam's*. In fact, *Cocktails at Pam's*, which premiered at the 1986 Fringe, has been revived at five-year intervals ever since, and two of the cast members, Leona Brausen and Davina Stewart, have appeared in all four productions. The *Edmonton Journal* reviewer remarked, "Edmonton's most talented and accomplished actors are always involved, and there is a lineup to see the show for the fourth or even the first time" (Babiak C3). Similarly, Darrin Hagen's *The Edmonton Queen: Not a River Boat Story* is based on his bestselling book, which in turn was based on the 1996 Sterling Award-winning play (for Outstanding New Fringe Work) of the same name. It is a piece of Edmonton history, a personal account of the city's underground drag scene in the 1980s, written and performed by Hagen, who explains in the show, "None of the names have been changed, because there are no innocents… but occasionally, the outfits I describe are nicer than what we were actually wearing."

Beyond the remounts of its "own shows," however, the 2001 Fringe featured only a very few by published Canadian playwrights: *The Terrible But Incomplete Journals of John D.* by Guillermo Verdecchia; *Seeds* by Gordon Pengilly; and *DeadBox* by Ron Chambers. It is often the unfortunate fate of Canadian plays to have a successful run and then disappear from our stages. Even after publication, rave reviews, and awards, many plays do not receive subsequent productions. The Fringe, then, might be a suitable place to mount previously published plays and introduce them to new audiences. One might even assume that the desire for a hit would lead companies to present plays with a proven track record. Instead, the Fringe relied heavily on a roster of well-known Edmonton "names." As one local newspaper put it, "Even a quick perusal of the festival guide underlines the crush of familiar names associated with productions—Trevor Schmidt, Darrin Hagen, Chris Craddock, and Marty Chan—on top of a few creators who are almost synonymous with this event" (Bouchard 6). Based on this "crush" of familiarity, one might suspect the festival has become something of a closed circle, difficult to break into from outside the city.

It quickly becomes evident that the most important criteria for success at the Fringe are a certain amount of familiarity and promotion by the local media, and that these two are closely linked. Some of the shows are on tour and rely heavily on positive reviews from previous stops in their Fringe publicity, but the best guarantee of popularity is a rave review from the Edmonton media; once a show has been granted the status of a "must-see," audiences dutifully line up. I would argue that Edmonton reviewers suffer from an affinity for the previously known, the familiar name, the actor or author who has already been declared "worth watching." This makes it increasingly difficult for newcomers to get much (positive) notice, and it makes the choice of play that much more crucial. This is not a new situation. Reviewing the Fringe in 1988, Anne Nothof observed, "Whether because of immediate identification and recognition factors, or because of loyalty to the locals, the audience response to [an Edmonton comedy troupe] was more enthusiastic," and "The sell-out shows, for which loyal fans were willing to hold the line for two hours or more, were the unusual offerings of Edmonton groups who have attracted a kind of cult following" (88). I do not think this is a problem exclusive to the Edmonton Fringe; I have heard actors say similar things about other Fringes, that shows by known companies from the host city fare the best, and that audiences seem reluctant to see a show that has not already been declared a hit. One can justify supporting local talent to a certain degree, but the second part of this equation—the pressure to have the work deemed a popular hit—is simply limiting.

Remounts of previous Fringe hits are one symptom of this pressure. There is also the unique genre of the Fringe sequel. For example, *DeadRats on Arrival* in 2001 was a sequel to a 2000 Fringe show introducing the band The DeadRats, which in turn is made up of a number of familiar Fringe performers (Dave Clarke, Paul Morgan Donald, Peter Moller, and Vladimir Sobolewski). The *Fringe Program* description for *Roommates 2.0* by Wes Borg and Shauna Perry explains that "*Version 1.0 of Roommates* was a sell-out hit at the 1993 Fringe" (32). *Die-Nasty: The Live Improvised Soap Opera* has been playing at every Fringe for years; the *Fringe Program* calls it "legendary" (30). Jeff Haslam, a very popular Edmonton actor who has been part of fifteen Fringes and also appears as the Fringe mascot, created an entire play for his Die-Nasty character. *Citizen Plate*, which premiered at the 2001 Fringe, continues the trend of actors beginning to write, but also demonstrates that part of the popularity and audience enjoyment for this kind of show comes from the recognition factor. Some performers, such as Zandra Bell, come back every year with a variation on their one-person show. Playwright and actor Chris Craddock is described in the program as a "Fringe Fave," and his new show *Moving Along...* is described as being "like his previous hits" (41). These shows were all counting on audience recognition and familiarity to guarantee large and enthusiastic crowds, and all succeeded. According to the Fringe's own publicity materials, only 8% of the Fringe audience is made up of out-of-town patrons, making it very much an Edmonton event (*A Twenty-Year Legacy*). The Edmonton audience member, and the repeat-Fringer, are rewarded; when Fringe-goers recommend shows to one another, it is often by mentioning what the creators did at previous Fringes: "[Y]ou should see this one, because their show last year was good."

There are other, related aspects of this "previously known" quality. There are productions of relatively well-established non-Canadian plays which are most often British. For example, in 2001, there were two productions of Pinter plays, *Betrayal* and *The Lover*, and one of *Closer* by Patrick Marber. Although the members of English Suitcase Theatre, which did *Betrayal*, are based in Winnipeg and Vancouver, they have been at the Edmonton Fringe consistently since 1987. Their well-received shows have made them another kind of "known quantity," so much so that England's Stark Naked Theatre, which presented *Closer*, billed themselves as including "three former English Suitcase members" and "Fringe veterans" (*Program* 6).

The reviewer who does try to draw some distinction between popularity and critical assessment finds him or herself in a self-made quandary, since the spectator is so relentlessly positioned as a consumer looking for a guaranteed commodity. A case in point was *Pigs*, the third in a Fringe trilogy written and directed by Zhauna Alexander. Andrew Hanon writes, "No matter how much critics implore the public to steer clear of her plays, she keeps packin' 'em in." And Alexander replies, "Of course sex sells…. If we use that to get people out to the play, how is that wrong? It's not like we're lying. We never advertise things we don't deliver" (qtd. in Hanon). Adam Houston's review of *Cocktails at Pam's* made this dilemma explicit by explaining that, "a packed house thought it worthy of a standing ovation, so I yield to the will of the people and bump up the rating a notch higher than it deserves" (Houston 3). But the media, along with the producers of the *Fringe Program*, are the prime culprits in placing so much emphasis on knowing what to expect, thereby influencing not only what audiences go to see, but also what theatre artists choose to produce.

Of course, some of the new plays presented are "one-offs," put together for the sake of commercial appeal or topicality, and that can be a virtue. However, for some new plays, regardless of where they come from, it would be healthier to label them what they are: works in progress. After scripts are read and workshopped in play development programs, for example, they can proceed to a Fringe production as the next phase in their growth. But their appearance at the Fringe would have to be understood as part of their larger process, without the illusion of being a finished product, and with a more realistic acknowledgement of how plays are created and (ideally) nurtured along through multiple phases. Likewise, when unknown theatre artists look for a play to take to the Fringe, they can select a Canadian play that audiences are not already familiar with. But will the Edmonton Fringe, its audiences, and reviewers welcome them? There has to be a sense that there is a place for them at the Fringe.

In a festival as large as the Fringe, there is room for everyone, and there is no reason the work of a first-time actor-turned-playwright, the remount or re-working of a Fringe favourite, and the production of an "older" Canadian play cannot happily coexist. Theatre artists win their place in the festival first, even before their offering has been determined, so it is not as if the organizers can be held accountable for the final lineup. Rather, I am arguing that a climate exists which tends to encourage certain choices, and that what might be touted as a celebration of the margins (it is called the Fringe, after all!) is driven by a desire for the familiar. One could call for a Fringe of the Fringe, another festival entirely for those feeling excluded. My point, though, is that the existing Fringe might be encouraged to serve another function beyond commerce and entertainment. Because of its organizational structure, it is an ideal opportunity for introducing works in progress, experimental projects, and unfamiliar plays. It is an established event with a huge audience, and it could be integrated into a system of play development across the country.

(2001)

Works Cited

Babiak, Todd. "Slurp up something fizzy at the end of the world." *Edmonton Journal* 18 August 2001: C3.

Bouchard, Gilbert A. "A Playwright's City." *See Magazine* 16–22 August 2001: 6.

Hanon, Andrew. "Critics be damned." *See Magazine* 16–22 August 2001: 9.

Houston, Adam. "*Cocktails at Pam's* 3 and a half stars." *See Magazine* 21–26 August 2001: 3.

Matwychuk, Paul. "These must be plays." *Vue Weekly.* 16–22 August 2001: 10.

Nothof, Anne. "A View from the Fringe." *Canadian Theatre Review* 54 (Spring 1988): 88–89.

Program. 20th Annual Edmonton International Fringe Theatre Festival, 2001.

Scott, Shelley. "Confessions of a Virgin Bride: Review of the 1999 18th Annual Edmonton International Fringe Festival." *Canadian Theatre Review* 102 (Spring 2000): 82–84.

The Ethnic Playwright's Challenge:
An Exploration of the Issues that Non-Caucasian Writers Face

by Marty Chan

Years ago, I remember the Pepsi challenge. This blind taste test asked Coke drinkers to distinguish their favourite pop from its archrival, Pepsi. Most times people couldn't tell the difference. Without the benefit of labels, people thought the two colas tasted the same.

Can the same be said for playwrights? Are all writers essentially the same bottle of pop with different labels? Is there a distinction between a visible minority playwright and a Caucasian playwright? Will an ethnic writer always be known as "that ethnic-hyphen-Canadian writer"?

I want to say there is no difference. I want to claim that all writers are revered and abused equally, regardless of race. I want to believe that writers are judged simply by the quality of the words we write. But that would be naive.

I feel obligated to say that there is a difference. I feel compelled to admit that I will always be viewed as a minority first, artist second. I feel that I have a duty to say that even in today's progressive society, an ethnic playwright's work will be judged by both cultural and artistic standards, while non-ethnic writers only have to worry about an artistic standard. But that would be whiny.

Truth be told, I have yet to find a satisfying answer to the playwright's challenge. Some days, I swear on a stack of David Henry Hwang plays that theatre is colour-blind. Other days, I wonder if I can change my name to Marty Foster. What makes this issue frustrating is that there is no clear answer; either side of the argument has plenty of proponents and proof.

Take the process of writing a play, for example. The act of writing is equally exciting, hellish, inspiring, and maddening no matter who you are or what your cultural background.

When I wrote *Mom, Dad, I'm Living with a White Girl*—my signature Asian play—I started out with a question. How would traditional Chinese parents react to their only son moving in with his white girlfriend? As I thought about the situation, I generated more questions. What if the son was so afraid of his parents' reaction that he decided to keep his living arrangements secret? What if his parents found out and they forbade him from living with his girlfriend? How would his lover react to this news? What if she told him to disown his parents? Who would the man ultimately stay with?

To answer these questions I drew from a wide range of sources including my own life, interviews with interracial couples, and articles about multiracial issues in North America. More importantly, I relied primarily on my imagination to come up with the answers. Further questions popped up as I thought about the story and the characters, and I kept coming up with answers until I finally stumbled upon my play.

I wished I could have laid claim to a more dignified method of writing, but stumbling was the most apt description. I felt my way through the dark until my hand flicked on the switch that lit up my first draft.

Fearing that I was alone in the dark, I asked a few of my contemporaries about how they started their plays. Some started off with a character. Some began with a powerful visual image. A few came up with a scene first and built the play around it. Others proposed "what if?" questions to get them a starting point to their first draft. Other than minor variations, there was no real difference between how they wrote a play and how I created mine. One notable difference was that they refused to admit they stumbled to their first draft.

But a more important distinction was the research process. I did less formal research for *Mom, Dad, I'm Living with a White Girl* than a non-ethnic playwright would, because I raided my family experiences to create the play. By the same token, a mother who writes about her daughter's death doesn't need to search far for the feelings of a parent who has suffered a tragic loss. If I tried to tackle this topic I would be in the same boat as other childless writers. Ethnic or not, we would all be rowing in unfamiliar waters.

Lack of personal experience should not prevent a writer from tackling a subject. It simply means that the writer will have to conduct more research to create plausibility.

For example, three years ago I wrote *The Bone House*, a thriller about serial killers. I had never committed murder in my lifetime (I came close with a few directors), but I read about such killers and their motivations and I simulated them in my play. All it took was some research and a whole lot of imagination. The result was a play that had audiences literally screaming in the aisles.

The success of *The Bone House* proved to me that writing was an intellectual endeavour, not a cultural one. Race was neither a boon nor a burden. However, when trying to achieve authenticity, a playwright must choose whether to be a dramatist or a historian. More often than not, these two hats cannot fit on the same head.

I wasn't surprised that playwrights shared similar creative processes. I long suspected that the solitary nature of the job attracted like-minded passive-aggressive personalities such as myself. I believed the differences between writers would appear when we crawled out of our caves. In particular, I feared that visible minority playwrights would be treated differently in workshops.

To confirm my suspicions, I sat in on the workshop of a Caucasian writer so that I could compare his sessions to workshops of my own work. I expected to see major differences, but to my surprise, I found no difference at all. Workshop participants treated him with the same tenacity and cruelty that they treated me.

Let me digress. If you've never seen a workshop from a playwright's position, here's a rundown. Remember the interrogation scene from *Marathon Man*? Sir Laurence Olivier has Dustin Hoffman at his mercy. He used a dental pick to extract from Hoffman the answer to the question: "Is it safe?" Hoffman says he has no idea what Olivier is talking about. Big mistake. Olivier jams the pick into Hoffman's exposed tooth, and then asks again, "Is it safe?"

Now imagine that you're Dustin Hoffman and Olivier has been joined by six more interrogators. They ask a million questions, all of which you must answer. If you fail to respond to them, they slam their instruments of torture into your cavity-ridden teeth. That's basically what a playwright endures in a workshop. Okay, I'm exaggerating, but give me a break; I'm a writer. That's what I do for a living.

Hyperbole aside, the workshop is pretty much the same as Dustin Hoffman's interrogation session. Playwrights subject their scripts and themselves to the probing questions of people who are coming to the play for the first time. The sessions are torturous, but if the playwrights survive, they will find ways to strengthen their script so that future probes will expose fewer flaws. Just for the record, playwrights don't develop thicker skins from these sessions; they just file away names for revenge later.

In the workshop of *Mom, Dad, I'm Living with a White Girl*, the actors' questions become nauseatingly repetitive. Every single one of them asked about their character and who that person was. They wanted to know about motivations of all the character's actions. They questioned transitions. They basically ripped apart my script scene-by-scene, moment-by-moment, word-by-word.

In the workshop that I spied on, the playwright suffered the same barrage of questions even though his play had nothing to do with Asian angst. In fact, some questions were identical. The workshop participants wanted to know why the characters did what they did. By the end, the playwright had that same shell-shocked look that I had after my session. At that point I realized that we were kindred spirits who shared a common bond that transcended race; we were both Dustin Hoffman against an army of Laurence Oliviers.

I also realized that my job as playwright was to make the characters and story as clear as possible. The workshop helped me do this by illuminating the murky puddles that pockmarked my script. My racial background was neither shield nor crutch in the sessions. If the story didn't make sense or if the characters were too shallow, no claim of cultural authenticity would protect me from the barbs of the keen actors. Like other playwrights, I was harassed and inspired into creating a stronger play. Love or hate them, workshops were colour-blind.

The play development process appeared to have passed the playwrights' challenge. All writers shared the same joys, successes, miseries, and failures when they went from the blank page to the finished script. And they faced similar interrogators in workshops. When they emerge from the development process, writers come out with the same unifying emotion: relief.

But the journey does not end here. Once their scripts are complete, writers join the gruelling marathon race that hopefully leads to production. Not everyone crosses the finish line. In fact, only the strongest reach the end. When I signed up for the race, I hoped that my Chinese-Canadian background would not handicap me, but I soon discovered that ethnic differences can and do dictate where runners finish.

Early in my career, I produced my own scripts at the Edmonton Fringe Festival. My goal was to attract the attention of artistic directors, critics, and the general public. None of my Fringe shows had anything to do with my Asian background because I wanted to avoid being stereotyped as the Chinese-hyphen-Canadian writer. I deliberately tackled non-Asian characters and stories to prove that I was a writer first, minority writer second.

My first self-produced play was *Weeping Moon.* In the story, a father had difficulty accepting the fact that his teenage daughter had committed suicide. The characters were Caucasian, and the play dealt with the father's overwhelming grief and subsequent recovery.

The reactions to the play were humbling. Few people came out to see the show; fewer enjoyed it. However, one particular comment stood out. An acquaintance of mine complained that the story didn't work for her because she had expected to see something closer to my Asian heart. She remarked that the characters, while played by Caucasian actors, seemed to have a Chinese sensibility. I informed her that the story was actually inspired by a real-life incident that happened to my Dutch girlfriend's parents. But my acquaintance insisted that I'd have more success if my next play dealt with Asian themes.

Her suggestion infuriated me, and spurred me to write *Confessions of a Deli Boy,* a play about a million rickshaw rides away from anything remotely Chinese. This light and frothy Fringe show was a romantic comedy about a Jewish song and dance man trying to break into Hollywood movies in the 1950s, who ends up falling in love. The play was full of cheesy songs and cheap gags, and had absolutely nothing to do with being Chinese. I was sure no one would ever look for grains of rice within this sugary confection.

I was wrong. Two critics argued the play's merits. One reviewer liked the show. The other did not. In the course of their discussion, the critics agreed on one thing; they were more interested in seeing me write a play about why a Chinese-Canadian playwright was creating a show about song and dance teams in the 1950s.

Once again my cultural background played a factor in how my writing was judged. I started to feel that my face was a burden around my neck. Some time later I was relieved to see a Caucasian writer receive the same criticism. W.P. Kinsella was accused of appropriating Aboriginal voices when he wrote his short stories about the Hobbema reservation.

Witnessing the furor over Kinsella, I wondered why in Canada did we want to practice literary segregation. As a Chinese-hyphen-Canadian, I did not want to limit myself to only Asian stories. I believed that writers were free to express themselves as long as they didn't promote hatred of others. I had hoped that the words could be judged—as opposed to the writer.

Years ago, I had the chance to put this belief to the test when I came across a writing contest. The competition claimed that all plays were to be judged on their own merits. The organizers required all script entries to be anonymous. The author's name would accompany the script in a sealed envelope to be opened only when the winners were selected. Eagerly, I submitted *Mom, Dad, I'm Living with a White Girl,* hoping only my words would be judged and not me.

On the day I received the notification letter, I lost both the competition and my naïveté about playwrights being treated equally. A juror's typewritten note accompanied the rejected script. The juror expressed concern that my play might come off as racist unless I was Chinese. I was shocked. Here was a competition that prided itself on judging the work alone and not the playwright, yet my racial identify came into question when the adjudicator viewed my script.

Granted, the juror's comments were probably well intended and reflective of today's politically sensitive climate. Also, if I truly wanted the script to be judged on its own merits, I probably should have submitted a play that was completely devoid of Asian content. But that said, if we live in a tolerant society, why did my race have to be an issue at all?

After this experience, I began to suspect that I would never enjoy the same freedoms as non-minority writers. I worried that I would always be stereotyped as the Chinese-hyphen-Canadian writer. I feared I would land in an ethnic artist's ghetto, where my voice would be considered valid only if it had a Chinese accent (and yes, I'm aware of the irony of bemoaning this fear in an issue devoted to Chinese-Canadian theatre).

My fears were not completely baseless. Even after Cahoots Theatre Projects' sold-out run of *Mom, Dad, I'm Living with a White Girl* in Toronto, and Firehall Arts Centre's successful run in Vancouver, I was told by countless producers that the play only worked in those cities because they had a large Asian population. They claimed that the play didn't have market value in any other centre. Fortunately, those naysayers were proved wrong. The play has been produced in Winnipeg, Saskatoon, Edmonton, Richmond, Nanaimo, and Kamloops. Audiences of all races have flocked to the play and proven that the show can work without a large Asian audience.

This success has its drawbacks. Now producers approach me looking for an Asian story told by an Asian writer. They are like Caucasian diners in a Chinese restaurant, looking for something exotic. When I offer a non-Asian story, their eyes glaze over like I'm reading them the phone book. Producers see me as the "resident Chinese expert," and my fear of living in the "ghetto" has come true. I'm not blameless in this dilemma either. I have accepted offers to write Asian stories, and my only defence is that writing an Asian story sure beats starving.

I soon became convinced that not only did ethnic differences exist but they also mattered. Then I examined the careers of my Caucasian colleagues, and discovered I was not the only victim of typecasting. A writer's breakout play is often the one that categorizes the writer. I know of audiences who expect only romantic comedies from one writer, heart-wrenching dramas with poetic language from another. Those writers are more than capable of crossing over to other genres, but they have been branded as the romantic playwright or the dramatic writer. They are stuck in a similar ghetto to mine.

Furthermore, to be fair, there are just as many people who ask for good stories as there are people who look for Asian stories from me.

In the end, I'm no closer to answering the question about whether or not visible minority writers can be treated as artists first, minorities second. Upon reflection, my essay does seem to answer the question: "Is there a bitter, over-sensitive playwright in the house?"

At the heart of my ramblings is a bigger question: is race an issue in Canada? I know Canadians make a big deal about making sure that race is not an issue. I've seen enough employment advertisements and grant applications that claim to encourage cultural diversity and equal opportunity employment. I've heard enough people swear to me that they are racially tolerant. Didn't "tolerate" used to be associated with some-thing undesirable, like pain? Just a question.

To be honest, when I look back to how I was treated as a playwright, I can find examples when my race was tolerated and examples when I was embraced as a writer. The situations differed greatly. In fact, the only common denominator in all my encounters was that they would be different depending on whom I was talking to. Some people assumed I was the resident expert on all things Chinese. Other people saw me as a good writer. One guy thought I was delivering his Chinese food. The individuals themselves decided whether to treat me as a Chinese-hyphen-Canadian writer or just as a writer.

I think I have finally arrived at the answer to the playwrights' challenge. In the Pepsi challenge, not everyone thought the two drinks tasted the same. Some preferred Coke to Pepsi, others converted to Pepsi. The outcome depended completely on the individual's personal tastes. I guess the same can be said of the playwrights' challenge. Some will look at labels, others will judge only the play.

In the end, if asked if there is a difference between an ethnic playwright and a playwright I'll have to say, "It depends."

(2002)

Wrestling with Regionalism in Atlantic Canada:
The Playwrights Atlantic Resource Centre
by Bruce Barton

I will preface my discussion of the Playwrights Atlantic Resource Centre (PARC) with the following caveat. Although I spent more than ten years of my adult life on Canada's East Coast, and held extended residence in three out of four of the Atlantic provinces, I was acutely aware throughout that time of my C.F.A. status. "C.F.A.," for those who have never visited Newfoundland, stands for "Come From Away." The term is shortened to "From Away" in the Maritimes, but the condition—and the multiple attitudes it evokes—are, for all intents and purposes, the same. As a "From Away," one is regularly reminded, in sometimes conspicuous but often subtle ways, of the depth of history, personal and cultural, from which one is not so much cut off as set safely at arm's length. A "From Away" can experience the East Coast; but it is the experience of the visitor—and, if you're lucky, the guest. And this, of course, also shapes the degree to which—and the ways in which—one can actually *know* the East Coast.

Similarly, my relationship with PARC has spanned the past seven years and involved participation at numerous levels of the organization. My first contact came in 1996, when I served as one of the dramaturges at PARC's annual playwriting colony, held that year in Charlottetown. Since then I have served on the PARC board as a provincial representative, a vice president, and from 1999–2001, as president. As well, I participated as a playwright in the 1999 Moveable Feast, developing a work that went on to productions in Charlottetown and Halifax. Yet despite my engagement with PARC over this time, I am constantly reminded of the complexity of its short history prior to my entry into it (and, for that matter, since), of the considerable gaps in my knowledge and understanding of its evolution, and of the multiple narratives that overlap, intersect and, quite regularly, contradict one another in the telling of its story. I am fairly confident, however, of two things: a) the fact that, as Canada's only mandated *regional* playwright development organization, PARC has consistently been defined by a determined, if not unquestioned, inclusivity that inspires and motivates its organizers while simultaneously stretching its personnel and finances to the breaking point; and b) the fact that manifold interpretations of "community" play a central role in PARC's ongoing efforts toward self-definition.

PARC was officially formed in 1991, in what emerged as a year of significant transition for, in particular, Nova Scotian theatre history. Fifteen years earlier, a group of Nova Scotian writers had successfully established the Dramatists' Co-op of Nova Scotia, an offshoot group of the Writers' Federation of Nova Scotia. With a mandate to develop both Nova Scotian writers and an appreciative audience for local drama, this organization provided training, workshops and public reading opportunities for its members, as well as a script copying and distribution service, professional representation and numerous audience development initiatives. In particular, Co-op members emphasized the development of a local community made up of accomplished artists and committed spectators (although tension between conflicting definitions of community had regularly monopolized its internal discussions).

Significantly, however, all of the Co-op's activities were informed by a clear emphasis on increasing production opportunities for its members, with the staging of plays as the definitive measure of the organization's success. The hindsight of history is never quite 20/20 and the factors that led to the Co-op's demise are myriad. However, concurrent with its dissolution were a couple of initiatives that seemed to address, while splitting in two, its production-oriented development philosophy. In 1990, one year after the Co-op submitted an unsuccessful funding proposal to establish an Atlantic Fringe Festival, a separate bid, organized by Co-op member Ken Pinto, was approved. That festival, which began in 1991, celebrated its twelfth anniversary in 2002, and remains the single most direct, accessible and effective route to production for new and established playwrights in the region, with over 240 shows in five venues during its 2002 schedule. [1] Also in 1990, there had been an enthusiastic turnout at a meeting of the Atlantic Caucus of the Playwrights Union of Canada, held in Halifax. The regional interaction and perceived commonality of interests and obstacles served as a catalyst, and a committee headed by Wanda Graham of Nova Scotia and including representatives of all four East Coast provinces (Jane Wilson, PEI; Kwame Dawes, New Brunswick; and Pete Soucy, Newfoundland) was struck to explore the possibility of establishing a playwrights' resource centre in Atlantic Canada. While Graham has described the expression of regret from some Dramatists' Co-op members about the shift away from a distinctly provincial profile and agenda, [2] there was clearly growing enthusiasm throughout Atlantic Canada for an initiative that would be regional in structure and mandate. Graham travelled across the country to gain first-hand knowledge of the structures and activities of Canada's other play development organizations. Based on her research, and with a start-up grant of $15,000 from the Canada Council, the Atlantic Playwrights Resource Centre (APRC) opened its doors for business in April 1991. (It was some years before the title was rearranged to allow for the more user-friendly acronym, PARC.)

PARC's stated, threefold mandate, as is the case with most organizational mandates, is both unrealistically ambitious and intentionally vague:

> to assist in the professional development of Atlantic Canadian playwrights;
> to undertake promotion of indigenous work and the medium generally;
> and to document all Atlantic region works.

Conspicuous is the emphasis on professional development—as opposed to any set measure of professional status as a base criterion for membership, such as that utilized by the Playwrights Union of Canada (now Playwrights Guild of Canada). This apparently intentional ambivalence had also proven a point of sometimes heated discussion within the ranks of the Dramatists' Co-op, and emerges directly out of the difficult, perhaps irresolvable task of establishing a fair and effective definition of professional status within the dense, diverse fields of production opportunities in the region. Equally noteworthy is the flexible reference to "indigenous work" (as opposed to "indigenous drama," which, if taken at face value, would imply a degree of commonality across the dramatic writing of the four Atlantic provinces that extends beyond geographic proximity).

All of PARC's initiatives have attempted to facilitate these praiseworthy aspirations through an appreciation for, and an apprehension of, the challenges posed by a region characterized by extremes of climate, geomorphology and culture. Similarly, most of its activities address the heightened isolation and insulation experienced by many East Coast writers. "Home Delivery" is a "long-distance" dialogue established between writers and dramaturges; the print newsletter and its contemporary sibling, the listserve, provide ongoing information on contests, production opportunities, member activities and other development information from within and beyond the region; PARC's maintenance of a growing online databank of regional writers and plays provides both a vital archive and a widely accessible showcase for regional works. Yet while these services reflect the fundamental separation of PARC's constituent provinces, it is what is regularly referred to as PARC's "flagship" initiative, the Moveable Feast, that most fully demonstrates the organization's determination to foster a community of regional playwrights, if not an "indigenous" regional drama.

The Moveable Feast playwriting colony, which originally spanned a week and which now extends over ten days, is the focal point of PARC's energies, resources and profile. As its name suggests, the event travels throughout the region, ideally rotating among the four Atlantic provinces on a yearly basis. Scripts are selected from each of the four provinces in the region and are workshopped throughout the Feast with professional dramaturges and actors. While the dramaturges are regularly selected from among Canada's most widely recognized, there is generally an effort made to utilize as many local performers as possible, in yet another calculated compromise between local and regional interests.

As noted, the dedication to the Feast among many of PARC's members, its board and its executive director, is frankly, remarkable. And the Feast's utility, in terms of attracting membership and funding, is indisputable. But more important, for many in PARC the Feast represents the physical manifestation of the organization's commitment to its regional status, as writers from every province in the region converge on the same location, engage in closely related processes and participate in a final, public sharing of their efforts. Feeling at times a bit like a modest summer camp for unemployed adults, the Feast nonetheless represents a rare opportunity to overcome the physical barriers of distance in an immediate, collaborative experience. That these are the terms so frequently used to describe the event by its organizers *and* its participants is testament to its impact. However, the Feast is also a temporary focal point to PARC's overall programming—one which demonstrates both the strength of "community" it can effect, and the need for that community's constant maintenance.

Clearly, the obstacles to PARC exerting a truly regional influence are multiple. The most concrete of these is the issue of finances. Following the completion of the initial funding, which afforded PARC the vital services of an administrative officer, the organization was run by a volunteer board. As with most arts organizations in this situation, a small number of individuals—such as Wanda Graham, Bev Brett, Catherine Banks, Gyllian Raby and, in particular, Paula Danckert—provided Herculean contributions. The results of this situation were inevitable: impressive but inconsistent activity; selfless commitment and individual burnout; and periods of remarkable activity combined with lapsed continuity. In 1998, however, PARC received operating funding from the Canada Council for the Arts for the first time, and the current Executive Director, Jenny Munday, was hired on a part-time basis. Under Munday's energetic stewardship, PARC has demonstrated an unprecedented degree of activity, consistency and full regional presence. But, ironically, the acquisition of minimal operating funding resulted in the loss of Council sponsorship for such initiatives as the Moveable Feast. Indeed, all of PARC's activities beyond the basic operation of its small office are now funded through individual project grants secured from public and private sources. Not surprisingly, this has been the focus of the organization's trials over the past five years.

As arts funding continues to shrink across the region, support for regional initiatives has all but evaporated. Of all the Atlantic provinces, only Nova Scotia has provided PARC with any ongoing base funding—albeit at the extremely modest level of just over $3,000 a year. Two years ago this amount was cut in half and, along with a handful of small theatre and dance groups, PARC was told that it would be phased out of sustaining funding entirely the following year. The move was framed as being of benefit for PARC: the removal from sustaining funding would, PARC was told, improve its chances in the project-funding category. However, the fact that two project grant applications went unfunded in that same year gave those words of encouragement a rather hollow ring.[3] Rather, the decision seems more directly related to the argument already openly stated by the provincial arts funding organizations in the three other Atlantic provinces, with funding for local initiatives drying up, provincial support for projects dispersed across the entire region did not enter into consideration. By adopting such an ambitious geographic scope in its services, PARC had unwittingly positioned itself outside of feasible funding categories.

However, there is another, more abstract, if no less critical, actor in the success or failure of PARC's regional mandate, and this relates to PARC's stated commitment to the idea of a regional theatre community. In few areas across this country does the term "community" carry more significance than on the East Coast. Uncommon degrees of isolation and insulation from the next village, let alone the next province, result in heightened awareness of local interdependence and communal identity, even within the largest of Atlantic Canadian municipalities. Thus the repeated reference to community in the organization's public relations material is as intentionally productive as it is problematic.

In a *Canadian Theatre Review* article in 1997 on the role and position of Rising Tide Theatre in Newfoundland's cultural scene, Heather Jones attempted to qualify Alan Filewod's generalized rejection of the term "community" in reference to professional theatre. In an earlier *CTR* editoral, Filewod had suggested that

> community has no meaning, it has become merely an index of power. Whoever invokes it, in government, in manifestos or in funding offices, draws strength from it but depletes its meaning. In consequence, the very word "community" has become as bankrupt as its rhetorical predecessor, "the people"… (Filewod 3)

While Jones concurs that "the rhetoric of both the left and the right [...] has made a political plaything of the term 'community,'" she also argues that "[i]n Newfoundland the term community is healthy and thriving not despite, however, but because of its politicized contexts." Jones further cites Rising Tide Theatre's Artistic Director Donna Butt, who asserts that "community here has always been political, class and economy driven, yet also firmly grounded in the place itself and in the conditions of everyday life" (Jones 38).

Although coloured by a characteristic and paradoxically gritty romanticism, Butt's contention is supported by the overwhelming presence of the collective model in Newfoundland theatre history. While Helen Peters, among others, has extensively documented the multiple external and internal artistic influences on the collective process in Newfoundland,[4] it is also difficult not to find a strong parallel between theatrical collaboration and self-conscious social cohesion. And while the collective movement, *per se*, is no longer an operative presence in Newfoundland theatre, a considerable amount of the drama currently staged by the artist-managed Resource Centre for the Arts in St. John's retains a collaborative production process that actually incorporates development to an uncommon degree. And it is precisely this communal allegiance to Newfoundland theatre practice—or, more specifically, to that of St. John's—that acts as a deterrent to regional (that is, "Atlantic") identification.[5]

While Newfoundland certainly represents Atlantic isolationism in its most extreme form, it is by no means unique in this respect. But the motivation behind such "separatist" inclinations is neither common nor simple. In some instances, it emerges as an indirect defence of local interests. Thus, speaking at a Symposium on Theatre in Atlantic Canada at Mount Allison University in 1986, Chris Heide, a founding member of the Dramatists' Co-op, expressed a skepticism about regional generalization:[6] "I'm not at all convinced that there is an 'Atlantic Canada.' To the best of my knowledge the term was invented by Ottawa bureaucrats in the late sixties to suit their purposes" (qtd. in Knowles 246). In other instances, distance is the direct product of prioritized internal funding policies. After the loss of a full three-quarters of its funding in the past few years, Theatre PEI has devolved into an earnest but largely facilitative service organization. With the disappearance of the majority of that theatre's independent programming, PARC has watched the decline of its strongest ally, its closest collaborator and its greatest source of public relations on Prince Edward Island. And in other situations, the failure to connect regionally seems primarily the consequence of vast, under-populated physical distance. Thus, Charlie Rhindress, the Artistic Director of Live Bait Theatre in Sackville, New Brunswick, near the border with Nova Scotia, remains highly active in PARC's administration and programming, but PARC has been frustrated in its attempts to establish connections with other New Brunswick professional theatre organizations in considerably more distant Fredericton.[7]

At the same time, however, the increasingly national and international influences on, and aspirations of, an emerging generation of dramatists in Atlantic Canada appear to provide sufficient encouragement to look beyond provincial barriers for opportunities in development as well as production. In contrast to the resistance or disinterest expressed by some (though certainly not all) of their more senior counterparts, these new writers seem keen to explore the possibilities of regional cross-fertilization. Thus, Robert Chafe of St. Johns' Artistic Fraud theatre company has attended the Moveable Feast in both 1996 and 2001. PEI's quickly growing ranks of young, self-producing dramatists are proving equally eager to make use of PARC's programming, both on and off *that* Island. And PARC is once again making inroads into the intensely active university theatre communities at the University of New Brunswick and St. Thomas University in New Brunswick. It would be simplistic, however, to isolate age as a determining factor, as one of the most exciting developments last year was the inclusion of an Acadian play, also from New Brunswick, originally by established artist Laval Goupil and translated by Glen Nichols as *Dark Owl*, as part of the Moveable Feast. And by offering increased flexibility in the new play development processes made available, PARC seems alert to the potential for generating linkages—indeed, communities—defined by affinities of form and technique rather than simple geography, between practitioners from throughout the region. Correspondingly, PARC is becoming adept at tapping into provincial coffers through its regional representatives who, as resident artists, initiate independent grant proposals within their own borders as the local organizers of events coordinated by PARC.

As part of a major review and revisioning of its operations, goals and objectives over the past year, the PARC board and its executive director took a long, close look at the feasibility of maintaining its regional mandate. The outcome was a restated commitment to serving the entire Atlantic region. However, an altered, more complex understanding of community has emerged—one that acknowledges the fluid, discontinuous and mutable boundaries that surround and separate, but also connect and overlap within what are in fact, multiple communities. In the article by Heather Jones already cited, one of her Newfoundland students, in reference to the border between Quebec and Ontario, observed, "I couldn't believe that two provinces could be so close together!" (38) And it is the startling, energizing proximity of the Atlantic region's distinct communities that will continue to define PARC's unique position among play development organizations in this country.

(2003)

Works Cited

Atlantic Fringe Festival. Official website. http://www.atlanticfringe.com.

Barton, Bruce. "Redefining Community: The Elusive Legacy of the Dramatists' Co-op of Nova Scotia." *Theatre Research in Canada* 21:2 (Fall 2000): 99–115.

Filewod, Alan. "The Spectre of Communi**" Editorial. *Canadian Theatre Review* 82 (Spring 1995): 3–9.

Graham, Wanda. Email to author. 16 October 2002.

Jones, Heather. "Rising Tide Theatre and/in the Newfoundland Cultural Scene." *Canadian Theatre Review* 93 (Winter 1997): 38–41.

Knowles, Richard Paul, ed. *The Proceedings of the Theatre in Atlantic Canada Symposium.* Centre for Canadian Studies. Mount Allison University, Sackville, New Brunswick, 1988.

Lynde, Denyse. "Writing and Publishing: Four Newfoundland Playwrights in Conversation." *Canadian Theatre Review 98* (Spring 1999): 28–46.

Peters, Helen, ed. *Stars in the Sky Morning: Collective Plays of Newfoundland and Labrador.* St. John's NF: Killick Press, 1996.

---

[1]   See Atlantic Fringe Festival.

[2]   Wanda Graham was extremely generous with her descriptions of the early days of the organization during the preparation of this article, particularly in a lengthy email to the author. See Graham.

[3]   Ironically, before PARC could be entirely excluded from sustaining funding, the Nova Scotia government abruptly dismantled the Nova Scotia Arts Council and replaced it with a Nova Scotia Arts and Culture Council, which reserves permanent representation for government officials in adjudication processes. In the midst of this transition, PARC successfully secured $16,000 in sustaining funding from the Nova Scotia Division of Cultural Affairs, and is eligible for future applications to this branch of government.

[4]   See Peters, "Introduction: Development," xiii–xliii.

[5]   In a recent conversation with Denyse Lynde, Pete Soucy—who had been central in the drafting of the original constitution of PARC—stated: "And because we're again, sort of removed, you know, from everybody else in Atlantic Canada, it's more or less their organization. PARC is really a Maritimes organization more than an Atlantic one" (Lynde 31).

[6]   These comments, published in 1988, predate the creation of PARC. However, Heide was clear about his reservations concerning a regional, as opposed to provincial, organization during early discussions concerning the founding of APRC.

[7]   However, the relationship with Theatre New Brunswick is obviously shaped by numerous additional complications involving that organization's current financial and administrative challenges.

Questioning the Text
by Rachel Ditor

I work as a dramaturg and director in Vancouver, British Columbia, Canada, and like many of my Canadian dramaturg colleagues I work almost exclusively in the development of new plays. This means that I spend most of my time talking to playwrights, and as I am contracted by a number of local theatre companies, I'm in touch with a wide variety of theatre artists creating work in varied styles. Regardless of the variety of style and content in the plays I work on, in the early stages of my discussions with playwrights we often find ourselves talking about story and how to craft or refine it. I have found this to be equally true of plays that are not narrative driven. I often focus the issue of story with writers by asking, "Where do you want to take me?" The journey can be primarily emotional or intellectual or anything that a writer can imagine and pull off, but in a broad sense this is what story has come to mean to me: what's the ride of this play?

Am I right to perceive that this question is relevant to all of the plays I work on? If so, does this imply that there is something universal about the mechanics of constructing and receiving story? Everything I have learned in the theatre I have learned through practice first, and so in an attempt to pursue these questions I set myself a seemingly very basic task for the 2001–2002 season: to identify how story pulls an audience through a play. Could I clock my experience as an audience member and note each point of engagement or distancing that I experience as the *receiver* of a story? Would this illuminate the mechanics of story for me in a new way and inform how I assist a playwright in crafting the ride of his/her play? I know not all people experience any one story in the same way, but could I codify my own experience and use that to extrapolate some larger lesson about experiencing story?

I found myself facing the 2001–02 season with three very different freelance dramaturgy jobs ahead of me to which I could apply my questions about story. The first project was a student production of *Hedda Gabler* at Simon Fraser University. They had engaged a professional director from a local company, Norman Armour (Rumble Productions), and he in turn hired me to dramaturg. The second project was a new play, *Flop*, created and performed by the Electric Company, a local collective theatre company that is known for its tremendous sense of spectacle and unwieldy scripts. In the third project, I was engaged to dramaturg and direct the posthumous premiere of the unfinished script of *A Season in Purgatory*, by the late Michael David Kwan, for the Gateway Theatre. What follows is a condensed version of my quest to track how I received story as I worked on these projects.

Hedda Gabler

The director, Norman Armour, generously handed over the entire first week of rehearsals to me for tablework—the form and content of which was left to me to define. I wanted to immerse the cast in the play; I wanted to open the play up, to make it accessible and ownable, but to hold off decision-making until they were on their feet exploring. I wanted them to use the research materials made available, not to look for the "right" answers, but rather for conversation, to search out specific arguments. What kind of process could I construct that would bring them to the place where I was, having at this point spent months researching and reading various versions of the play?

In the end I decided that I would dub everyone around the table "dramaturg"; that together we would question the text. We read the play aloud, and every time we completed a french scene (i.e., scenes delineated by the exiting of a character or the entrance of a character), we would stop reading and take a few minutes to write down any and all questions we had about the scene. I requested that they write down *all* the questions that occurred to them in that moment, even if they knew an answer was forthcoming in the text. Then we went around the table and everyone read their list of questions. The director, designers, stage managers, and I participated equally. I made the goal very clear: we were collecting questions, *not* answering them. They would answer them on their feet, in rehearsal.

Below is the list of questions generated in response to Thea Elvsted's arrival in act 1, pages 71–74 in the version by playwright John Osborne.

TEXT

MRS ELVSTED: …I'd better tell you now: Eilert Lövborg is here as
　　well.
HEDDA: Lövborg? He's here?
TESMAN: He's not! You hear that, Hedda?
HEDDA: I hear very well, thank you!
MRS ELVSTED: He's been here for a whole week. Think of it. In a
　　place like this. All on his own. And surrounded by the dregs, you
　　can be sure.
HEDDA: But, Mrs Elvsted, my dear, what has all this got to do with
　　you?
MRS ELVSTED: (Frightened; quickly) He's been the children's tutor.
　　Looked after them, in fact.
HEDDA: Yours?
MRS ELVSTED: They're my husband's children. I don't have any.
HEDDA: Oh—stepchildren.
TESMAN: (Unsure) I don't quite know how to put it—but was he
　　reliable? That is, could you depend on his, well, way of life and all
　　that, regular and so on, to be put in charge of, care of, children?
　　Um?
MRS ELVSTED: For two years past there's been nothing. Nothing to
　　concern oneself with at all.
TESMAN: Is that so? What do you think of that then, Hedda?
HEDDA: I'm listening.

MRS ELVSTED: There's been nothing, believe me. Not in any way at all. But now he's here, in a big town like this. And with so much money on him. I'm just so afraid for him, that's all.

TESMAN: But why didn't he stay up there with you and your husband?

MRS ELVSTED: Once his book had come out, he didn't seem able to contain himself any longer.

TESMAN: Yes, of course, his book, it came out. Auntie was telling me...

MRS ELVSTED: All about the development of culture. Oh, civilization itself, and on such a scale! That was a couple of weeks ago and everyone's been buying it or talking about it ever since. It's roused such attention, I can't tell you.

QUESTIONS

- What kind of place is implied in the line "in a place like this"?
- How did Lövborg come to the Elvsted's?
- What was Lövborg teaching?
- Why didn't Lövborg tell Thea where he was going? How did they part?
- What is Thea's life like with her husband?
- Who is Thea's husband and how long have they been married?
- What is the implication of stepchildren? Can Thea not have children? Is her relationship with her husband non-sexual?
- How many stepchildren does Thea have?
- Why are they concerned about Lövborg's reliability? What do they fear might happen to children in his care?
- Why does Tesman keep checking that Hedda has heard Thea's news? Is he trying to make some sort of point to Hedda?
- How much money does Lövborg have on him? Has the success of the book made him wealthy? Is he famous now?
- Why is she frightened? What happened last time Lövborg was in town?
- What does Hedda want from Thea?
- How does Hedda feel about Thea's arrival?
- Did Thea and Tesman ever sleep together? How close was their relationship? Why did it end?
- Is there a flirtation between Thea and Tesman? Chemistry crackling in the air?
- What is the history between Thea and Hedda?
- When does Hedda decide that Thea is hiding something? What gives her that clue?
- How do others react when Hedda says things that are cruel?

Now, a different cast would likely come up with different questions and, frankly, I often found myself less interested in the actual questions they asked and more engaged with the way in which this seemingly tedious exercise of questioning completely absorbed their attention. The questions opened the play up and shone some light in the dark corners and crevices, and illuminated for the cast the great number of meaty choices that the play offered them as actors. My instruction to not answer the questions around the table but to hunt for answers on their feet in rehearsal allowed the table work to remain specific yet exploratory—the questioning never reduced the play.

Here was the first piece of my answer about how story is received: the act of questioning *completely absorbed their attention.* The students were very good at not anticipating answers. Even though they knew a question was going to be answered during a later scene, or even in the next line, they posed it anyway. As a group we were moving through the play, or the play was moving through us, question by question.

Flop

Flop was an exploration of failure; in retrospect I can say that that statement applies to the content of the play as well as to its process and product. I expect this was my own doing as much as anyone's and, like any true failure, much hard-won knowledge was gained by the experience. The Electric Company (comprised of Kim Collier, David Hudgins, Kevin Kerr, and Jonathon Young) is renowned in Canada for its unique sense of physicality, spectacle, eclectic interests, and for its propensity to tell large, unwieldy stories. I had worked with the company before with success so we thought we'd try it again, and for this project the company had also hired an outside director, Katrina Dunn (Touchstone Theatre). By engaging an outside director as well as a dramaturg the collective was investigating an adjustment to their creative process. Could they sharpen their sense of narrative structure by bringing in artists who were not also writing and performing in the show?

I was put in charge of creating and facilitating a process that would help the collective refine the script. We entered into the first leg of rehearsals after we had held a few readings of progressive drafts of the script. I could hear in the script evidence of many points of disagreement about the basic story among the members of the collective that would have to be worked through if *Flop* was going to tell a coherent story. How could I use what I had observed about questions having the ability to pull an audience through a play to help make the ride in *Flop* clearer?

I thought we would benefit from a rigorous line-by-line questioning of the text as I had used with *Hedda Gabler*. I thought this was a good choice for two reasons: it would illuminate where there was actual agreement about points of story and characterization within the collective, and where opinions diverged, and it could help us track the experience, or the questions, of the audience, which would illuminate for us information that was missing from the script or was unintentionally self-contradictory.

To help us differentiate between questions that pertained to disagreement within the writing team and questions that attempted to track the course of the audience's interest and engagement, I created two categories into which we would organize our questions: Internal (questions for the collective to solve in the next draft) and External (questions the scene poses to the audience). Within the External category we distinguished between questions that were appropriate (questions we are intending the audience to ask) and questions that we don't intend to be posing. In other words, what story did we *want* to tell, and what story might we *appear* to be telling, despite our best efforts? Below is an example of a scene (which is in fact a paragraph of stage directions) and the questions that came out of our discussion about it.

The basic set-up of the play is that the architectural team of Cooper, Crowne, and McLure has been commissioned by the enigmatic Ruby to build her a spectacular flying house. The play begins moments before the grand opening and launch is due to commence. We have just witnessed Ruby secretly sabotaging the project by cutting important wires. The playing space is bare except for a very large beam hung in mid-air upstage center. The playing style is highly physical.

Excerpt from *Flop*, draft 4, act 1, scene 4: The Project

> Wind, rain, thunder sound effects are now out. Ruby happily puts her scissors away and re-tapes the tube. She suddenly notices a movement at a nearby window. She captures another bird, plucks a feather and releases it into her hidden place. Suddenly she hears the men approaching.

Questions from *Flop*, draft 4, act 1, scene 4: The Project

INTERNAL QUESTIONS
"She suddenly notices a movement at a nearby window."
- How do we plan to make it clear that she's at a window? Mimed? Gobo? Frame?
- Is this an outside window, or is she looking down into the Aviarium? (Her *hidden place*.)

"She captures another bird."
- What is her relationship to the birds?
- Does Ruby interact with the bird?
- What does the Aviarium look like?

EXTERNAL QUESTIONS
We intend the audience to ask…
- Did the storm stop? Why?
- What is her relationship with the birds? What do they mean to her?
- Why did she capture and pluck the feather from the bird?
- What is that room?

We hope the audience isn't asking...
> • What the hell is she looking at?
> • Where is she in the building?

Breakout Aviarium Discussion: General Questions
> • How do we communicate the Aviarium?
> • Who discovers it? When?
> • Do the architects know about it, or not? Did Ruby create this space secretly?
> • Is this about liberated space, or housing flight, i.e., cages?
> • Do we conflate the Addition with the Aviarium? Are these two rooms actually the same space?
> • What does it mean to connect with this space? Is this finding inspiration, or strength?
> • Do the men acknowledge this space to each other?
> • Is this the one successful space that they have created?

In our conversation around the table, questions would spark intense debate angling for resolution. It quickly became clear that individual assumptions about form, content and characterization diverged wildly. It was also clear that in the past disagreements within the collective about story were subtly skirted and/or leapt over by the generating of a new idea that moved sharply away from the problem area, and opened up completely new territory (and new problems). In *Hedda Gabler* everyone was excited by the way the questions opened up the play and made it richer than before. In *Flop* the act of questioning the text appeared to accomplish the opposite— reducing the world of the play and highlighting old and new (there was a director at the table for the first time) dysfunctions in the group dynamic. Was this process of defining the story a necessary evil, or was I needlessly making everyone miserable? Yet, when I made suggestions about ending this process and trying something else the group expressed a strong desire to push through.

In the end *Flop* had a clarity of plot that their other work had lacked. There wasn't anyone I asked who couldn't recount the basic story for me point by point. But *Flop* didn't engage the audience emotionally. People didn't invest in the characters' aspirations and were left untouched by their weaknesses, downfall, and rebirth. In searching for clarity we created an environment in the rehearsal hall that didn't promote emotional risk and honesty, and this was evident in the show.

Although I had found a useful tool in deciphering story through a series of questions, I was missing a step somewhere. The emotional heart of the story was so abstracted as to be impenetrable; a dense and confusing plot was made coherent, but to what end? My next query about story was, how do you get a question to occur to a person in the audience as emotion?

A Season in Purgatory

The play *A Season in Purgatory* takes place at a prison in Beijing during the student uprising at Tiananmen Square. The prison is deserted except for the Warden, a young Investigator sent to "close the file" on the remaining resident and Prisoner 565 (Madame Mao). As Prisoner 565 tries to reconcile herself to death she tells stories to the young Inspector about her past loves, including her relationship with her husband Mao and his son, Ahnying.

Mr. Kwan's estate was in favour of producing the show as written, though when the author died, there had been plans afoot for a new draft. I had permission to edit and rearrange text as I felt necessary, but not to generate new text. The play seemed far from being ready for production since the primary narrative engine, the quest to discover the true identity of Prisoner 565, didn't work. The cat was out of the bag by act 1, scene 4. The play had nowhere to go after that. No amount of editing and rearranging of the text would make the play work as a mystery, so I would have to find another throughline to drive the action of the play.

Over the course of the year I did my best to acquire enough information to delve into the world of the play and make informed changes. I spent the better part of a year getting up to speed on Chinese history, particularly as it related to events in the play. I also tried to get to know the author in absentia, through his other published works, many of them autobiographical (including the stunning *Things That Must Not Be Forgotten* that recounts his childhood in China during World War II).

Once again I decided to employ the method of questioning the text, but this time with an added goal: I wanted to clarify the story in order to identify a protagonist and begin the process of crafting an emotionally truthful story about that character.

This time I only spent one day reading through the play with the cast and going around the table collecting questions. In addition to the cast of three, my invaluable assistant dramaturg, Jo Leddingham, the stage manager and two staff members from the theatre's marketing department were present. The designers, technicians, and Simon Johnston, the Artistic Producer of the Gateway Theatre, came to join us whenever they were available. Having been immersed in research it was very refreshing to hear questions from people who were new to the play, such as those from the marketing and technical staff. I knew that if, at the very least, I wanted to communicate any kind of coherent story I would have to pay attention to their questions in particular and make sure my edits and rearrangements of text were going to answer some of the basic confusion their questions revealed.

Once I had looked over the accumulated questions I decided to use the list differently; my assistant dramaturg and I used the checklist to communicate queries to each other, and it became a document of our running conversation in rehearsal.

Below is a sample of this checklist drawn from text at the top of the play. The boxes were left open until tech week when I watched a run and checked off questions when I could see the answer in the play. If I couldn't find the answer to the question during the run the box was left unchecked. Below the question is a summary of the running dialogue between Jo and me.

Excerpt of checklist from *A Season in Purgatory:* act 1, scene 1

☑ Why does the Warden need someone else "to close the file"?

> RD: Answered by Warden in act 1, scene 17. Is this too long to wait?
> JL: Support for given circumstances can be in Prologue.
> RD: Great idea. Let's look for quotes we can use for slides that give
>   context and sense of changing political tides.
> JL: Something from the Courtroom quotes?
> RD: Maybe. Also, we need to look for ways to highlight Warden's status
>   with the Minister.

☑ What is implied in "to close the file"?

> RD: Okay to not have this answered at the top. A good question to
>   have the audience ask: Is the Investigator there to kill her? Still, we
>   know why Kwan thought she was a threat, but this isn't really in
>   the play.
> JL: Should we print his notes in the program?
> RD: We could but the answer still needs to be in the play itself. Ideas?

☑ Who is Prisoner 565?

> RD: No pay off for this question to function as arc of the whole play.
>   We know by act 1, scene 4.
> JL: If this isn't the overarching question of the play, what is?
> RD: What if this play is about the fate of the Investigator? Jo, look for
>   a beginning, middle, end for him and we'll compare ideas.
> JL: I'll try story arcs for everyone.

❑ What is the connection with the Tiananmen uprising?

> RD: When do the public announcements from the Square get
>   connected to the interrogation of Madame Mao inside the prison?
> JL: Quote on page 4, act 1, scene 2.
> RD: Too early for this information, no context for it. Who connects the
>   dots in this play? Any mileage from this as a reveal? Or do we need
>   to know this up front?

I knew that last box needed to be checked off; the question had occasioned a lot of discussion around the table when the play was new to people. During rehearsals I had lost sight of its importance to the play as a whole. During tech week I focused my attention on solving this issue and finally crafted a solution. My checklist gave me perspective on the story—something that I often have difficulty maintaining at the start of tech when I've spent so much time looking at the trees that I need a little help seeing the forest again. The questions brought me back to Day One and allowed me to see the play fresh, the way an audience member might.

The draft of the play I was working with did not, on the surface, support an emotionally truthful story for the young Inspector, but I knew that merely editing for clarity wasn't going to provide enough of a ride for a satisfying evening. In the end the cuts and rearranging of the text had thrown into high relief a latent and compelling mother-son drama. It wasn't until I was watching the dress rehearsal that I realized that the mother-son dynamic in the play was also present in, and in fact central to, the first installment of Kwan's moving autobiography.

•

I did learn something about the mechanics of how story engages an audience and I do think it is a lesson that can be applied to any story.

I observed that the myriad variations on the question "What will happen next"? serve as the basic architecture on which the dynamic relationship between the story/storytellers and the audience is built.

The continual planting and answering of questions is story. This process can be obvious or barely perceptible, a question and answer exchange can take hours to unfold or can happen in the blink of an eye. In any story the difference between a moment on stage feeling satisfying or arbitrary is directly related to whether the question, which that moment answers, has yet occurred to the audience. And although question and answer is, in a sense, the microcosm of beginning, middle, and end, I have found it a valuable concept in discussion with playwrights whose work aims to subvert or reject a linear structure as an organizing principle.

Further, in the plays that successfully take someone on an emotional journey or ride, the questions and answers will have occurred to that audience member first as emotions. For example, when Hedda Gabler burns Eilert Lövborg's manuscript, the emotional *ride* of that moment might be curiosity to repulsion, or impatience to relief. If a person isn't invested in that moment the basic question and answer dynamic is still present but might be as simple as *"Is she actually going to burn the book? ...Yes, she is."*

And of course this game of question and answer begins at home for most audience members. The conscious question: *Should we see that show?* The question as emotion: *Where will it take me?* The answer...

(2003)

The De-Ba-Jeh-Mu-Jig Method: Making Stories
by Shannon Hengen

At his father's side, he learned that it is the story-bearing nation, not the arms-bearing nation, that will triumph over racism and tyranny.

(Herriort 79)

After nineteen consecutive years in existence De-ba-jeh-mu-jig Theatre of Wikwemikong Unceded Indian Reserve won, in the summer of 2002, recognition from Canadian Heritage as the site of a national arts training program, joining the ranks of such other organizations as the National Theatre School and the Banff Centre; and so De-ba-jeh-mu-jig will have funding for interns to train at De-ba-jeh-mu-jig in their permanent facilities on Manitoulin Island in Northern Ontario as well as funding to develop those facilities. De-ba-jeh-mu-jig will receive the annual contribution specifically because of its non-European organizational style (Berti, Personal interview).

The views of current Artistic Producer Ron Berti figure largely here, for it was under his guidance that, in 1995, the theatre developed the Four Directions creative process that moved the company's management style and method of script development beyond what he calls a European model: that is, an Artistic Director at the helm who sifts through manuscripts, chooses a season and works within the typical three-week rehearsal time per production. Among the major Aboriginal companies in Canada that have received annual operating funds from the Canada Council, only De-ba-jeh-mu-jig has developed a style that arises from the culture itself (Berti, Class lecture). De-ba-jeh-mu-jig's uniqueness, especially the Four Directions creative process, was celebrated by the Art Gallery of Ontario (AGO) in Toronto when the theatre became Artists in Residence from 23 February to 14 March 2003. Daily improvisational performances occurred at a venue called Audrey's Place, a set that reproduced the home of Audrey Debassige Wemigwans, current Associate Artistic Director of the troupe and vital citizen of the Wikwemikong Community.

As well, the company presented storytelling and studio activities at the Art Gallery of Ontario and in Toronto schools, and collaborated in events with other Native arts groups in Toronto. The theatre's appearance as Artists in Residence at the AGO represents the first such appearance of a theatre company at a museum or gallery of that size.

The result of some five years of work, De-ba-jeh-mu-jig's Four Directions model of creation shifts focus away from the final product and towards the artist whose whole person—intellectual, emotional, spiritual and physical—is believed to be engaged in making the show. "How can you create with only a part of yourself?" Berti asks, and continues: "We maintain a huge responsibility to our artists" (Class lecture). This process embraces traditional wisdom and teaching—company elders form an integral part of it—and is illustrated by company members as a kind of organism (to replace the concept of an organization). The organism includes Native and in some cases non-Native arts workers and theatre practitioners necessary for shows to come to be and then to find venues and audiences. Near its centre are animators who are always from the culture and who have followed the path of Best Medicine; finally, at the organism's very heart, is the creative process itself.

Actors' and writers' lives directly inform what evolves into each show. De-ba-jeh-mu-jig productions can start, for example, with improvisations around a theme, or with a traditional story, as has occurred in two recent mainstage productions, *The Dreaming Beauty* (by Daniel David Moses) and *Ever! That Nanabush!* (based on the series "Legends of Nanabush," as retold and illustrated by Daphne Odjig), when the company then makes the stories their own. For the summer of 2002 production of *Ever! That Nanabush!* the group worked with storyweaver Muriel Miguel, founder of New York's Spiderwoman Theater, in order to bring themselves into the legends (Dbaajmaataadaa 4). As a visiting animator, Miguel taught the actors how to weave each legend through every part of their bodies, through whom and what they are and believe, Berti explains (Personal interview).

Born out of necessity, the De-ba-jeh-mu-jig method responds to the fact that in its first eleven years, the company had made its way through all of the known talent in the Aboriginal theatre world. Its Artistic Director/Playwrights had included founder Shirley Cheechoo, her successor Tomson Highway (whose work there was aided by his brother René), Larry Lewis and Alanis King. By 1995, no such personages were applying for the job of Artistic Director, and few manuscripts were arriving. De-ba-jeh-mu-jig's many illustrious alumni had moved to the cities, and so the group made a conscious decision, Berti states, to invest in local talent, to create from what they are all about on the Island rather than measure themselves against a southern Ontario standard, to "turn their chairs around" and compare themselves to the rest of the country north of the Island. He concludes that this decision has been "extremely empowering" to the company (Personal interview).

And so ended the era of putting up one new show every summer and touring it in the fall, travelling to Toronto, if possible, to qualify for a Chalmers or any of the other awards that require performances in Toronto. De-ba-jeh-mu-jig made a commitment to develop local talent and to market their skills where most needed—especially communities to the north of Manitoulin Island. De-ba-jeh-mu-jig now offers, through its Best Medicine Troupe of young people, workshops that result in "custom shows" that "reflect the specific themes of your conference or gathering" (Dbaajmaataadaa 1). The troupe also conducts on-site training residencies with youth or adults such as the one at remote Summer Beaver, a fly-in community, in 2002 (Dbaajmaataadaa 3).

At the heart of De-ba-jeh-mu-jig's work is storytelling, implied in the theatre's name, which is a Cree-Ojibway compilation meaning the tellers of tales. Berti states that a recurring question for the company is, "Where does storytelling meet contemporary theatre?", the answer to which comes out of the shared experience of the De-ba-jeh-mu-jig staff as it produces each year's main stage show (Personal interview). Critical writing also responds to Berti's questions, such as the one implicit in Drew Hayden Taylor's article, "Storytelling to Stage," in which he writes that theatre [...] has become the predominant expressive vehicle for Canada's Native people. I believe the reason is that theatre is just a logical extension of storytelling. To look back at the roots and origins of traditional storytelling [...] it's about taking your audience on a journey through the use of your voice, your body, and the spoken word.

The tradition of storytelling would seem to have clear links with the stage, and indeed in 2002 at the Stratford Festival Aboriginal playwright Ian Ross, in the notes to his play *Bereav'd of Light*, opens with the statement that

I grew up, as most people do, hearing stories. Some of these stories were fictional, some real life, and some were of things that happened a long time ago; but all were communal, and all were connected to the land. *Bereav'd of Light* is my invention of one of the stories I heard growing up. (9)

All playwrights could make scripts out of the stories of their youth. But a crucial element distinguishes Aboriginal storytelling, an element that links traditional tales directly with the De-ba-jeh-mu-jig method. UBC anthropologist Julie Cruikshank, in her two books that recount and analyze her experience of recording oral history in the Yukon territory, where she lived from the early 1970s until 1984, details how the traditional legends told her by the three female elders whose lives she transcribed were inextricably linked with the women's personal lives. In the first of the two books, *Life Lived Like a Story*, Cruikshank explains: "From the beginning, several of the eldest women responded to my questions about secular events by telling traditional stories. The more I persisted with my agenda, the more insistent each was about the direction our work should take. Each explained that these narratives were important to record *as part of* her life story" (2).

Our notions about autobiography need to be queried in relation to the telling of these tales in this way, Cruikshank argues, but so must our ideas about the role of stage stories in an Aboriginal theatre group, for much is at work when De-ba-jeh-mu-jig produces contemporary and traditional Aboriginal legends in a culturally sensitive milieu.

In her second book, *The Social Life of Stories*, Cruikshank argues that although we (non-Natives) like to believe that indigenous knowledge is essentially uncomplicated (53), we might consider instead that it is defined differently in Aboriginal terms, as a relational concept more like a verb than a noun, more a process than a product (870). She writes that "Indigenous storytelling assumes a relationship between speaker and listener. A listener becomes knowledgeable by hearing successive tellings of stories and may mull over, reinterpret, and absorb different meanings with each hearing" (144).

Not uncomplicated, this knowledge is subtle and earned, and connects well with a concept of theatre as a place where one's own and one's people's stories are told and retold so that both the people and the stories gain new direction. Traditional stories change over time, taking their form and content from the contexts of each new generation of tellers. With the dying out of the tellers of these tales in their original languages, Aboriginal communities can adapt such non-traditional modes of retelling as staged performances to keep the stories alive.

Two of our best-known commentators on Canadian theatre, Alan Filewod and Ric Knowles, both address the subject of Aboriginals or Aboriginal writing in Canadian theatre and so point towards possible links between the two methods. In Filewod's analysis of important moments in Canadian theatre, *Performing Canada*, he critiques the first theatrical performance in what is now Canada, Marc Lescarbot's 1606 river spectacle, *The Theatre of Neptune in New France*. Filewod writes that the play

> was both a performance and a quotation of a more authentic [old world] performance that could never be realized. This was a defining moment that would be played for the next five centuries, a moment in which the theatre enacted an imagined authenticity even as it confirmed the extension of empire by transmuting the work of colonialism into spectacle. (xiii)

Hence the subtitle of Filewod's monograph, *The Nation Enacted in the Imagined Theatre*. For five centuries we have had theatre driven by a colonized Imaginary whose impossible project has been to make itself and its audience, Canada, real. Canadian theatre, Filewod states, "summons two historically unstable terms to create a third site of crisis" (x). But Aboriginals viewed that first spectacle. Filewod claims that "Neptune's Aboriginal supplicants were probably portrayed by Frenchmen, but, as Lescarbot tells us, they were watched by the settlement's Aboriginal neighbours. What did they make of this moment? ...Two sets of eyes saw two very different events," he concludes wryly, as the enacted Natives offered their world to the King of France along with their devotion to him, and his descendants (xiv).

We might imagine that a traditional indigenous story does survive that relates and comments upon that very spectacle, however obliquely. And in relation to the story from the other sets of eyes we might gain perspective not only on life in New France in the early seventeenth century but also on social and cultural experiences of Natives and non-Natives in Quebec now and in the future. Or that is the promise of Aboriginal storytelling.

In the section of his *The Theatre of Form and the Production of Meaning* entitled "Playing Indian," Knowles affirms an established theoretical view that orality can destabilize more dominant forms of recording events and experiences (148). Julie Cruikshank rehearses the writings of Mikhail Bakhtin, Walter Benjamin and Harold Innis, for example, all of whom argued for the power of oral traditions to destabilize commonsense categories, to promote non-confrontational ways of re-evaluating hegemonic concepts and to encourage dialogue rather than monologue (*Social Life* 154). Knowles elsewhere in his monograph describes the newest and best historiography from mainstream culture in a way that links that practice with oral traditions:

> At its best, contemporary history writing recognizes that every "received" historical fact has been shaped and reshaped from conflicting

imaginations, mental projections and mappings that bear particular cultural, ideological and political inscriptions. Such writing acknowledges and incorporates into its analysis an understanding of history as necessarily conditioned by an accumulation of the ideologies, assumptions, and (conscious or unconscious) interests of recording and interpreting consciousnesses from both the present and the intervening past. Historiography, then, becomes the ongoing process of remaking history, of "making it new," as fiction or as myth and therefore of shaping a culture's pasts, present, and future. (122)

There, on new territory, academic and Aboriginal Canada meet, and the meeting ground is method. For such ground to be fruitful, it seems we need what US philosopher Kelly Oliver[1] in her book *Witnessing: Beyond Recognition* describes as recognizing difference as that which is beyond immediate recognition (9). Furthermore, only where all subjects have full address-ability and response-ability, Oliver states, will full subjectivity be possible (7).

A kind of trust is needed for the witnessing that Oliver describes, and it is in a spirit of trust that De-ba-jeh-mu-jig works. One sign of the company's success, Ron Berti believes, is the tone of mutual respect and acceptance that the Four Directions method has fostered in recent years. Another sign is the permanent home that the company will occupy starting next spring. That space represents one of a very few permanent locations for a culturally specific theatre company in Canada outside the two dominant cultures (English and French), Berti states. All other such companies "struggle with access to stages and work in basements and third-rate places," to quote him (Personal interview). But culturally specific theatre companies are alive and well, nevertheless: they are not following the European model, do not feel reflected in or supported by the Canadian Theatre Agreement, and so he predicts that "a major shift is coming soon." Mainstream theatre and the culture that upholds it will have much to learn from that shift, from both the content that results and the method that produces it.

(2003)

Works Cited

Berti, Ron. Personal interview. 1 August 2002. Wikwemikong, ON.

———. Class lecture. English 4686: Aboriginal Drama. Laurentian University, Sudbury, ON. 22 November 2001.

Cruikshank, Julie, in collaboration with Angela Sidney, Kitty Smith and Annie Ned. *Life Lived Like a Story: Life Stories of Three Yukon Native Elders.* Lincoln, NE and London: U of Nebraska P, 1990, 1991.

———. *The Social Life as Stories: Narrative and Knowledge in the Yukon Territory.* Lincoln, NE and London: U of Nebraska P, 1998, 2000.

"Dbaajmaataadaa, De-ba-jeh-mu-jig Theatre Group Newsletter." Issue 1. April–June, 2002. www.debaj.ca.

Filewod, Alan. *Performing Canada: The Nation Enacted in the Imagined Theatre.* Vol. 15. Kamloops: Textual Studies in Canada, 2002.

Herriot, Trevor. *River in a Dry Land: A Prairie Passage.* Toronto: Stoddart, 2000.

Knowles, Ric. *The Theatre of Form and the Production of Meaning: Contemporary Canadian Dramaturgies.* Toronto: ECW, 1999.

Oliver, Kelly. *Witnessing: Beyond Recognition.* Minneapolis, MI: U of Minnesota P, 2001.

Ross, Ian. "Sharing History, Sharing Humanity: Playwright's notes." Playbill. *Bereav'd of Light* and Other Plays. Studio Theatre Season, Stratford Festival, Stratford, ON. 2002.

Taylor, Drew Hayden. "Storytelling to Stage: The Growth of Native Theatre in Canada." *TDR* 41.3 (1997): 140–41, 144–52.

---

[1] I would like to thank Margaret McArthur for recommending Oliver's work.

The Cartography of Drama: Dramaturg's Notes to Part Three,
The Swanne: Queen Victoria—The Seduction of Nemesis
by Paula Danckert

The Canadian play is a relatively new art form. Considering that the Stratford Festival is 52 years old and that most regional theatres are yet to reach that ripe age, it is quite astonishing then to realize that Canadian theatre is and, more specifically, Canadian plays are, younger than many of their patrons. This puts theatre in a time frame where the audience and the artist are speaking directly to each other.

Culture and history go hand in hand. They are fraternal twins, coming from the same source, DNA linked. But they don't always share the same birth date. Canadian plays came very recently to the theatre, and along with them came the playwright. Until this arrival it was a rare occurrence to have the playwright in the rehearsal hall. More likely he was dead or possibly living in another country, and not because he had moved there from Canada. This is not a vote for nationalism. I am merely pointing out how extraordinary it was when, 30 years ago, someone in the theatre began to imagine that the living Canadian playwright might be as valued a source of interest and inspiration as, say, Shakespeare.

Theatre is collaboration. Shakespeare lived, breathed and wrote in a theatre with a company of actors. A new play is, more often than not, created with the playwright, a director, designers and a company of actors. Sometimes a dramaturg is involved. Though the theatrical practices and conditions of past and present have little in common, the impulse to create new work is shared through time. It cannot be made silent. A new work of art is a conspiracy, regardless of when it is made. It is dependent on the artists' needs to create as well as to interpret. It relies upon the commitment and the intrigue of an audience. Its existence is subject to desire and will. This assemblage is a dialogue; it is the dramaturgy of the creative process. Artistic expression is a language; if it is not practiced it cannot live. Contemporary art practice keeps the work of the past alive and thrusts new thought into the future. This correspondence makes art immediate and eternal. It is the call and response of the imagination to the subject. It can occur anywhere at anytime.

This relationship with art, in the theatre, could only happen fully when it included the work of the Canadian playwright. Canadian plays gave us something to return, in response, to other cultures. The presence of the playwright deepened the connection between creation and interpretation, between artist and audience. It made us richer. Culture makes a country's relationship to the world reciprocal. The writer gives us our fiction wherein we might discover who we are. Without our own plays we miss an opportunity to be original, to find our true selves. Necessity brought the playwright back to the theatre. Not because the theatre lacked for great plays, but because culture demanded it. We cannot live on history alone.

Along with new plays came new ways of working in the theatre. How to work with the playwright and how to support a process of writing had to be learned. There is no existing system in society to fully support the development and creation of a new work of art. Money to write is scant. Yet the process of constructing a play from an idea or an image into a full production takes years of dedication and craft. It is a process of transforming blind faith into vision. It is a broil of guesswork pitching the playwright from instinct, suspicion and certainty, into language, character and story. Steering the course from beginning to end is often tumultuous. This is dramaturgy.

The work of the imagination is noisy. A dramaturg can bring new ways of listening to the process. The work of the dramaturg demands an inherent understanding and respect for what the playwright is trying to accomplish. It is about knowing the difference between something that is ambiguous because it is incomprehensible and something that is ambiguous because it is yet to be understood. It is tracking the where, why and how of the action according to the knowledge and needs of the characters. Dramaturgy involves a thorough examination of all elements of the drama: story line, character dynamics, sequence of events, time frame, historical background, and, of course, language. Through these applications, techniques have been developed for supporting the writer in the constructing of a play: text analysis with playwright and dramaturg, readings with actors, public readings, staged readings, workshops, and improvisation. These are the practices that help transform a text into a play. During this evolution, many Canadian theatre artists did great justice to the messiness of invention and experimentation before sorting out what can now be called a methodology of play development, or Canadian dramaturgy.

Dramaturgy is argument, it is psychology, it is imagery, it is research, and it is design. It is the means for building fiction. It is how we arrive at interpretation. Dramaturgy is a reference point for every part of the writing process. It is the alleyways, the backroads, the uncharted terrain of the story. Dramaturgy is the cartography of drama. Production dramaturgy takes this process into the rehearsal hall and works it in 3D.

This production marks the completion in an eleven-year process of building *The Swanne*. But process is the refusal of finality. Art lives. Its currency is the engagement with the imagination. This is the gathering place of exchange, where past, present and future meet. Where the material world is left behind and another reality occurs: culture's time zone. It is the vicinity of the artist where history and fiction share their lineage. It is the continuum of culture, the constant and ever changing power of art.

(2004)

Dramaturgy: Forging Definition
by Peter Hinton

We gather round a text which yields meaning
Reluctantly.
We try to perform its contradictions.
We do not smooth,
And yet it occurs.
That must be the purpose of art.
That must be art
Occurring.
Its discomfort is considerable
And yet we return.

Howard Barker, *Arguments for a Theatre*

As artists, we come to the theatre by accident or trauma. We remain out of fortitude and stubbornness. We return to each project with the knowledge that true discomfort is humanizing and that it is never too late for hope to stimulate change. Popular skepticism and a lot of contemporary theatre talk tell us that art has never changed anyone. We have seen the failure of a political attachment to culture and social change and prefer to abandon the idealism of the theatre we desire for the more practical concerns of the theatre we have. I have always believed in the innate power of the theatre to change people's lives because it changed my own. While the Canadian regional theatre embraces dramaturgy in terms of "audience," people seeing "their own stories," and writers writing about "what they know" and creating works "for the large stage," they fail to grasp the relevance of the independent dramaturges, who encourage writers to think unashamedly for themselves, pursue stories that have yet to be claimed and nurture the courage in playwrights to write about what they do not already understand.

The dramaturge is an artist who intimately walks into the imaginations of others, knowing how softly or boldly to tread. She or he is well versed in tradition, knowledgeable and curious, able to see what is on the page and committed to a theatre that might not yet exist. The dramaturge is dedicated to the play, more than to the producing theatre, more than to the playwright, more, even, than to the ideas the play contains. Contentious and delicate—dramaturgy is a moral negotiation between an artist and the art. The dramaturge thrives on possibility not probability and fosters writing for "the large stage" that has more to do with the size of an ambition to question our society in action than with the number of sets of costumes.

In an age of political globalization and cultural specialization, it is not only difficult to create a living theatre but important to ask why we create new work at all. Why is there an ambivalence about discussing a passionate vision for the theatre that can actually distinguish success from significance? How many theatres produce virtually the same playbill, whether it is Vancouver or Halifax. How many theatres actually have a playwright as central and necessary member of their company? Is success measured by the means by which we expand and reinvent dramatic writing for the stage, or rather determined by a commercial agenda operating within a not-for-profit arts organization? Are theatres suspicious of having a playwright as a central and necessary part of the artistic team? Are the audiences complicit? Are playwrights frightened? What role does (or should) the dramaturge play in all this? Is the context in which we create new works changing so rapidly that we confuse lies with truth, reassurance with entertainment, and a message with moral inquiry? How is the theatre evolving if we cannot distinguish narrative from narration, commentary from action, directing from "letting the play speak for itself," opinion from criticism and dramaturgy from "fixing the script."

This is the cloudy, unspoken yet voluble terrain of dramaturgy. The dramaturge must first negotiate a way through the context in which work gets produced before any play begins. I speak to the individuals working with playwrights and participating in the creation of new plays for the stage—not "script doctors" or well-intentioned and perhaps useful editors, but the dramaturge who understands how the purpose of theatre must be part of the creative relationship. I also do not speak to the literary manager/dramaturge who creates educational programs and provides research and supplementary materials for theatres and directors working on the existing repertoire—a related but different job entirely.

The kind of dramaturge that I am talking about has a role that I have struggled to understand through most of my twenty years in Canadian theatre. It is a role I have both shunned and embraced. I have witnessed both inspiring and frustrating examples and have seen artists struggle for excellence within the field, while others claim the title with little or no qualification to do so at all. I have always been curious why a position that should be central to what we do consistently proves so hard to describe, is rarely perceived as necessary and so often is made invisible by our colleagues when compared to the more familiar and obvious disciplines of production. Maybe the purpose of the dramaturge and the ambivalence surrounding meaning in Canadian theatre are related. My mother, for example (whose theatrical experience could be best described as a subscription to the Royal Alexandra Theatre throughout the seventies), could understand what I did when I was an actor. She did not like it, but she could see me on stage, playing other people and mostly doing disagreeable things. As I started to direct plays, she got an idea that I had authority, made decisions about how things might be done. Playwriting, she more or less got the picture. But when it came to dramaturgy, she was at a complete loss. That was my mother. But I, too, have witnessed this same inability to articulate dramaturgy in the theatre. I think this has to do with the personal and highly subjective nature of what the discipline means. We have very few fine dramaturges, but that makes sense: Dramaturgy is extremely difficult and carries with it a very specific set of skills. Also, historically, the breeding grounds for dramaturgy have been various and numerous new play development programs, a haven for emerging directors, actors and other artists gestating during the pursuit of other ambitions. We have also misunderstood dramaturgy as an aspect or sideline of directing. We see the director as powerful, creative, autonomous—and the dramaturge as a mere helper or faceless aid in the creative process. So, for some, it has followed that a dramaturge is a director-in-training. As the adage goes, if you can't act, you teach, and, for many, if you can't direct, you dramaturge. Nothing could be further from the truth.

Perhaps after forty years, now that a Canadian theatre has been doggedly forged, the dramaturge will at last be more clearly defined and take a rightful, understood and respected place in the creative process. However, until the idea of dramaturgy embraces meaning in addition to craft, the dramaturge will remain part of the terrain of artistic administration rather than be an essential participant in the theatre.

The dramaturge is sometimes described as a "midwife" in the creative birthing of a new play, and just as midwives have been dismissed and unvalued in Western society, our theatre has created the lie that great ideas are the product of one imagination. We long to further the notion of creativity as a singular and isolated event of creative genius. We love the myth of plays popping out of the heads of writers, like Athena from the head of Zeus. The act of writing is more often slow and agonizing; a play reveals its meaning "reluctantly" and is constantly informed by a group of artists working together. Theatre, by its nature, is a collaborative art form, and yet we are still seduced by the image of the playwright alone at a computer in the late hours of the night envisioning all the characters and events of the play unfold. It's that picture of Shakespeare surrounded by Falstaff, Lear, Hamlet and Juliet, without Thomas Middleton, Ben Jonson or Richard Burbage's arguing over content and form. A similar engraving of Dickens comes to mind, and it is probably from the nineteenth century that we still carry this idea of the singular genius. Where else but from the great period of the novel do we still carry this misconception that writing for the theatre is the same as writing a book of prose fiction? And if it isn't the singular genius of the playwright, then again it is the director. We resist the notion that great theatrical ideas happen through the alchemy of many forces at work. Actors implicitly understand the dramaturgical process, for they, more often than not, are left with the responsibility of integrating the polarities of far-reaching ideas with the brutal specificity of playing an action on stage. A great benefit of new play development is that we have a national community of articulate actors, who are as well versed in dramatic ideas as in the creation of character. A play is not a play until it is acted before a public. A simple truth, but a confounding reality to all playwrights. The nuts and bolts of dramaturgy—"We gather around a Text." Partnership and collaboration are not a liability to dramatic writing but are central to the very essence of what the theatre demands.

However, responsibilities can be as blinding as they are informative. When the actors, the director, the designer or producer is dealing with the specifics of resources, personalities and time, the dramaturge can keep a perspective on the overview of the creative vision—a sense of purpose. I am often amazed, when working on a classical text, by the lengths to which all involved will go to honour (let's say) Shakespeare's intent: to make a five hundred year-old joke about the possible threat of Spanish invasion work for an audience today: while on a new play, a difficult emotional transition is challenged and questioned, and sometimes a rewrite is demanded. The dramaturge has the perspective to support the creative solutions that honour both the difficulty of intent and the refinement of the script when needed.

Dramaturgy reminds us why the story is worth telling, ensures that it is one that others might like to see and is aware of all the people involved in making it. It is the art form of relationships. Relationships are the dramaturge's professional currency. Relationships are why not all dramaturges work successfully with all playwrights. There is a resolutely undemocratic aspect to this work. The playwright must select a dramaturge with care, and the dramaturge must assess honestly his or her commitment to the playwright. The fact that so many theatres have saddled new-play development programs with regional representations and notions of fairly representing as many different playwrights as possible has reduced the dramaturge to "reader" and limited the full potential of the role.

This is common in a theatre that is suspicious of art, not interested in new works truly being new and replaces an artistic vision and body of work with activity. How many companies boast of relevance in terms of numbers of scripts in their play-development programs, rather than of a commitment to the artists they choose to work with, and the audience that eagerly follows that work? Again, the smaller independent theatres tend to work more along these lines than any of the larger regionals. The Tarragon Theatre, with Jason Sherman and Judith Thompson, Alberta Theatre Projects with Eugene Stickland, and Factory Theatre with George Walker, are examples where the vision of a theatre can best be defined by the work of a playwright (all, coincidentally, theatres that have a strong dramaturgical focus in relation to the artistic direction). Yet, I can barely think of one regional with a playwright or producing vision identified in such a way.

Remember the days when Buddies in Bad Times was dramaturge-free? I think Sky Gilbert recognized the inherent danger of unidentified dramaturgy and feared the potency of the theatre would be diluted or reduced by such interference. Indeed, in a profession where many dramaturges are self-appointed or are appointed for reasons other than those concerned with the complexities of art, we forge another myth, that of the teacher/dramaturge. I confess—one of the reasons I resisted identifying myself as a dramaturge for so many years was because it all seemed so un-sexy. Somehow removed from the essential core of creation, a disapproving warden (scissors and glue in hand), making sure things did not get out of hand. Many people think of the dramaturge as a level-headed and objective voice: the editor or critic or preview audience. But new play development is not a focus group, and even though most theatre companies on the surface would agree, I wonder what those forms I am asked to fill out at public play readings and workshop events are about. "What did you like about the play? Describe the play in one word. What is a question you have about the play?" Guilty of participating in such exercises, I have come to wonder what this information ultimately means. In one theatre, audience comment forms like this one are posted like wallpaper in the lobby! In fact, working there as a director, I was asked by the artistic director when I would read the audience comment forms so that I could make adjustments to the production for the next performance. Gone the under-standing of a quiet and expectant audience; gone the agony of restless movement, nervous laughter and telltale coughing; gone the experience of participating in a new play. Here, the measure of theatrical experience was defined by public taste and ignored consideration, reflection and content. In this world, where vision is replaced by activity, the presentation of a new play is turned into an "event," in the fear that without such a sense of occasion, no one will come. Surrounded by forums and talkbacks and issue-related panels, the theatre is forced to play talk-show, and dramaturgy, as a process, is reduced to the single purpose of making a play comprehensible for an audience in one viewing. We do this at our peril. Dramaturgy is dangerous, the line between tradition and convention is a fine one and clarity can be the enemy of original thought. I long for a theatre that makes me want to return. A great play contains that rare quality of gripping narrative, with the knowledge that it's meaning cannot be grasped in one viewing and will reveal itself to you over time. A play is an experience you live with and process—slowly.

Dramaturgy divines meaning from the well of a shared imagination. This involves bringing the playwright's voice from the private to the public sphere, aiding innermost visions of our society to come to light. Dramaturgy does not interpret; it reveals. For the process of dramaturgy is not only a question of understanding somebody else. It is a question of becoming your fullest self through the story the playwright has to tell. It is not about you but rather about a quality of articulated wisdom made necessary through life and experience.

It is not another way of understanding theatre: it is theatre. Real theatre makes us nervous or elated. Simply understanding a play in regard to its content and then working with that is to domesticate the wild purpose of art. Dramaturgy excavates a buried secret; it is, by its nature, in search of discovery, opposed to conformity, refining why we do what we do.

Our theatre is largely a director's theatre, and we must be cautious of an overly interpreted *mise en scène* that creates shadow worlds of meaning, an echo of existing conscious knowledge. The challenge of dramaturgy is not to duplicate the playwright's creativity through interpretation but to insist the play be experienced immediately.

For the past five years, I have had the pleasure of working alongside a dramaturge who has helped me define what I think dramaturgy can be. Paula Danckert is the artistic director of Playwrights' Workshop Montréal (PWM). For four years, she was the program dramaturge at the Banff Playwrights Colony. For many years, she has been on the faculty of the National Theatre School, teaching primarily in the playwriting program. Paula's new play development work is enriched by her diverse experience in the fields of radio production, sound design, contemporary dance, directing and dramaturgy. She has collaborated with writers from coast to coast, developing their scripts from initial creation through to productions that have crossed Canada. I have worked with Paula as a dramaturge, director and playwright. Most recently, Paula was production dramaturge when I directed Marie Clements's *Burning Vision* for Rumble Theatre and Urban Ink in Vancouver, for the Festival de Théâtre des Amériques in Montreal and for the Magnetic North Theatre Festival in Ottawa. And since 1998 she has been the production dramaturge on my trilogy of plays entitled *The Swanne* for the Stratford Festival of Canada. I have also, throughout this time, worked with her on countless projects at PWM. Paula is essentially about forging relationships. She eschews the notion of development activity in favour of a long-term commitment to writers and unshakable faith in finding a solution to dramatic problems. Her vision of play development is flexible, responsive to the demands of plays and playwrights as they evolve and constantly under consideration and re-evaluation as the world around us and the theatre around us shifts and changes. She is neither the serving midwife nor the objective authority, although her command of ideas and bedside manner are exemplary. She fashions herself as a creative partner, an adult working in tandem with all the members of the theatre in support of the play—challenging, confrontational, comforting and inspiring all at once. She works specifically, line by line, and mines the full dramatic potential from character, narrative, metaphor, language, image and ideas. It may be that because Playwrights' Workshop is not a producing company, Paula has the opportunity to fulfill the potential of dramaturgical purpose; she has, through her working practice, further defined dramaturgy as both a respected function of theatrical process and the environment critical for the art form's flourishing.

Paula is one of a handful of dramaturges that I believe are truly making a difference to the way in which we create new work and meaningfully contributing to the quality of the new work we create. I think her own definition, culled here from her production notes to Part Two of *The Swanne*, best expresses what the essence of dramaturgy should be.

> It is to engage the imagination in full dimension. It is an endeavour that includes all of the arts: music, dance, visual arts, and language. The purpose is to inspire argument and inquiry into the deepest concerns of humanity, such as equality, identity, responsibility and love. To consider our own lives and our own world in new ways [...] To make theatre is to create opportunity for a society to discuss its own orchestration.

Dramaturgy embraces the moral properties of the theatre; not only does it ask, "What are the stories we have to tell?" It also explores the ways in which we tell them, with courage and intelligence, and really demands why they must be told to begin with. Ultimately, the dramaturgical process asks the question—"Will art make any of us better?"

(2004)

Work Cited

Barker, Howard. *Arguments for a Theatre*. 3rd ed. Manchester, UK; Manchester University P, 1997.

Pure Research
by Brian Quirt

Definition of insanity: "Endlessly repeating the same process, hoping for a different result." (frequently attributed to Albert Einstein)

Pure Research[1] came out of a conversation I had with former Theatre Centre Artistic Director David Duclos in 1997. At the time, the Theatre Centre operated a program called R&D—research and development—which successfully generated a wide range of innovative new works. But the title was inaccurate. We did a lot of development, but did not really do any research; product was the goal of every process. So I asked how the program could accommodate the sort of research, for example, that a high-tech company conducts, which may or may not result in a new item on the shelves. What would a program dedicated solely to theatre research look like?

Out of that conversation came two years of research workshops at the Theatre Centre (1998–9). One of my favourite sessions was led by Darren O'Donnell, who explored acupuncture as a potential rehearsal tool. Darren and an acupuncture therapist designed treatments to elicit specific emotional responses in their performers and tested the results in scene work. Darren concluded that it was a promising, but powerful, tool—subject to misuse and requiring substantial further testing before it could be used in a rehearsal process. I loved this workshop because it explored a single idea, in depth, within a safe and supportive environment. The idea did not have to work. The opportunity to fail was built into the program, as it must be in any research-driven process. By offering artists a place to explore outlandish or unusual ideas, the research program might, occasionally, reveal something wonderful. In the process, artists could learn about their work, themselves, and their craft.

The results from these two years were not well-documented, however, and the program never generated enough momentum to ensure its survival. I realized that if the Theatre Centre could not keep it alive, then this important program had to find a new home. David supported my desire to re-establish the research program as an activity of my company, Nightswimming.[2] I retitled it Pure Research.

Here is what it currently looks like. Pure Research supports theatrical experiments that are not production-oriented (that is what defines them as *pure*). Our intent is to pursue *primary, practical* studio research into issues of form and performance. We provide space, money, and resources to artists conducting pure research into provocative theatrical questions. A call for proposals is distributed in October, and the workshops take place the following May. Successful candidates are offered three days in a fully-equipped studio theatre. There are funds available to hire personnel (often actors, but past participants have included directors, writers, sound designers and DJs, among others), plus a small budget for expenses. Each workshop is thoroughly documented and written reports are posted on Nightswimming's website.

As dramaturg, my role is to select proposals (along with Nightswimming Producer Naomi Campbell), work with the researchers to develop their experiments, attend all sessions and edit the reports they submit afterward. We are trying to isolate and indulge those moments in rehearsal when someone says, "I wish we could explore X, Y and Z, but we don't have time." We provide that time. Pure Research is designed to encourage artists to follow their instincts and make discoveries rather than generate new or explore existing material (text or movement) in ways that they have tried before.

Pure Research's goals are very broad (to increase the amount and quality of theatre research in Canada) and very specific (to offer me, as a dramaturg, the opportunity to work with and/or observe the investigations of skilled artists as they gnaw on an issue of their choice).

And did I mention that every Pure Research session—at both the Theatre Centre and, last year, at Nightswimming—has been fun? Pressure comes only from the desire to learn; the joy of discovery; the act of searching for answers with time and freedom on our side; time in a theatre not fixing something, not rushing something, but digging deeply. Research invigorates and inspires.

In 2003, its first year, Pure Research took the form of two sessions, each comprising a total of twenty-four hours, over a period of two weeks. Kate Hennig conducted a workshop in the use of voice and sound as a rehearsal tool for actors; Martin Julien worked with two singers to examine the extent to which pitch, key and other musical devices influence our understanding of narrative. Both sessions were full of high pleasures (spending an afternoon with Martin and his actors discussing the semiotics of the musical voice) and juicy insights (seeing passages of Shakespeare come to exhilarating life during Kate's vocal exercises). The workshops were challenging and the reports are intelligent and searching documents recording Kate's and Martin's productive experiments.

> When I think back to my week guiding a Pure Research project, what sticks with me most powerfully is the feeling, or "tone," of the room. In spite of the fact that we, as participants, collectively covered a lot of material—delved into many arcane theoretical concerns; utilized dozens of musical and textual sources; staged and choreographed many experiments in spatial and acoustic design—there seemed a great sense of expansiveness and relaxation in the theatre. The discussions were free-flowing and good-humoured; each day's accomplishments were significant yet never overwhelming in their demands. Somehow, we found a productive middle ground between the structured rigour of the academy and the production pressures of the professional theatre. It felt to me like a new environment. The big question, I suppose, is: Whither research? What is the next step of application? How do you share what you've learned and provoke continuing explorations? (Julien)

One of the most fascinating discoveries that first year was that applicants found it difficult to articulate precise research questions to separate inquiry from product. Many tantalizing creative projects were submitted—generally a show at an early stage of development—in which the proposed research directly related to the eventual execution of the piece. That is fine, of course, but it is not the point of our program.

Are we asking for the wrong things? Have we not found the right words to frame the application process? As Martin suggests, "Can *pure* theatre research exist?" Or is the drive for product so powerful that it is nearly impossible to identify theatrical issues outside the context of creating a new piece of interpreting an existing one?

These questions have become incorporated into the program; through Pure Research, I am conducting research into research. And despite the challenges the program poses, terrific projects continue to appear. Guillaume Bernardi articulated a very specific need in his application to Pure Research 04: to examine, outside the rehearsal process, the moment of transition from speaking to singing and from singing back to speaking. As he wrote in his application,

> My initial impulse in applying to Pure Research came from the strong desire (a need actually) to tackle a concrete, two-faced stumbling block that I encounter regularly in my work. Actors struggle when I request that they deliver their text in a more "musical" way; when I work with singers in my opera projects, they feel challenged when I ask them to deliver the recitative with more sensitivity to words. Those very concrete rehearsal challenges [...] reflect a bigger, more crucial issue: What is the territory that lies between speaking and singing? In rehearsal there is never enough time to really deal with this issue, but in the space opened by Pure Research, I would like to chart that territory with both pragmatic and practical goals. (Bernardi)

A happy by-product of the program is that it has emphasized research and led to new approaches in our own, ongoing creative work. Even though Pure Research was not created to foster particular results for the company, I have discovered that it feeds Nightswimming's work in unpredictable ways, exposes us to ideas and individuals that our own work might never otherwise encounter. My instinct says that it is transforming our approach to play development in general. While Kate's and Martin's experiments have not yet had immediate repercussions in our own theatre practice, Pure Research has encouraged Nightswimming's development process to be more adventurous and more open to instinct and serendipity. Through Pure Research, I have developed a great tolerance for the unknown. I have embraced patience as a tool. I have come to value performance research as both an end in itself (as in Pure Research) and as a starting point for creation.

Without Pure Research, I fear that our world would move inexorably closer to the product-oriented side of the play-development equation. I struggle to resist the temptation to make the Pure Research projects more applicable, more like conventional developmental workshops. To counter this, I am designing our ongoing developmental work to look more like Pure Research, using the program to shift our developmental processes toward the "purer" end of the spectrum, where I believe we will find more interesting places to begin new pieces of theatre. Increasingly we are suggesting the Pure Research model to artists we want to commission, encouraging them to explore ideas rather than propose topics for a new work. The result is that we have found ourselves conducting what are—in essence—*applied research* sessions. The challenge we face is the same as that faced by artists who submit to Pure Research: to keep the emphasis on *search* not creation.

For example, in the past two years, we spent twenty half-day sessions with actor Andy Massingham, exploring slapstick and pratfalls as a way of generating movement phrases. We refused to worry at the time about creating product; our work was almost entirely about *how* to create rather than *what* to create.

> Brian allowed me *carte blanche* as to the creation of *Rough House* (the show that evolved out of this work). I was instructed to take my time and keep in touch occasionally. Terrific. Julia Sasso suggested that I film myself improvising, as a way of developing material. So I created an archive of all the falls, rolls, and slapstick bits I had been doing all these years. More than "researchals" than rehearsals. I resisted looking at the tape until the end of the third session. It was full of chaos; as a cohesive whole it seemed hopeless, yet an uncanny thread started to weave its way through the anarchy. The difference between making it happen and letting it happen was asserting itself. I did my best not to stand in its way. I didn't know what I had, but I was elated. (Massingham)

In July and November 2003, we conducted research workshops with playwright Claudia Dey, who wanted to watch her writing being explored by a choreographer, an actor and two dancers. She brought a new text to each workshop, and by the end of each two-day session we had a staged version of it. But in neither case was that product meant to be part of the eventual work. By working with a different choreographer each time, we forced ourselves to find new ways of physicalizing Claudia's dense, poetic text.

> I learned that the moments that feel somehow "right" are often indescribably so—they just are. Once those accidental discoveries are made, the moments are marked. And so the experiment becomes the thing, the performable thing, the eventual show. This transition from discovering to actually marking moments is achieved through a combination of detailed and vigorous rehearsal that at the same time remains open to all possibility. It is one part craft and one part instinct. Initially the process seems murky, ill-defined—and eventually you realize that a code is being devised. (Dey)

In October 2003, we conducted a two-day research workshop with choreographer Julia Sasso and a group of fourteen actors and dancers. The focus was very specific; to explore her choreographic process by testing a series of exercises with actors and dancers together. We did not know what the results would be; generating new material was not the point; the movement that was created during the two sessions—while wonderful—would not be used in a future piece. But we learned that certain choreographic exercises were very effective with actors, that the physical barriers between actors and dancers did disappear and that Julia's approach to movement would work in this new context. This knowledge then inspired the design of our next process—the creation of a new piece incorporating both actors and dancers.

The most effective Pure Research workshop eliminates expectations and allows the search for discovery to govern the process. Success is proportional to the purity of intention (the determination to ensure that the research is free of developmental goals). You cannot enter the research expecting certain results or with an eye to an eventual product. Doing so immediately skews the process and taints the research: you can never be free of a desire to shape the results unless you do not know what the results should be. It is akin to an improvisational performance in which you accept that a few gems will be generated among the dross. We have been elated to find that purity of intention and elimination of expectation are producing substantial benefits in our actual developmental work as well.

Underlying the program is my belief that we need more spaces in which to search and research. It comes back to faith—I believe that the cumulative information from Pure Research, over time, will be valuable for the company and the community. Each session offers specific insights and provokes new ideas that will blossom later; it challenges conventions and demands creative thinking.

Get rid of the phrase, "Will it work?" and replace it with "Try this" and "What if...?" Replace fear with possibility. *Make knowledge itself the product and see what happens.*

Part of what I have discovered by doing Pure Research is that, to my surprise, no one else is doing it. Our universities are home to thousands of research investigations each year, but few of them relate directly to the performance issues that our theatre companies face each day. How can we bring together our needs and their resources. Established theatres are entirely focused on producing new work and, at times, on developing new work, but rarely think about how they create new work, about *theatre,* society or ideas. Who, other than dramaturgs, will insist that our theatres make time and money available for this research?

Pure Research is a tiny, imperfect, incomplete program. It makes up two of my favourite weeks each year. Can Pure Research be truly "pure"? Yes, although it seems that even I cannot prevent myself from applying it. A colleague recently asked me about a new process we are starting, "Is that a Pure Research project, or a new show." My answer: "Yes."

(2004)

Works Cited

Bernardi, Guillaume. Pure Research application. 1 December 2003.
Dey, Claudia. Email to the author. 8 January 2004.
Julien, Martin. Email to the author. 4 January 2004.
Massingham, Andy. Letter to the author. 15 December 2003.

[1] Pure Research application forms and full reports can be read on Nightswimming's website (see www.nightswimmingtheatre.com). Pure Research 03 included two research sessions.

> • *Beneath the Poetry: Magic Not Meaning*, by Kate Hennig—an exploration of intuitive and metaphysical connections between voice and text.

> • *Voice, Music and Theatrical Narrative*, by Martin Julien—experiments regarding the influence of live vocal musical sound on the uses and meaning of narrative within a theatrical context.

Pure Research 04 took place May 10–21, 2004, at Toronto's Theatre Centre. It featured sessions by Guillaume Bernardi and visual artist Heather Nicol. Reports on their research [were] posted on Nightswimming's website in September 2004.

[2] Nightswimming is a Toronto-based dramaturgical company that commissions and develops new works of theatre, dance and music but does not produce them itself. Nightswimming seeks out established theatre companies as partners in an extended developmental process leading to production. See www.nightswimmingtheatre.com.

Navigating "Turbulence": The Dramaturg in Physical Theatre [1]
by Bruce Barton

Certainly, it is a familiar observation that few theatrical terms are more fluidly evocative or problematic than "dramaturgy." The range of possible definitions of the term is practically as broad as the number of its practitioners is great, and most contemporary discussion on this topic has productively moved beyond attempts to categorically determine and fix its "correct" objectives and/or techniques into a consideration of its effective variety and potential. Yet most understandings of the concept include two basic characteristics of sound practice: 1) an effort to establish and maintain a degree of critical objectivity; and 2) a deep commitment to the creator(s) involved, the project, and the art and craft of theatre. Further, while highly elastic in terms of specific strategies, a central role of dramaturgy is to question habit, to complicate unreflective expediency, and to dig beneath the surface of unearned presumption.

In terms of developmental dramaturgy, while these seemingly simple precepts are considerably more complex in application, the situation becomes even more complicated when the role of writer is fragmented and dispersed among a collaborative body of creator/performers utilizing found, adapted, and invented text within a physically-based devised process of discovery. The role of text in a creative process that foregrounds what Eugenio Barba has described as a "dramaturgy of changing states" is charged with anxiety and ambivalence, as inherently ambiguous and instinctual physical movement wrestles with the conventionally delimiting constraints of symbolic language, generating what Barba effectively calls "turbulence." Within the context of this increased level of indeterminacy, it is not surprising that the role of developmental dramaturgy is an elusive and mobile target. Is it, in fact, possible to distill a specific aspect or set of activities out of the development of new physical work which can confidently be called dramaturgy? Or is physical theatre creation not, perhaps, itself the most explicit expression of dramaturgy (developmental and production) possible?

My attempt in this article to come to terms with these questions will proceed through a series of related considerations. In the first section I address the general context of inquiry—in this instance, Canadian theatre—through a brief description of common dramaturgical objectives and practices employed in this country. In the second section I consider the specific context of this study: the influences, motivations, and strategies of the Toronto-based devised theatre troupe, Number Eleven, with which I have worked as a dramaturg on multiple occasions. In the third section I narrow the focus still further through the depiction of my experience as dramaturg on Number Eleven's creation/production of *The Prague Visitor*. In the article's conclusion, I attempt to summarize and generalize my observations to this point and consider the implications therein for the broader context of developmental dramaturgy—both physical and text-based. Are there lessons to be learned from the experience of physically-based developmental dramaturgy that can be capitalized on generally in a variety of developmental contexts?

A "Developing" Nation

While the strategies employed and objectives pursued by Canadian dramaturgs are similar to those practiced within many other nations (particularly the US), the relative amount of developmental as opposed to production dramaturgy is uncommonly disproportionate—to a degree that conspicuously underscores a disconnect between these two spheres. Influenced by a broad cross-section of factors ranging from a historic national inferiority complex to unrealistically truncated contemporary production schedules and budgets,[2] the vast majority of dramaturgical activity in this country concerns itself with new play text development.[3] The effect of this situation has been both positive and negative: while there are currently an unprecedented number of professional productions of Canadian plays (albeit most of them clustered in Toronto and, to a lesser degree, Vancouver), this focus on development has also resulted in what playwright Elliot Hayes described, as early as 1986, as "The Workshop Syndrome."

A survey of the pages of *Canadian Theatre Review* across the nearly two decades since Hayes proposed his pessimistic definition of "[w]orkshopitis" (36) yields a remarkable (and depressing) consistency of tone and position. Playwrights of highly diverse backgrounds, orientations, and reputation equally lament a near automatic resort, on the part of producing companies large and small, to a standardized workshop format of new play development that is repeatedly characterized as well-intentioned but ill-suited and unresponsive to the individual playwright's needs and interests. Specifically, in a process that rarely involves the input and priorities of designers and technicians, the playwright whose work is being workshopped regularly experiences a critique of her play as text, and is thus cut off from a discussion of her play as production.[4] Granted, practically all the established theatres that stage new Canadian drama in Toronto have also recently built into their programming the public presentation of scripts as the culmination of a workshop process. However, the value of these developmental processes—ostensibly reserved for the playwright—is fragmented and diffused in this context through a prism of diverging and, at times, conflicting priorities. Factors such as promotion, operational funding requirements, and artist and audience development jockey for pre-eminence, and the practical circumstances of performance—of such potential relevance to an evolving writer and playtext—often take on a separate life outside the developmental context.

Relatively constant within all text-based new play development in this country—and in this Canada is hardly unique—is a matrix of economic, commercial, aesthetic, and organizational constraints that ensure that the playwright's task is largely finished precisely at the moment when the script shifts from a verbal (if not necessarily literary) document to the proverbial blueprint for performance. And, in keeping with a relatively neat and generally enforced distinction between developmental dramaturgy and production dramaturgy—again, not unique to Canada—the dramaturg of new play development is regularly "excused" from the process at much the same time as the writer, and thus similarly disconnected from the realization of the very theatricality that it has been her job to prompt and prioritize at all times throughout the evolution of the text. What, arguably, distinguishes the Canadian situation is that in a context in which text-based production dramaturgy is practically nonexistent, the dramaturg's exit from the process is often final and definitive (unlike, for instance, in many American contexts in which the dramaturg switches between developmental and production activities).

Under these conditions, the distinctions between text-based developmental dramaturgy and developmental dramaturgy within a physically-based devised theatre environment are inevitably exacerbated. Admittedly, "physically-based" and "devised" theatre are sufficiently broad categories to incorporate a wide range of very different objectives, techniques, and styles. However, for the purposes of this argument, the terms identify an approach to theatrical performance for which text is a secondary component—in the sense that text is often secondary both chronologically in the development process and in communicative significance. Rather, the elements of visual and aural presentation, as well as the work's engagement with narrative, emerge out of a set of processes that are based in movement, improvisation, physical discipline, and the set of creative instruments understood and experienced as *instinct* and *intuition*. It is, in a sense, an opportunistic form of theatrical creation which, to a sometimes alarming degree, relies upon an engagement with coincidence and the unpredictable through a heightened sensitivity to possibility and a rigorous ability to exploit its gifts. It is a form of theatre which, as Barba contends, "must forge [its] own fortuitousness" (59).

Given these conditions, it is not surprising that the strategies employed in an orientation to text-based developmental dramaturgy that operates, through material necessity, prior to and at a distinct distance from the activities of theatrical production will be ill-suited to a transfer into the arena of devised theatre creation. However, my own experience and that of a small but growing number of Canadian dramaturgs working in physically-based theatre [5] suggests that the obstacles are more closely related to the orientation adopted than to the strategies employed.

A Dramaturgy of Changing States: The Theatre of Number Eleven

As a playwright and dramaturg as well as a theatre researcher, my experience of developmental dramaturgy prior to my involvement with Number Eleven Theatre was predominantly text-based. With developmental experience in multiple professional and academic theatre contexts, involving both emerging and established authors, I had acquired, through practice and training, a variety of strategies and approaches to the fostering of new written work. However, in 1998 I attended a theatrical production that altered my understanding of the potential parameters of dramaturgical activity. Staged in the dynamic (if economically desperate) confines of the Khyber Klub in downtown Halifax, Nova Scotia, the work was Number Eleven's *Icaria.* [6] Led by director Ker Wells, a founding member of the now defunct but deeply influential Primus Theatre (of Winnipeg, Manitoba), the company included Primus co-member Sondra Haglund, as well as Varrick Grimes, Alex MacLean, and Elizabeth Rucker—the latter three all alumni of Primus training programs. Having never seen a

Primus production, and only minimally familiar with their modes of training and performance, I was not prepared for the level of physical intensity, rigour, and innovation that each member of Number Eleven brought to the execution of the demanding, wildly physical, yet intricate *Icaria*. Incorporating characteristics of mime, *commedia dell'arte*, acrobatics, martial arts, choreographed dance, orchestrated choral work, and "kitchen sink" naturalism, the production emerged as a stylistic jigsaw puzzle, its many pieces expertly constructed into a complementary, cumulative whole.

Equally remarkable was the irresolvably elusive and eclectic use of diverse textual styles and sources that made up the symbolic mosaic of the play's narrative. For while a succinct synopsis of the play's "story" is conceivable, its recounting results in a misrepresentative diminishment of the performance to a degree far exceeding that in the situation of traditional, text-based production. Swirling around a basic scenario depicting a young girl's recollections of her distracted and disaffected mother, her charismatic and abusive father, and her idealistic and ultimately suicidal brother, *Icaria* unquestionably created a deeply moving sense of context, character, and resolution. Described by Halifax *Daily Mail* reviewer Ron Foley MacDonald as "part circus, part nightmare" (31), the work tapped into primal, intuitive elements of anxiety and aspiration that, for this spectator, were seldom accessed in my regular visits to the theatre.

The most immediate influence on the art and craft of Ker Wells and Number Eleven is the legacy of Primus Theatre and its founding director, Richard Fowler. Yet an understanding of this lineage comes most accessibly through an appreciation of the Odin Teatret of Eugenio Barba, where Fowler had studied extensively and with which he maintained an ongoing professional and developmental relationship. As Lisa Wolford has noted,

> One might suggest that the Odin influence in Primus's work is most visually discernible in relation to the use of masks and stilt characters in certain productions, yet such an influence can also be traced in the group's rehearsal methods and process of developing performance text, the rejection of a naturalistic performance style in favour of overt theatricality, and a preference for what Ian Watson describes as a concatenate plot structure over a more conventional, linear narrative. Even more significantly, however, such an influence is reflected in Fowler's conception of a theatre ensemble as a living entity. (40)

As Fowler himself has asserted, "The members of Primus Theatre are precisely that, members, the articulating limbs of a living organism" (qtd. in Wolford 40).

Further, while Wells is respectfully uneasy about citing increasingly distant influences, the "idea" of Jerzy Grotowski is also, inevitably, a conscious presence in Number Eleven's practice and ethos. "Discipline," "integrity," and "honesty"— frequent and elusive, yet also deeply resonant terms and concepts throughout Grotowski's writings—enter into Wells's discussion of both the company's process and its objectives, along with a conscious insistence that every idea and every image be entirely "earned" in the moment (Interview).[7]

However, it is Barba who has offered an explicit and tantalizingly suggestive, if elusive, incorporation of dramaturgy into the dynamics of physically-based work. There are, according to Barba, three different dramaturgies within physically-based theatrical performance, and while they occur simultaneously, they can—indeed must—be developed separately. The first is "an organic or dynamic dramaturgy, which is the composition of the rhythms and dynamisms affecting the spectators on a nervous, sensorial and sensual level" (59). The second is a "narrative dramaturgy, which interweaves events and characters, informing the spectators on the meaning of what they are watching" (59). Identifying these first two dramaturgies in a performance like *Icaria* is relatively easy; describing the precise relationship between them is more difficult. To a degree, it is possible to find a basis for the distinctions between text-based production dramaturgy and developmental dramaturgy in the first two categories proposed—the former regularly attending to the "nervous, sensorial, and sensual level" of performance, and the latter traditionally focusing in large part on the narrative "interweav[ing of] events and characters." Indeed, separated from Barba's third category, these first two classifications evoke a typology of co-existent yet distinct dramaturgical categories of physically-based devised work, running parallel to that which distinguishes between development and production in text-based work.

Yet it is, perhaps, Barba's final dramaturgy that provides a bridge, a means and opportunity for exchange between the concepts of composition and realization, thereby opening an avenue toward an understanding of authorship and, by extension, dramaturgy, in physically-based work. The third, most challenging—and, for the purposes of this discussion, most important—category is the "dramaturgy of changing states, when the entirety of what [is shown] manages to evoke something totally different, similar to when a song develops another sound line through the harmonics" (60). Although physically-based devised performance is often tightly choreographed and painstakingly rehearsed, the dramaturgy of changing states operates without "technical rules," "distill[ing] or captur[ing] hidden significances," and producing "leaps from one dimension to another [...] from one state of consciousness to another with unforeseeable and extremely personal consequences, both sensorial and mental" (60). Connecting, combining, and thereby bypassing the physical and intellectual domains of the first two categories, Barba suggests, the dramaturgy of changing states taps into a spectator's instinctual interpretive capabilities.

The result or, more accurately, the product of the dramaturgy of changing states, Barba contends, is twofold: on the one hand, "enlightenment," and on the other, what Barba calls "turbulence." Intriguingly, turbulence is proposed as the more significant of the two outcomes. Only apparently a "violation of order," turbulence is, in fact, "order in motion" (61), disrupting "continuity, rhythm, and narrative," forestalling unity and complicating meaning: "The dramaturgy of changing states... has nothing to do with the written text, with the dramaturgy of the words, in the way that the vibratory quality of the singing voice has nothing to do with the score" (62). Thus, the dramaturgy of changing states extends beyond the text and indeed, perhaps even the text/performance interface, into a territory in which the communication occurs physically and visually through productive disruption and facilitating interruption.

Drawing on methods acquired while in Primus, further developed through training opportunities with Barba and other associated practitioners, the individual members of Number Eleven begin the development of a project in isolation. Each conducts her own research and creates initial scenes—or, more accurately, patterns of movement and voice, often inspired by found or created text and songs. Under Wells's directorial eye and sensibility, and working from the raw material of the individually created sequences, the company begins the long process of establishing connections, resonance, and interpenetrations of meaning. The initial text fragments and physical patternings may be transposed, modified, or discarded through the progress of this work, as the emerging meaning of the piece is developed largely through the evolution of a physical dialogue between the performers, the director, and the shared space through which they move. Thus, while the company is not a collective in the full sense of this term (as the troupe's director, Wells conspicuously leads the activities of development and rehearsal), its approach is, from the outset, definitively collaborative.

Understandably, the experience is as intimidating as it is liberating, and the company must be able to withstand prolonged periods of uncertainty and abstraction. But the objective is not what, for instance, Erin Hurley has described as the self-consciously postmodern "pastiche of unreconciled movement vocabularies" (29) of Quebec's Carbon 14. Rather, once again, Barba is an evocative—if ultimately insufficient—filter through which to consider their process:

> Confusion, when it is sought after and practiced as an end in itself, is the art of deception. This does not necessarily mean that it is a negative state, one to be avoided. When used as a means, confusion constitutes one of the components of an organic creative process. It is the moment in which material, prospects, contiguous stories, and diverse intentions become con-fused, i.e., fuse together, mixing with one another, each becoming the other face of the other. (62)

This final image provides a potential avenue into the complex issue of composition—and thus developmental dramaturgy—in physically-based work. However, I find the metaphor of "mixing" or "fusing" of elements, "each becoming the face of the other," inadequate to describe the dramaturgical processes employed in much of this type of physical theatre, in that it evokes a modernist anticipation of ultimate organic unity. Rather, in the work of Number Eleven, it is precisely the turbulence—the productive disruptions and facilitating interruptions—between the multiple physical vocabularies in place, and between the physical and textual channels of communication, that regulate narrative progression.

Instead I propose a metaphor that posits a site of meaning that is, on the one hand, more rowdy and unstable, and on the other, more visceral and substantive. That metaphor is "collision"—the fundamental act and condition identified by Sergei Eisenstein in the creation of montage. Montage, Eisenstein asserts in his mid-twentieth century writings on the formal attributes of film, is conflict—it is "the collision of two given factors [from which] arises a concept" (37). While the "factors" are material, the "concept" is psychological and emotional. Of particular significance is Eisenstein's insistence that montage is not a linear process. In this, he set himself in opposition to his contemporary Pudovkin, who (Eisenstein contended) defined montage as a "linkage of pieces" into a "chain" of signification (thereby fulfilling, one might conjecture, traditional Aristotelian "inevitability"). Rather, for Eisenstein, montage is explicitly characterized "[b]y conflict. By collision" (37).

Granted, Eisenstein was attempting to establish a "unified system for methods of cinematographic expressiveness that shall hold good for all its elements" (39). In this, he seems to ascribe to filmic processes a degree of symbolic stability approaching that of the Japanese ideogram that provided both his inspiration and his overtly systematic model. But, as Patrice Pavis, among others, has argued, any attempt to restrain theatrical signification within a controllable and fully decipherable process of "communication" represents both an impoverishment and a fundamental misinterpretation of the performance context. [8] Yet, when relieved of such totalizing intentionality, the concept of montage intersects with the conditions of physically-based creation at a number of central points.

Montage's conceptual proximity to more arbitrarily symbolic systems of expression (i.e., verbal and written language) emphasizes the ways in which it both resembles and deviates from traditional forms of composition (specifically, in this context, theatrical text-based writing). The model in which distinct material units are forced into a collision that produces psychological and emotional concepts accurately describes the physical process employed within Number Eleven's compositional strategies—albeit in a manner far less contained and predictable than Eisenstein anticipated. The troupe's ongoing process of creating initially disconnected and unrelated sections of movement and text that are then, in a very real sense, brought into thematic, spatial, and rhythmical collision, parallels—in terms of strategy and objective—Eisenstein's pursuit of psychological and emotional concepts. And both approaches to meaning effectively embody (and, perhaps, provide welcome concretization to) Barba's proposed "dramaturgy of changing states, when the entirety of what [is shown] manages to evoke something totally different, similar to when a song develops another sound line through the harmonics." Montage, literally embodied within physically-based devised theatre, does indeed connect, combine, and bypass the spectator's physical and intellectual interpretive strategies, tapping into an instinctual—and potentially transformative—model of communication.

A Dramaturg in Devised Theatre: *The Prague Visitor*

Since my fateful introduction to the work of Number Eleven Theatre, our paths have crossed repeatedly, and Wells and I have developed a strong dramaturgical relationship. It is the nature of Number Eleven's work that they continuously revisit a project, entering into lengthy periods of refinement and revision, leading to a remount production. As such, *Icaria* has been recreated four times, with multiple runs in Montreal, Toronto, Halifax, St. John's (Newfoundland and Labrador), and New York

State, in addition to a Northwestern Canadian tour that included numerous stops in Northern Ontario as well as in Winnipeg. Following the first production of *Icaria*, Sondra Haglund left Number Eleven; Jane Wells—Ker Wells's sister and a Primus-trained performer—joined the company at that time and has appeared, along with Grimes, MacLean, and Rucker, in all subsequent company productions. I have seen all five separate versions, and have provided occasional, though minimal, dramaturgical input (restricted largely to issues of textual revision) as the work has matured.

It was not until the summer of 2002, when the company began its next creation, *The Prague Visitor*, that the challenge of defining a specific dramaturgical role emerged. After approximately six weeks of creative work, a staging of *The Prague Visitor* was offered as a public workshop at the Festival of New Theatre, hosted by the North American Cultural Laboratory (NaCl) at Highland Lake in the Catskill Mountains of New York State. As a participant in the festival's Internal Exchange—an intense week of physical theatre workshops, discussions, and performances—I was in residence at NaCl in the days leading up to the workshop performance, and I attended three consecutive rehearsal runs, as well as the public staging.

The Prague Visitor tells an elusive and fragmentary tale of a young man who travels (apparently from North America) to Prague to take up a position at the "Central Registry." The city unfolds and folds back in again, repeatedly, through a series of interactions and exchanges with a wide variety of other characters, some momentary and others deeply embedded in the production's maze-like weaving of history, fiction, and fantasy. Following each movement through the piece, Wells and I met to discuss its evolution in terms of its structural integrity and thematic evocation, and the dramaturgical input these conversations yielded influenced the development of the production in both conspicuous and implicit ways. In particular, we discussed the mutable relationships between the actual historical figures that each of the per-formers had chosen to explore and the fluid characterizations that were emerging through the developmental process, as Wells navigated a course at the edge of the gravitational pull of historical "veracity." Yet our conversations and my contributions appeared to me, in the moment, as unsystematic, even arbitrary, in their focus. While my experience of the work was immediate and visceral, the traditional dramaturgical frameworks of structure, characterization, language, etc., often emerged as awkward and anemic in this robust context. At the same time, those aspects that seemed most evocative of comment—almost all of which related to the physicalization of the work's intentions—seemed to lie outside the sphere of a traditional developmental dialogue.

Invariably, these debriefing sessions focused as much on our process as on the work itself. Indeed, the paradox of verbally analyzing theatrical processes that are first and foremost physical in their inspiration and intention became a central issue within the entire Internal Exchange event, as practitioners of physically-based performance sought a vocabulary to articulate that which they experienced and expressed as largely intuitive and instinctual. Yet what became clear throughout the multiple intersecting conversations—both organized and informal—was that this general sense of disequilibrium was not the product of a context or process antagonistic to dramaturgical inquiry. In fact, the situation can be understood as precisely the opposite.

After a hiatus of several months, during which the members of the company applied themselves to a variety of other activities, Number Eleven returned to *The Prague Visitor* in January 2003. Reopening the "package" that they had initially constructed the previous summer, they consciously challenged the patterns and interpretations that had emerged with (according to Wells) unsettling ease during that first period of development. Seeking to scrutinize the existing material for habitual reliance on past accomplishment, the company (unwittingly) engaged the work's dramaturgy of changing states, critiquing and disrupting its tentative "continuity, rhythm, and narrative." Meaning was to be challenged at each step in an effort to ensure that the performance's coherence and meaning were fully earned in the moment, rather than through a resort to habitual or shortcut solutions. It was into this purposefully destabilized environment that I was once again invited as dramaturg. I attended weekly run-throughs for the nearly three-month period of the company's exploration, with each viewing followed by an extended one-on-one discussion with Wells.

Unlike a more traditional arrangement, my engagement with the production did not begin with a preliminary session with the director in which he laid out his "vision" and aspirations for the piece. Wells is consciously and systematically resistant to such premeditation. While the company had prepared for the initial work on the production through a series of vocal workshops focused on Yiddish folk songs, and had established a variety of thematic source materials (in particular, several actual historical figures and a group of four short stories by Franz Kafka), fundamental issues of narrative and mise-en-scène were to be "imagined physically," so to speak, through the collective work of the company. Obviously, this approach significantly decreased the amount of front-end dramaturgical preparation I could bring into the beginning of a developmental process that resists—indeed, discourages—practically all gestures of prefabrication. From the outset, I was aware that my involvement would require a higher level of active engagement and accelerated response than had been demanded of me in my experiences in text-based developmental dramaturgy.

Nonetheless, Wells's primary concern, from the very earliest stages of development, is with what he calls "story." Indeed, the director has asserted that story is the only objective that can justify not only Number Eleven's creative process, but the act of making theatre itself (Public Forum). Not entirely averse to the level of abstraction attributed to the writings of Barba and Grotowski, Wells suggests that Number Eleven's compositional approach amounts ultimately to a search for the "best" story to be "discovered" within the particular conditions of a specific creative project. For Wells, however, the range of factors that culminate in a work's story is broad and variable, beginning with the source materials and extending through the physical space and place of creation, the length of available development and rehearsal opportunities, levels of physical and mental conditioning, clarity of individual and group focus, and the often random contributions and accretions of input that occur throughout the process, to name only the most conspicuous elements at play. In this context, Wells agrees, assertions of a single "correct" story are counter-productive.

Rather, what Wells terms the "best" story would seem more accurately to be a composite understanding of narrative that overlays multiple, explicit, and conspicuously "spectacular" (and, thus, performative) modes of communication: dense, poetic, and disjunctive passages of verbal text; tightly choreographed individual and group spatial negotiations; scale, rhythm, and tempo of semi-autonomous physical movement; *a cappella* aural variation, recitation, and song. Wells is insistent that these elements must ultimately combine to produce an identifiable thematic focus and a progressive development of event and character. Clearly, however, these familiar narrative preoccupations are pursued through a highly unconventional and intensely physical struggle with material that is experienced viscerally as well as understood intellectually, and which is selected and generated in large part with an emphasis on its inherent resistance (physical as well as conceptual) to generally accepted strategies of dramatic storytelling.

Proceeding without the determining foundation of a previously scripted narrative and/or systematic formal characteristics, the coherence and logic of the work evolve largely outside of the signifying momentum of pre-existing thematic or structural conventions. [9] For Wells, issues such as plot structure and characterization are inseparable from the physical, spatial, and aural qualities through which they are expressed—and can only be composed (or discovered) from within their realization. And while this collaborative process of making meaning shared between story and its delivery is hardly unique to either devised theatre or the work of Number Eleven, an immediate consequence of this approach in terms of dramaturgical input is the impossibility of sustaining distinctions between development and production.

As is the case with most practitioners of physically-based devised theatre, the members of Number Eleven employ a heightened degree of discipline, rigour, self-reflection, and self-evaluation. As a consequence, the function of the dramaturg—to question habit, to complicate unreflective expediency, to dig beneath the surface of unearned presumption—is, in fact, inextricably woven into the company's understanding of creation. This, of course, brings us back full circle, to the questions posed at the outset of this article. Within such a dense and integrated dramaturgical environment, what does the role (if there is one) of the individual dramaturg (if there is one) look like?

In the effort to describe the necessary reorientation, it is useful to turn to a comparison offered by Wells. As dramaturg, he suggested, my observation of weekly run-throughs was in a sense analogous to viewing video recordings of him "wrestling with a crocodile." It is fine, he noted, for a dramaturg to watch closely and suggest that "You probably shouldn't have put your arm in his mouth like that." This would certainly be useful (if somewhat obvious) advice if the next day the director was to do combat with the same crocodile in precisely the same way. But the nature of Number Eleven's collaborative, physically-based creation is, as described above, fundamentally determined by a far greater engagement with unpredictability. What would be considerably more useful, Wells continued, would be to have someone standing immediately beside him to advise, "Okay, now, don't put your arm in the crocodile's mouth"; or, more immediately effective, "Look out, here comes the crocodile"; or, of perhaps even greater utility, "Wait, it's not a crocodile at all, it's an ostrich!"

In this playful analogy, I have come to realize, Wells has neatly (if metaphorically) captured the elusive concept of a dramaturgy of turbulence. Ultimately, truly effective dramaturgy of physically-based work (or, at least, that based upon similar principles as Number Eleven's activities) must likewise demonstrate that its merit is, like the creative act itself, earned in the moment. "For a process that takes such a long time," Wells notes, "things happen fast." Within this context, the potential for deep dramaturgical insight may only be realizable through a surrender of the safety of physical and imaginative distance and by means of a fundamental relocation to within the spatial, rhythmical, and conceptual site of collision. An effective dramaturgical presence in this type of work, then, can be seen as one that bears immediate witness and which, through the commitment of its intimate attendance, embodies the fundamental tenet of communal objectivity within the collaborative unit. Even more problematic, however, dramaturgical input—traditionally the stuff of relative critical remove and reflection—may also need to occur "in the moment" at which the opportunity to distinguish and exploit the difference between a crocodile and an ostrich (figuratively speaking) offers itself. Pregnant with communicative potential, these literally pivotal instances are also likely not to be repeated or recreated.

Having developed the level of mutual trust and respect that Wells suggests is a prerequisite for the type of creation Number Eleven practices, the next stage was to begin exploring a dramaturgical relationship that is invited inside the deeply personal space of the creative moment. In January 2004, the troupe remounted *The Prague Visitor* for a production at the Glen Morris Studio Theatre of the Graduate Centre for Study of Drama, University of Toronto. The company had continued to develop the project during a month-long residence, again at NaCl in New York State, during the summer of 2003, and this process was continued in Toronto that December. Throughout December and leading up to the staging in January, I returned to my role as dramaturg, although in a significantly modified capacity.

Rather than only attending specially scheduled weekly run-throughs of the show, I was also present on a more frequent basis to observe the far more characteristic and instructive fragmentary process of exploration and discovery. The nuances of creative strategies that invite and enthusiastically capitalize on emergent tangents (which, in more traditional practice, would perhaps be understood as diversions or digressions) revealed a mutable hierarchy of priorities in which precise repetition is punctuated by excursions into the realms of opportunistic experimentation and courted contradiction. Physically and imaginatively relocated into a markedly tighter proximity to the director—and, thus, to the turbulent sites of the project's generative material collisions—my role became more fluid and multifaceted. In literal terms, my position on the rehearsal hall floor, seated beside Wells, provided us with a shared visual sense of the evolving work, as well as a relatively common experience of its physicality. Equally important, this location facilitated the ease and immediacy of our exchange with a minimum of interruption or distraction for the performers. Combining this level of access with the privilege of moving throughout the rehearsal space allowed me to construct a composite perspective, which could then be shared with Wells as the rehearsal continued. Wells's method of operation proceeds within a perpetual stream of questions—some to specific actors, but many posed generally to the company:

"How about...?"; "What if...?"; "Can you...?". And with a surprising absence of disturbance (attested to by both the director and the performers), I was invited, as dramaturg, into the creative dialogue in what was, for me, an unprecedented level of engagement.

Within such a dynamic, pretensions of distinguishing between developmental and production concerns were largely abandoned, as—even more than in our previous weekly meetings—discussions of character, language, and structure were blended with considerations of design, performer interpretation, and choreography. Depending on the state of the performers' concentration, Wells and I would either privately or openly discuss choices related to issues such as blocking, timing, and the appropriate dimensions of text (length, pitch, tempo, accessibility). For example: the atmosphere of *The Prague Visitor*, given its thematic preoccupations, is one of increasing enclosure and entrapment. Wells and I discussed multiple avenues to this effect, including a section of the work in which the performers literally bind the playing space through the use of retractable strapping. Similarly, we discussed the progressive creation and collapse of operative space through character placement, in order to emphasize the unpredictable and increasingly constrained access to movement on the part of the central character. A key piece of setting in *The Prague Visitor* is a mobile door, set in a simple frame, which is constantly relocated about the playing space. In direct response to the performers' evolving, exploratory relationship with this property, Wells and I discussed its critical symbolic qualities, its defining relationship to the production's spatial registers, and its dominant influence on the piece's narrative progression and meaning.

Thus, added to the more detached observations that characterized my previous work, was a much more heated and immediate level of interaction, including focused queries and comments inserted into the director's moment-to-moment construction of the play's spatial and aural configurations. While these are not uncommon considerations within the context of production dramaturgy, their centrality within the company's developmental activity once again rendered such categorization beside the point. In a context in which the defining conjunctions of meaning are generated by often sudden and unpredictable collisions of mobile material, the impressions of the dramaturg's second perspective was accessible at the moment of impact (i.e., at the moment of most immediate potential).

Throughout this activity I was constantly reminded of the fundamentally self-critical and reflective nature of Wells's approach, and that of all the members of the company. My presence did not seem to introduce a heretofore absent function into their process, but rather afforded a localization (and thus, perhaps, stabilization) of an element of self-examination operative within each stage of their development process. The collaborative nature of their work accommodates a degree of curiosity and questioning that continually encourages reflection on their own and one another's contributions (director as well as actors). This recognition provides at least a partial explanation as to why my immediate presence did not result in disruption for the performers, whose relationship with Wells during development is deceptively intense (given the degree of levity that characterizes their interaction) and had certainly never before accommodated this kind of outside participation. The dramaturgical role responded to the existing framework of the company's process; all my comments and suggestions were addressed to and filtered through the director, providing both a visible critique and an ultimate reinforcement of his creative authority. Ultimately, it seemed as if my physical presence, while a new and unfamiliar material component of their process, quickly emerged as a pre-existing and entirely familiar conceptual component in their understanding of that process. However, the fact that they are moving so quickly—imaginatively as well as physically—requires that the dramaturg get in close, hang on tight, and be prepared to dance.

Conclusion—And New Questions

Clearly, this experience generates many questions—about both the specifics of these circumstances and the broader issues of dramaturgy in and beyond physically-based theatre. As I suggested at the beginning of this article, my experience suggests that effective dramaturgy in a physically-based devised context is less about radical new strategies than it is about a consciously altered orientation to the work—an orientation that more accurately focuses and accentuates a dramaturgical function that is, arguably, inherent in much physically-based creation.

The first stage in this reorientation involves scrutinizing and problematizing the distinction between developmental and production dramaturgy. This common act of categorization, which capitalizes upon and solidifies a practical, yet limiting and lamented, divide exhibited in most text-based dramaturgy in North America (and to an extreme in much of Canada), quickly reveals itself as untenable within a mode of performance that refuses to recognize such a division of theatrical spheres. In an approach to performance in which issues of structure and characterization are not "translated" or "embodied" but rather discovered through physicalization, the acts of creation and realization—and, by extension, development and production—are inseparable.

The second stage of this transition calls for a heightened sensitivity to the inherent tension between critical objectivity and personal investment—a tension that must, of course, be perpetually renegotiated in all developmental processes, whether textual or devised, but which becomes exponentially more difficult and insistent in a creative context in which "things happen [so very] fast." To be fully effective within the type of devised creation practiced by Number Eleven, the dramaturg must relocate herself much closer to the turbulent center of the creative act and to the sites—actual and potential—of the productive collisions of the montage-based process's raw materials. This tightened proximity is measured in multiple ways—temporally, spatially, in terms of collaborative status—and each represents both a concession to the prerequisite of personal investment and a threat to the traditional expectation of relative dramaturgical distance and objectivity. At the same time, however, the type of interactive, collaborative, query-based practice of devising theatre practiced by Number Eleven is itself defined by a heightened degree of collective and self-examination and reflection—by, in a sense, an internalized dramaturgical objectivity. Certainly, this is not to suggest that objectivity is either easily purchased or a constant given in such practice; the velocity and intensity of the creative process also, ironically, provide fertile soil for habitual behaviour and unchecked subjectivity (in the guise of "instinct" and "intuition"). However, the cumulative and unavoidably collaborative nature of Number Eleven's creative strategies provides a system of checks and balances that, when successful, effectively challenges such unearned solutions and repeatedly reinstates conspicuous self-critique.

Nor, necessarily, is the underlying premise here that physically-based devised theatre practitioners are "naturally" more dramaturgically-minded than practitioners working in more traditional theatrical forms (although this, too, has often been my experience). Rather, the assertion that emerges is that physically-based devised theatre, which is regularly developed without the central plan of a pre-existing playtext, enforces a heightened degree of self-reflection and self-evaluation upon practitioners. And just as the categories of "development" and "production" are thoroughly compromised within this work, so too do rigid role designations weather assault. The engaged dramaturg in physically-based devised work is drawn directly into the site of creative collision, and thus toward the status of "creator." Such proximity, both physical and conceptual, brings heightened opportunity and increased demands of self-consciousness and respect for the artists' integrity.

There are, to be sure, multiple implications in these observations for the practice of dramaturgy—developmental and production—in a variety of other contexts, including more traditional text-based work. These merit detailed discussion, and represent the next stage in my own practice and research. However, a number of preliminary observations are possible. As I have noted, the stability of designated roles is necessarily and productively challenged in physically-based devised work, and the inherently collaborative nature of the processes involved allows for, perhaps even demands, a flexibility of self-definition and an evolving exchange of responsibilities and rights. In this, devised practice departs significantly from much text-based developmental dramaturgy—in theory, if not always in practice. While the level of collaboration between text-based dramaturgs and playwrights can be extensive, one only needs to consider the friction between associations such as the Literary Managers and Dramaturgs of the Americas and the Dramatists' Guild (or the Playwrights Guild of Canada) to be assured of the investment, personal and institutional, in clearly defined territory. Reconsidering the formalized relationships between playwrights and dramaturgs to systematically accommodate more fluid segregation of activity and ownership is thus a subject as volatile as it is potentially productive.

Less controversial is the topic of timing. Experience with physically-based devised development unquestionably argues the benefits of increased presence and engagement on the part of the dramaturg. Granted, "things happen fast[er]" in this context, in terms of the need to quickly observe, analyze, and incorporate the understanding that emerges within the physical and conceptual collisions of physical practice. Playwrights have more time, and are not under the same constraints of physical volatility. Nonetheless, the potential for ideas and assumptions on the part of a dramatist to settle and solidify prior to even having heard his or her writing spoken aloud (let alone enacted) is significant, and more frequent, systematic exposure to the eyes and sensibility of a trusted dramaturg can effectively promote increased levels of self-reflection and self-evaluation.

A related issue—one that returns this discussion full-circle—pertains to the thoroughly discussed distinction between development and production. As noted, the material factors that lead to the demarcation of these areas are substantial and not likely to be significantly altered over a short period of time (even if the institutional will was in place). Most dramaturgs know that the divide is artificial and counterproductive. But most dramaturgs are also pragmatic, and have learned to work within the systems that house them. A consequence of this is that much professional dramaturgy is too efficient—too well adapted to working conditions that prioritize literary expertise (the domain for which the tools and resources are at hand) and downplay the distant, unpredictable, yet inevitable necessities of production. Developmental dramaturgy in physically-based devised theatre contexts is forcibly confronted with the impossibility of making such distinctions. Ultimately, however, most devised work results in a text—a living, multimodal performance text, but a text nonetheless. Physically-based development is, undeniably, an act of composition. Infusing more traditional text-based developmental dramaturgy with a constant, conspicuous appreciation of—and impatience for—the playtext's realization can only enhance and emancipate a dramatist's art and craft.[10]

While these ideas for transfer beyond the physically-based devised context are preliminary, the power of this type of theatre practice to challenge and inform our understanding of and approaches to dramaturgical practice is unquestionably significant. The inherent curiosity, self-critique, and creative unrest that characterize much of this type of theatre stand as undeniable reminders to constantly reconsider the normalized activities, categorizations, and institutional structures that define our vocation.

(2005)

Works Cited

Barba, Eugenio. "The Deep Order Called Turbulence: The Three Faces of Dramaturgy." *The Drama Review* 44.4 (T168) (Winter 2000): 56–66.

Eisenstein, Sergei. *Film Form: Essays in Film Theory.* Trans. Jay Leyda. New York: Harcourt, Brace & World, Inc., 1949.

Filewod, Alan. *Performing Canada: The Nation Enacted in the Imagined Theatre.* Vol. 15. Kamloops: Textual Studies in Canada, 2002.

Gilbert, Sky. "Dramaturgy for Radical Theatre." *Canadian Theatre Review* 87 (Summer 1996): 25–27.

———. "Inside the Rhubarb! Festival." *Canadian Theatre Review* 49 (Winter 1986): 40–43.

Grotowski, Jerzy. *Towards a Poor Theatre.* New York: Simon and Schuster, 1968.

Hayes, Elliot. "Stasis: The Workshop Syndrome." *Canadian Theatre Review* 49 (Winter 1986): 36–40.

Herst, Beth. "Opting In: Theory, Practice and the Workshop as Alternative Process." *Canadian Theatre Review* 84 (Fall 1995): 5–8.

Hurley, Erin. "Carbone 14's Intelligent and Responsive Body." *Canadian Theatre Review* 109 (Winter 2002): 26–31.

Knowles, Ric. *The Theatre of Form and the Production of Meaning: Contemporary Canadian Dramaturgies.* Toronto: ECW, 1999.

Knowles, Richard Paul. "Voices (off): Deconstructing the Modern English-Canadian Dramatic Canon." *Canadian Canons: Essays in Literary Value.* Ed. Robert Lecker. Toronto: U of Toronto P, 1991. 91–111.

Lazarus, John. "A Playwright's Guide to Workshop Survival." *Canadian Theatre Review* 49 (Winter 1986): 27–29.

MacDonald, Ron Foley. Review of *Icaria.* Halifax *Daily News* 28 Nov. 1998: 31.

Pavis, Patrice. *Languages of the Stage: Essays in the Semiology of the Theatre.* New York: Performing Arts Journal Pub., 1982.

Rubin, Don, ed. *Canadian Theatre History.* Toronto: Copp Clark, 1996.

Salter, Denis. "The Idea of a National Theatre." *Canadian Canons: Essays in Literary Value.* Ed. Robert Lecker. Toronto: U of Toronto P, 1991. 71–90.

Smith, Peter, and Lise Ann Johnson. "240 Cups of Play Development." *Canadian Theatre Review* 87 (Summer 1996): 11–13.

Taylor, Kate. "Shiny new stuff for the stage." *The Globe and Mail* (Toronto). 19 Oct. 2002: R15.

Wells, Ker. Personal interview. 11 Oct. 2003.

———. Public Forum, North American Cultural Laboratory's Festival of New Theatre, Highland Lake, NY. 15 Aug. 2004.

Wolford, Lisa. "Seminal Teachings: The Grotowski Influence: A Reassessment." *Canadian Theatre Review* 88 (Fall 1996): 38–43.

Wylie, Betty Jane. "A Playwright's Guide to Workshop Survival." *Canadian Theatre Review* 49 (Winter 1986): 24–26.

---

[1] This article is one of two connected inquiries based on the creative processes of Toronto's Number Eleven Theatre. The focus of this article is the role and function of the dramaturg in Number Eleven's creative work and other, related approaches to devised theatre. The second article, entitled "Mining 'Turbulence': Authorship Through Direction in Physically-Based Theatre," is a more narrowly-focused, detailed, and theoretically-based analysis of the relationship between direction and authorship—"authorship through direction"—in the compositional strategies of Number Eleven and its founder-director, Ker Wells. The two articles emerge out of the same developmental experiences and share descriptive material; however, they proceed into distinct areas of study and present separate bodies of analysis and interpretation. The second article is currently in review at Legas Publishing for inclusion in their forthcoming book entitled *Directing and Authorship in Western Drama*, edited by Anna Migliarisi.

[Editor: since published in *Directing and Authorship in Western Drama.* Ed. Anna Migliarisi. New York, Ottawa, Toronto: Legas Publishing, 2006. 115–33.]

[2]   For a range of perspectives on this topic, see Filewod, R. Knowles, R.P. Knowles, Rubin, and Salter.

[3]   See Taylor for a journalistic overview of the current Canadian preoccupation with new play development.

[4]   For a variety of responses to this situation, see Gilbert, Herst, Lazarus, and Wylie.

[5]   This list includes, among others, Brian Quirt, Artistic Director of Toronto's Nightswimming developmental centre; Ross Manson, Artistic Director of Toronto's Volcano Theatre Company; and DD Kugler, Professor of Theatre at Simon Fraser University in Burnaby, BC.

[6]   The premiere of *Icaria* was staged in the Turret Room of the Khyber Klub on Barrington Street, Halifax, Nova Scotia, in November 1998.

[7]   All quotations from Ker Wells come from the interview identified in the Works Cited, unless otherwise indicated.

[8]   See Pavis, *Languages* 23–36.

[9]   This is not to suggest that Number Eleven's approach to composition and stagecraft is not governed by established values, strategies, and aesthetic priorities. As noted, the company's influences, ranging from Grotowski through Barba and Fowler, have directly resulted in an extensive and rigorous set of performance competences and vocabulary. Rather, I am suggesting that inherent in this training and skills set is a resistance to traditionally unifying and overarching conceptions of story, as well as to any systematic application of theatrical convention that establishes, *a priori*, signifying templates and practical guides to performance.

[10]   For an intriguing variation on the common workshop model, see the description of Playwrights' Workshop Montréal's "extended workshop" in Smith and Johnson.

Dramaturgical Strategies:
Articulations from Five Toronto-Based Theatre Artists [1]
by Pil Hansen

In the autumn of 2003 I initiated conversations about dramaturgical approaches, tools, and strategies with five theatre artists in Toronto working within contexts of cultural or artistic diversity. The conversations were part of an experimental PhD dissertation about dramaturgical practice and mechanisms of human perception that I was completing at University of Copenhagen in Denmark (Hansen 2006). I approached the Toronto-based artists from an "outside" perspective, and rather than enter into a critical analysis of their concepts and assumptions, my aim was to work with them to articulate their practices as potentially useful sources of inspiration for other dramaturgs. This article presents the product of these case-based conversations—namely, the articulation of dramaturgical practices that

> 1) facilitate other artists' creative processes through a focus on cosmology, cultural competences, and differences between the disciplinary specializations of the collaborators involved, and
> 2) consider the spectators' different cultural competences as a contributing factor within a performance.

The participating Toronto-based artists/dramaturgs were the following:
- Kate Lushington (British/Jewish, Canadian resident): dramaturg, director, and teacher;
- Yvette Nolan (Algonquin/Irish-Canadian): playwright, dramaturg, and Artistic Director of Native Earth Performing Arts;
- Brian Quirt (Canadian): dramaturg and director, Artistic Director of Nightswimming, and (then) head of the Canadian section of Literary Managers and Dramaturgs of the Americas (LMDA);
- Djanet Sears (British-Canadian, of African decent): playwright, director, teacher, dramaturg, Artistic Director of AfriCanadian Playwrights' Festival, and co-founder of Obsidian Theatre;
- Guillermo Verdecchia (Argentinian-Canadian): playwright, director, dramaturg, and (then) Artistic Director of Cahoots Theatre Projects.

Before I share the articulations, however, some additional context and terminology is needed.

While preparing for the interviews, a comprehensive literature review revealed that there existed an established vocabulary for the politics, institutions, and cultural boundaries of dramaturgy in Canada, but not for practical dramaturgical tools. [2] Once I was working with the dramaturgs I reached the level of tools through detailed questions about specific creative projects. On my route to this solution, information about institutional and non-institutional functions and issues surfaced. I quickly discovered that in the context of Toronto, dramaturgy is often considered to be "common knowledge" of theatre practitioners and thus not an independent profession with specific tools. Regularly, a director, producer, or playwright may take upon herself the dramaturgical function. As the above list indicates, the five participants wore a number of professional "hats," and their educational backgrounds generally emphasized practice.

As dramaturgs, these artists worked for their own independent theatres, organizations, or individual artists. They primarily associated dramaturgy with new play creation and considered the dramaturgical function as playwright advocacy. They also perceived a similar attitude within most institutionalized new play development in Canada, but criticized a tendency towards artistic standardization within this context. According to several of the dramaturgs, predefined processes of development—including one-on-one dramaturgy, workshops, readings, and staged readings—largely determined the type of work that could be imagined within these institutional frames. The dramaturgs' critique of these formats of development often focused on actors' interpretations of and judgments on the works in question, and on an incentive to arrange public readings that derives from commercial interests in marketing and box office returns rather than development of the work or artist. Another concern expressed was that the distance between the developmental context and the stage often becomes so significant that most of the developed plays never reach production.[3]

In the cases chosen by the dramaturgs as the bases for our conversations, development did not only involve playwright and text. Rather, it could also occur in a field between multiple artistic disciplines where the dramaturg's task is to navigate the process, rather than offer expertise in, for instance, dramaturgical structures. This shift in function gives rise to a shift of object—from text to creative process and exchange. Once this shift is made, elements of staging and devising are introduced into the processes of play development. Thus, on closer examination, the often repeated divide between developmental and production dramaturgy may be both inaccurate and (to the extent it hinders further integration) counterproductive.

However, my general observation is that to avoid falling between funding categories, it is often necessary to position the activity as either new play development or stage production. Inevitably, this reflects backs onto the discourses of dramaturgy and the dramaturg. Yet, because the material conditions of development can be understood as political, it is also possible to recognize these conditions and to make them explicit, with a strategic political agenda. Such an agenda potentially reframes the institution through repetition of practice, and operates as an active, rather than reactive, relation to material conditioning. This is the attitude that characterized the positions taken by the five dramaturgs.

Once in conversation, I introduced the artists to a few theoretical concepts, drawn from a cross-field between dramaturgy and cognitive studies of perception, that potentially could facilitate our communication. Among these were the concepts of *performativity, cultural and professional competence, optic, entries* and *filtration*.

- The first, *performativity*, derives from J.L. Austin's theory of speech acts and Judith Butler's gender theory. In very basic terms, speech acts refer to utterances or other kinds of exchanges that *act*, that do something. A classic Austinian example is saying "I do" in a wedding ceremony. Butler's examples tend to be more complex; her use of "performativity" relates, for instance, to how our everyday enactment of gendered behaviour reconstitutes and maintains certain social discourses about gender. Both examples refer to situations where an utterance or an activity becomes meaningful and affects reality because of collective traditions, behaviour, and memory: other people recognize your "I do" or your behaviour as that which enacts your entrance into marriage or a certain gender. In dramaturgy, the concept can be used both in considering how spectators may understand performance material and in anticipating how the material may affect the spectator.
- When I speak about *cultural or professional competence*, I basically refer to an individual's experience with different culture- or discipline-specific types of behaviour and discourse.
- Instead of the general and collective ways in which we may understand something, the concept of *optic* looks at how our attention, perception, and thus possible response, is shaped (conditioned) by environment and training (Cerutti 2501–11, Baddeley 1–10, and Damasio 68).
- Seen from a neurobiological perspective, we perceive through memory, and thus our reality is shaped by past perceptions (Edelman 102–10). *Entries* serve as memory triggers, as that repetition of sensory stimuli which makes us perceive a situation through certain previously established processes of perception.
- When I use the term *filtration* I am considering the possible effect of filtering a given material or situation through the specific optic of someone's training and memory.

During our conversation, several of these concepts were adopted by the dramaturgs and all of them shaped my frame of understanding. As such, they take part in the articulations produced.

My presentation of these articulations begins with the issue of power and work relations in connection with cross-cultural work. From this point, attention is then directed towards basic dramaturgical principles. This gradual shift offers some insight into how the field of potential tension between cross-cultural work and the tools of Western theatre is navigated. After these initial conversations I turn to the approaches, tools, and strategies of each dramaturg that move beyond the perceived limitations of established new play development practice. In the last section, I briefly summarize the strategies and comment on their relation to the theoretical concepts.

Basic Attitudes, Principles, and Tools

Kate Lushington and Djanet Sears share a history with playwright/actor Monique Mojica (Kuna Rappahannock).[4] It began at Nightwood Theatre in Toronto in 1993, while Lushington was the company's Artistic Director. During the succeeding decade the three women have served as each other's dramaturg(s) and have participated in each other's projects. From interviews carried out by Janice Hladki, it is clear that the three women prioritize reflection about power relations between themselves and in relation to their surroundings (Hladki 154). The latter is particularly evident with reference to issues of gender discrimination, racism, and cultural marginalization.[5]

When I wrote to Sears that I intended to ask how the three women had influenced each other and with what kinds of tools and approaches they entered each other's work, she replied, "We are friends. We respect one another. We respect each other's work. We share a love of theatre. How else can one begin?"[6] According to Mojica, this friendship forced them to confront their differences (Hladki 121). The concepts of respect and difference reappeared in my interview with Sears. She expressed the belief that human beings have an intrinsic need to tell stories—that stories provide nutrition for the soul. As a dramaturg, she attempts to help a writer find her own intrinsic preferences through categories such as style, form, and subject matter. For Sears, the author or the artwork holds the answers, not the dramaturg. For this reason, Sears's engagement with writers, as teacher or dramaturg, proceeds from an understanding of difference and a respectful relationship that is meant to preserve the writer's agency. One approach Sears uses to this end is a dialogue that explicates personal differences—thus emphasizing the point that there is no one correct way to tell a story. A related component of her own preferred writing process is to consult several dramaturgs on a single project in order to access diverging perspectives.

Lushington elaborated on her contribution to an individual playwright's work process through descriptions of a few basic (i.e., fixed) tools and several variable tools. All these tools were connected to her understanding of theatre, the individuality of playwrights (and thus their needs), and an anticipated audience relation. She described her function as "midwifery," which she understood as a responsibility to nurture the writer's confidence in her own abilities while helping her enter unknown territory. However, Lushington also emphasized that there are territories from which the dramaturg must stay at a respectful distance. One such boundary may coincide with the limitations of the dramaturg's *cultural competence.*

Brian Quirt expressed a similar attitude in the form of a dilemma. On the one hand, Quirt noted, one has to acknowledge one's cultural ignorance and ensure that culture-specific means of expression are not diluted due to lack of understanding. On the other hand, cultural sensitivity should not prevent an author from writing into a dominant culture if that is her wish.

I received a more forceful, but also somewhat conditional, response on this topic from Guillermo Verdecchia. He was critical of intercultural projects where specially trained performers from different cultures are brought together with the expectation that their means of expression can communicate on a "cellular" level of universally accessible language. Initially he explained that he does not work with performance techniques that lie outside of his *cultural and professional competence.* However, he added, if the work is grounded in collaboration that is built on shared experiences and political necessity, cultural competences become less important.

That political necessity is important for the dramaturg's choice of projects is a statement with which Nolan agreed. She explained that both of her traditions (Native storytelling and Greek drama) are about "guidelines," and thus she asks "How can a work alter my world?" and "Where can its necessity be found?" Her expressed preference was for works that have a "heartbeat," a centre that can be unfolded. Her approach was holistic and informed by her cosmology: "There is no way to unbraid the things that are woven into the fabric of me." This experience was transferred to her work with playwrights in the sense that she helps them reflect the cosmology they write from, and through that reflection they search for the "heartbeat." Drawing on Djanet Sears's words, the position may be expressed as follows: "I can pretend, but I cannot come from anywhere but here, my experience."

The dramaturgs marked the boundary of their agency, in terms of culture and preferences, with concepts such as difference, respect, and sensitivity. Meeting places between dramaturg and playwright that could transgress these boundaries were grounded in political necessity and a particular work relationship where power is balanced and trust is based on shared experiences or objectives. Although I partly leave the subject of cultural limits here, it is not my impression that the issues of cross-cultural collaboration were contained within the named boundaries. An indicator of the complex relation between such issues and dramaturgical approaches can be found in the fact that a shared (and often Western) theatre terminology, or language, was named as a precondition for the dramaturgical development of work.

Nolan stated that during the first week of a developmental process she usually establishes such a language. Sears's starting point when teaching is to extract Aristotelian concepts from dramaturgical textbooks such as Lajos Egri's *The Art of Dramatic Writing* (1946) and then redefine them with her students. Another basic principle that appeared in relation to several of the dramaturgs is the search for the "centre," "core," or "heart of story": "What is the piece about? Who is it about? And why?" Lushington explained that she tends to choose this approach when a project is short of time. When she works with inexperienced playwrights, she furthermore introduces basic techniques such as metaphors, images, and the principle of "show, don't tell." The latter is accomplished by asking the writer to try out the material on her feet, as an actor would. While working with the Chilean writer Carmen Aguirre on *Chile con Carne* (first produced 1995), Verdecchia used a similar method. A wide spectrum of anecdotes was interwoven by *filtering* it through a central character on stage in such a way that superfluous characters were eliminated and material that could be delivered in a non-verbal moment on stage was cut from the text.

Quirt and Nolan introduced basic principles at an even earlier stage of a creative process. To Quirt it was important to be clear about the initial impulse or idea, even if this changes during the process. Nolan noted that she encourages the playwright to write impulsively at the outset in order to create characters with more dimensions than the final composition can contain—dimensions that a director may unfold.

Approaches and Strategies

Thus far I believe that most of the basic principles and tools described are relatively familiar to dramaturgs with a literary orientation. The elements that move beyond such a perspective are a focus on process, working on one's feet, and reflections about cosmology and/or audience relations. In addition to taking a more thorough look at these aspects, I will now also pursue the question of how four of the Toronto-based dramaturgs attempted to re-imagine the frames of developmental work.

Brian Quirt

I begin with Quirt of Nightswimming because his thoughts about process and frames of developmental activity were particularly determined and explicit. In collaboration with the producer Naomi Campbell, Quirt aimed to further develop not merely new plays but also new developmental approaches. Nightswimming continues to commission and develop projects within theatre, dance, and music through long-term collaboration with individual artists.[7] During our conversation, Quirt began with the notion of searching out an original impulse or centre, proceeded through working with several centres, and concluded at "always fight against the reductive thinking that always brings things back to the centre." The implicit ambivalence of this movement can be understood through another of Quirt's statements. On the one hand, he regarded it necessary to undertake clarifying and at times reductive manoeuvres in order to ensure integrity and offer the spectator the possibility of discovering meaning. On the other hand, he stated that one should not clarify the work to a stage where poetic and *performative* potential is lost. This ambivalence is in part dissolved by Quirt's work methods because he facilitates the clarification through a creative process of development with generous time and space for exploration.

From the outset, Quirt's stated intention is to offer a level of freedom that allows for the author's needs to determine the direction as well as the time frame of the developmental process. He described attempts to create a space where the materiality of the text does not lock the work into a search for stability, but rather where the work can pursue the unstable as far as possible. Quirt deliberately sought out projects with needs that exceeded his *professional competence* in order to renew his tool kit, adding and changing tools through each project. A tool he often used is to *filter* text through actors—not by letting them read and comment, but by setting up criteria of improvisation and asking the actors to respond to a problem of the text in such a way that a dialogue is initiated between the author's writing process and research and the theatrical potential of the words. Each writer, Quirt noted, has different needs. For example, during development on *An Acre of Time* (first produced 2000), Jason Sherman asked Quirt if he could work on a particular acre of land with a Native actor in a process where he was offered developmental feedback but not production-oriented criticism. For another project, Claudia Dey wished to work with a cellist and, at a later stage, a choreographer and dancers.[8] These artists were not asked to comment, but rather to interpret and express through their own artistic means. This form of perceptual and discipline-specific *filtration* subsequently became an important part of Quirt's tool kit.

These tools and experiences were further developed through Quirt's own adaptation of Jane Urquhart's novel *The Whirlpool* (first produced 2000). His initial criteria for improvisation were that all dialogue had to be extracted directly from the text and that the theme of "voyeurism" (the original impulse) should be situated centrally by keeping all performers simultaneously present on stage. With actors and a choreographer, Quirt read the book out loud chapter by chapter and extracted relevant passages. The choreographer created visual images and staged movement in order to explore the relation between words and physical material that was communicated in choreographic moments. One of the central motifs they discovered was the whirlpool as a score for the development of the five characters' relative patterns of movement. At a later stage Quirt involved a set designer who highlighted landscape details, visual images, textures, materials, and colours found in the book. Her disciplinary *optic* enabled her to focus differently than the rest of the team; her material was organized around patterns of images. Referring to the motivation behind the involvement of the mentioned artists, Quirt said, "I want their tool kit." Instead of trying to change his optic, he added to his tool kit the experience of filtering through the optic of others.

For Quirt, it was very important that the process was shaped and reshaped through the playmaker/writer's shifting reactions and needs. In Quirt's examples, the process clearly influenced the material and the means of expression used. Thus it was important that the process was kept creatively flexible and that it was challenged and explored whenever it became repetitive.

Guillermo Verdecchia

The general point of departure named by Verdecchia was his broad artistic experience. He was not interested in the literary focus of what he considered traditional dramaturgy, but in theatre as a medium that unfolds in space and time. In the interview he also spoke about the theatre as a socio-economic environment and a space that, due to marginalization and low budgets, allows for a high degree of freedom of speech. He saw the special strength of the theatre as the *performative* possibilities of building a piece with the audience—using their knowledge, recognition, and reactions. In this connection, he drew inspiration from Lecoq actor training, with its global approach to the tasks of theatre creation (including props, set, light, sound, and more), to consider the spectators' responses to the various aspects of the performance. Thus, Verdecchia's primary focus was not on the process of creation, as was Quirt's; he was more attentive to performative strategies as part of a performance situation that is understood as a communicative process. This focus also remained present in our discussion of his work with text (his own and as dramaturg/director for others).

Verdecchia proposed that a good performance uses several strategies. While working with Aguirre on *Chile Con Carne*, Verdecchia used the previously mentioned attention to potential communicative effects and the tool of working with text "on their feet" to interweave a number of anecdotes from Chile and Canada. Through the gestalt and consciousness of a seven-year-old immigrant girl, a transitive combination of different realities made sense. Processed through the perceptual agency of the girl, her family and friends could hang up pictures of Communist heroes or live in Barbie castles without further explanation. Because the actions and their composition did not only draw on the memory of the girl, but also on the audience's memories, Chilean and non-Chilean spectators were invited to enter the performance, and were challenged, by different aspects of the work.

In Verdecchia's own writings/performances, he would apply humour to offer the audience a safe *entry* to the work, irony to make it ambiguous, reversion to raise awareness about what the situation implied and how the spectators were implicated, humour to win over the audience, and self-implication to earn the right to point at others: "I like the dynamic of performance where one moment the audience is laughing and the next I am asking them why." He continued, "I drop a bomb, win them over and drop another, constantly asking them to address assumptions, perspectives, privilege, and points of view." Verdecchia expressed his interest in the moment where a reversion (a call for perceptual reorientation) unarms the spectator's habit and opens possibilities of new perspectives or new critical competence.

In the plays *Fronteras Americanas* (Verdecchia, first produced 1993) and *The Noam Chomsky Lectures* (Brooks and Verdecchia, first produced 1990), the previously mentioned strategies appear as central elements. [9] In the latter project, in particular, a choice of dramaturgical structure was used to comment on social structures. Verdecchia and Daniel Brooks chose to abort narrative, character development, and smooth transitions in an attempt to increase the spectators' attention to structures that reach beyond the singular event or individual. Based on *Manufacturing Consent* (Chomsky and Herman) and the lecture as a frame of communication, the two performers wove a network of connections and comparability between global politics, media, theatre institutions, themselves, and the audience. A map reflecting connections between large commercial companies and media was, for example, exchanged with a map of sexual connections between individuals from the Canadian theatre community, including Verdecchia and Brooks. The two artists criticized images of truth created by media, and they pointed out economic and political interests in an attempt to awaken the audience's skepticism. When I asked Verdecchia if the performance also created its own constructed manipulation, [10] he answered:

> We got our say, a response, another version of events. Language is manipulative, performance is manipulative. It is part of being human; we are constantly manipulating our realities and one another. In that way it is a scalpel that cuts both ways, but there are not infinite levels of manipulation at play, it is not just fun for our little intellects. We can actually ascertain facts that have impact on us [...] I believe in truth with a little "t."

To Verdecchia the performative strategies were tools, a vehicle, and the destination was "reality." He employed several entries such as humour, references, and characters; he worked with a centre of story or a fundamental statement; and he installed a kind of closure: "The play had to end." Thus the performative strategies were combined with conventional manoeuvres and frames of understanding.

Kate Lushington

Lushington reported using the concept of *entries* in a related way. However, Lushington would call strategies such as a child's consciousness or the lecture as frame of communication "contractual principles": "To me it is all about set up and pay off and convention. If you create a consistent world you can go in any direction you want, and it does not have to be linear. It just has to follow some principle somebody can get and be carried along with." [11] She offered me an example from Joseph Chaikin of the Open Theater: in the performance *Trespassing*, on which Lushington worked in the 1980s, their contractual principle was the moment a person experiences a "burst brain." Within that moment, Lushington asserted, unstructured fragments and wreckage could make sense. She stated that there is always cause, effect, and progressive movement: "You can go back [i.e., in time], but you go back to a different place with different information." Instead of responding to linearity by fighting or following it, she considered it much more productive to investigate what it is that one can return to and how new information affects the space and the body in a transformative way. This is an investigation that leads beyond the writer's desk; it depends on the audience and the space and body of the theatre. Therefore, she stated, it is important to work on your feet and to think via your audience—or, at least, to try.

Lushington reported that psychological cause and effect did not interest her. Inspired by Chaikin, she spoke of working from the point of view that psychology attempts to separate mind from body and spirituality. Lushington stated that it is more productive to create from an embodied and corporeal reaction, which potentially can reunite these three components in expression. Her intention is to give the spectators permission to experience the joy of recognition, to follow the traces they can access, and to leave be the ones they cannot, without feeling that everything has to be meaningful.

Lushington proposed that such an approach can strengthen the possibilities of communicating across diverse *cultural competences*. One of the strategies she described is to ask an author whether the reason she, as dramaturg, did not understand the writer's text was its lack of clarity or her own lack of knowledge of the author's culture. In the case of the latter, she will ask the author if she is included in the piece's anticipated audience. If she is meant to be included, it remains necessary to consider the traces she *can* follow and to work towards both sufficient entries and a contractual principle that gives her permission to let go of the rest. Instead of the piece saying, "If you were a bit cleverer, or a bit more knowledgeable, or a bit more open, or a bit less racist, or whatever, you would get it," she aims for work where "everybody will get something different, but everybody has to get something similar too." One concrete tool for achieving this she described as follows: "My dramaturgy is to say: how few bits can you give people and still allow them to construct a picture?"

According to Lushington, the responsibility to deliver the necessary amount of "bits" and to let go of fully pre-interpreted expression falls to the artist. But it is the spectator's responsibility to accept the offer and go along without needing to understand everything. Lushington stated that an effective process invites artist, dramaturg, and audience to reflect on and challenge preconceptions.

Yvette Nolan

Nolan's primary statement was also directed towards a kind of "space in between"—in her own words, "the space in between the words on stage." A large part of Nolan's own plays make use of realism and Aristotelian dramaturgy. [12] Her subject material draws on Native experience and is delivered with a strong awareness of social and gender politics. A comparative tendency was at play in a number of the cases she chose for our dialogue. [13] She nevertheless expressed a deep interest in theatre and performance with quite different dramaturgies. We discussed forms that, in resonance with Nolan's cosmology, operate with multiple, simultaneous, and reciprocally transcendent universes through embodied imagery. Nolan explained that her connection with Chëyikwe Performance [14] over the previous five years had been a process of significant learning. Their performance *The Place in Between* (2004) was generated through improvisation on Native performance traditions. The process, as well as the material, consisted of a number of transformations between the earth world, the place in between, and the world of spirits: between body and animal, birth and death. In words, dance, movement, and images, the performers moved through three generations of medicine women. Nolan reported that during the process she continued to look for the rules of the different universes and the heart of the performance; but something in the devising process and close relationship between the means of expression and the mythological and ritual material gave her a greater trust in the space in between, that which is neither present nor absent in the words. When I inquired further into the cosmological aspect, Nolan mentioned the fundamental understanding that past, present, and future, the spirit world, dream world, and earth world, all exist simultaneously, are connected through place and speech, and affect each other. As Nolan explained, her realistic and political drama reflects this understanding in the sense that genocide, racism, life on the reserves, the forced placement of Native children in boarding schools, and the loss of language and culture are not just something Natives can leave behind. History is and remains part of their existence.

In her 2002 PhD dissertation *Mapping the Web of Native American Dramaturgy*, Christy Lee Stanlake states that "home" is a place where Natives both build and get caught in identity. Their answer to this conflict is not to break away from home, but to renew the home's geocentric identity (60). In the Hopi story of creation, the human being is created by the sun god Tawa and the earth god Spider Woman with clay/earth and song/language. This relation between materiality, articulation, and spirituality informs the concept of storying (105–13). The human being is nourished through the grounding in earth and the renewal, or transformations, of storytelling. Within this frame of understanding it is possible that theatre, through its combination of place, movement, and words (as opposed to the idea of a fictional space-time), can facilitate a renewal of geocentric identity and transcendentally-based history/becoming.

Nolan did not elaborate on the concrete dramaturgical principles and strategies this kind of cosmological approach may bring about, but she did offer a glimpse of her hope for the future of Native theatre and performance production: "We need to find a way to internalize all that [the history] and turn it into something good [...] We are moving on from the place where we just talk about our rooms, to a place where we are turning them into something else." Among the cases Nolan and I discussed, two possible, and possibly connected, directions were emerging. One of these was the offering of life guidelines through drama. The manuscript *O'Keefe* (Guno), which addresses violations at residential boarding schools, suggests that Native people may have become such fast learners that they are suppressing their own culture and each other. While the content reflected Native experiences, and the play offered a concrete solution to the presented problem through students' rediscovery of Native rituals, formally the text remained Aristotelian. *The Place Between* took another direction. The means of expression of the theatre were transformed through mythologically inspired material, dramaturgy, and work processes. The principle of transformation was a generative point of departure.

Syntheses

In summary, regarding the focus on process, Quirt described process as a creative component of the playwright's development and production. An emphasis on process was also manifested in the frames Lushington established: midwifery, the safe space, and contractual principles. While the first two of these frames concerned the process of creation, the latter anticipated the processes involved in performance. Verdecchia took a similar turn when he injected into developmental dramaturgy strategies an actor uses to "play" an audience.

In response to the previously mentioned critique of the workshop format, all of the dramaturgs aimed to renew the form of this developmental context. Lushington and Verdecchia worked the playwright through improvisation on her feet. Sears and Nolan set up rules for the actors' interaction in order to ensure that the workshop served the playwrights' needs rather than repeating a formal structure. Quirt pushed this project further and added a wider spectrum of artistic *optics* to the workshop, which the playwright could draw inspiration from or write into.

Regardless of whether the goal was to develop new frames for the individual's process or approach the performance situation as a process of communication, it is my understanding that these dramaturgs' application of tools in workshop contexts built on an engaged understanding and prioritizing of process.

When it came to the question of which was given priority—the playwright's cosmology or strategies to navigate the audience's experience—explicitly political concerns entered the conversation. Sears preferred to keep the audience at a distance until a manuscript was finished, and Sears and Nolan both asserted that it is only possible to perceive from the place of one's own ethnic experience. The other dramaturgs agreed with this assertion when the issue was cultural differences between artist and dramaturg, but when they opened the question of audience relations, they proposed that the dramaturg can use tools to look at the work from various perspectives. Verdecchia described reflecting upon the constellation of his audience in order to deliver his "sting" in a pertinent manner. Lushington spoke of aiming for clarification about the entries the work offers, and to whom. Quirt reported working from the hypothesis that audience members will always attempt to synthesize their experience through the search for a centre.

The fact that Nolan and Sears work within the most explicitly culture-specific fields situates them differently than the rest of the dramaturgs. Their work and their consistent articulation of its social and cultural politics contributes to the constitution and continuation of the categories "Native drama" and "AfriCanadian drama." Although they both produce work for mixed audiences, their primary political objective has been to bring culture-specific voices and faces to the stage. A consequence of this tendency may be that they focus on the strength of the voice and discourse before directing their attention to an audience—which is commonly drawn from dominant culture. In addition to this identity-oriented objective, the continued articulation of social and political conditions, as well as strong mission statements (consider, for instance, those of Cahoots Theatre Projects and Nightswimming), can be considered strategic attempts to reframe new play development and the institution of the theatre.

•

The introduction of the theoretical concepts (*performativity, cultural and professional competence, optic, entries*, and *filtration*) to these articulations of practice contributes an awareness of the perceptual mechanisms involved in the dramaturgs' strategies. From the outset, the concept of performativity brought into focus the questions of what the dramaturgs' methods, as strategies, potentially could do, affect, or set in motion. For instance, when repeatedly filtering text (as Quirt does) the differences between the cultural competences, discipline-specific training, and general optic of the participants are used to generate and realize creative potential. It is possible that the discrepancies between each filtration can lead to reorientation and the discovery of new possibilities, instead of habitual repetition of responses. When this is true, the process will affect the text, its possibilities of realization, and the optic of the participants. Another example is Verdecchia and Lushington's use of entries. When a dramaturgical composition includes a number of different entries, which trigger collective as well as individual memory, the spectator is invited to become a participant—to co-create the performance experience. The paths of perception that are activated through the entries will shape what the performance can be to the audience.

The complexity and flux of adaptation which mechanisms of filtration and perceptual openings add to these dramaturgical processes are countered by strategies that introduce limitations, an element of order, or a principle of organization. A common statement of all the dramaturgs was that even creative filtration should be controlled and facilitated through predetermined criteria, tasks, and the consistent midwifery of the dramaturg. Part of the motivation behind this position is to keep the playwright's ownership of the developmental process intact. Another factor that may inform this position is the fact that the product of creative processes tends to be more useful when it is generated within limitations; limitations are not only limiting, they can also encourage an artist to look for different solutions, simply because the usual ones do not fit within the limits. When a shift in focus is made from the process of creation and the playwright's cosmology to the performance situation, the contractual principle can have a similar effect. It delivers parameters that, in often implicit ways, re-focus the spectator's expectations and perception.

·

The articulations from the five Toronto-based dramaturgs reveal a number of approaches, strategies, and tools with a focus on complex processes that differ from the ordinary table-dramaturgy or play reading. The diversity of the strategies enunciated indicate that there is much to gain from articulation and exchange— including exchange with scholarship that, as with the concepts I contributed, can provide some insight into (and vocabulary for) the ways that dramaturgical strategies affect a process of creation or communication. Another possibility, one which I have begun to explore (Hansen 2005), is to combine the tools of this field with the (largely conceptual and analytical) tools of North European dramaturgs. Articulation can run the risk of locking dynamic practices into definitions; however, it can also function as an opening—a means of discovering potential connections to experiences from complementary areas of knowledge and praxis. As such, I hope our articulations can serve as a source of reflection and inspiration.

(2006/2008)

Works Cited

Aguirre, Carmen. "Chile Con Carne." *Rave: Young Adult Drama*. Winnipeg: Blizzard, 2000. 57–86.

Appleford, Robert. "Making Relations Visible in Native Canadian Performance." *Siting the Other: Revisions of Marginality in Australian and English-Canadian Drama*. Ed. Marc Maufort and Franca Bellarsi. New York: Peter Lang, 2001. 233–46.

Austin, J. L. *How To Do Things With Words*. Oxford: Clarendon, 1962.

Baddeley, Alan. "The Concept of Episodic Memory." *Episodic Memory: New Directions in Research*. Ed. Alan Baddeley, Martin Conway and John Aggleton. New York: Oxford UP, 2002. 1–10.

Banks, Catherine, A. *Three Storey, Ocean View*. Toronto: Playwrights Union of Canada, 2000.

Beaucage, Marjorie. "Strong and Soft: Excerpts From a Conversation with Muriel Miguel." *Canadian Theatre Review* 68 (Fall 1991): 5–9.

Breon, Robin. "The Adventures Of A Black Girl: An Interview With Djanet Sears." Performance program. Toronto: Harbourfront Theatre, 2003.

Brooks, Daniel and Guillermo Verdecchia. *The Noam Chomsky Lectures*. 2nd ed. Vancouver: Talonbooks, 2001.

Butler, Judith. Introduction. *Bodies that Matter: On the Discursive Limits of Sex*. London: Routledge, 1993. 1–26.

Cahoots Theatre Projects. Website. www.cahoots.ca. Accessed 13 Sept. 2008.

Cerutti, D.T. "Psychology of Conditioning and Habit." *International Encyclopaedia of the Social and Behavioral Sciences.* Ed. Neil J. Smelser and Paul B. Baltes. Oxford, UK: Elsevier Science, 2001. 2501–11. www.sciencedirect.com.my-access.library. utoronto.ca/science/referenceworks/9780080430768. Accessed 10 May 2008.

Chomsky, Noam and Edward S. Herman. *Manufacturing Consent: The Political Economy of the Mass Media.* New York: Pantheon, 2002.

Cottreau, Deborah. "Writing For a Playwright's Theatre: Urjo Kareda on Dramaturgy at Tarragon." *Canadian Theatre Review* 87 (Summer 1996): 5–8.

Coulthard, Lisa. "The Line's Getting Mighty Blurry: Politics, Polemics and Performance in *The Noam Chomsky Lectures.*" *Studies in Canadian Literature* 20.2 (1995): 44–56.

Damasio, Antonio R. *Fornemmelsen af det, der sker.* Trans. Bjørn Nake (from *The Feeling of What Happens*). Copenhagen: Hans Reitzels Forlag, 2004. 68.

Edelman, Gerald M. and Giulio Tononi. "Perception Into Memory: The Remembered Present." *A Universe of Consciousness.* New York: Basic, 2000. 102–10.

Egri, Lajos. *The Art of Dramatic Writing.* New York: Simon & Schuster, (1946) 1960.

Grant, Agnes. "Native Drama: A Celebration of Native Culture." *Contemporary Issues in Canadian Drama.* Ed. Per Brask. Winnipeg: Blizzard, 1995. 103–15.

Guno, Larry. *O'Keefe.* Later titled *Bunk#7.* Under development and unpublished. Toronto, 2003.

Hansen, Pil. "Dance Dramaturgy: Possible Work Relations and Tools." *Space and Composition.* Ed. M. Frandsen and J. Schou-Knudsen. Copenhagen: Nordscen, 2005. 124–42.

———. *Dramaturgy and Perception.* Diss. University of Copenhagen, 2006.

Harvie, Jennifer. "The Nth Degree: An Interview with Guillermo Verdecchia." *Canadian Theatre Review* 92 (Fall 1997): 46.

Haugo, Ann. "Colonial Audiences and Native Women's Theatre: Viewing Spiderwoman Theater's *Winnitou's Snake Oil Show from Wigwam City.*" *Journal of Dramatic Theory and Criticism* 14.1 (Oct. 1999): 131–41.

Hladki, Janice. "Knotting It Together: Cultural Production Across Difference." Diss. U of Toronto, 2000.

Knowles, Ric. "Marlon Brando, Pocahontas and Me." *Essays on Canadian Writing* 71 (Fall 2000): 48–60.

———. "The Hearts of Its Women: Rape, Residential Schools, and Re-membering." *Performing National Identities: International Perspectives on Contemporary Canadian Theatre.* Ed. Sherrill Grace and Albert-Reiner Glaap. Vancouver: Talonbooks, 2003.

Lushington, Kate: Personal interview. 3 October 2003.

Mendenhall, Marie Elaine Powell. "The Playwright's Path: An Analysis of the Canadian Play Development Process as Practiced by the Saskatchewan Playwrights Centre 1982–2000." MA Thesis. U of Regina, 2001.

Mojica, Monique and Ric Knowles. "Introduction." *Staging Coyote's Dream: An Anthology of First Nations Drama in English.* Ed. Monique Mojica and Ric Knowles. Toronto: Playwrights Canada, 2003. iii–viii.

Nightswimming. Website. http://interlog.com/~bquirt/aboutus.html. Accessed 10 Sept. 2003.

Nolan Yvette. "Selling Myself: the Value of an Artist." *Aboriginal Drama and Theatre.* Ed. Rob Appleford. Toronto: Playwrights Canada, 2005. 95–105.

———. *A Marginal Man.* Toronto: Playwrights Union of Canada, 1994.

———. *Annie Mae's Movement.* Toronto: Playwrights Union of Canada, 1998.

———. *Everybody's Business.* Toronto: Playwrights Union of Canada, 1999.

———. *Job's Wife, Blade and Video.* Toronto: Playwrights Union of Canada, 1992.

———. Personal interview. 16 October 2003.

——— and Valerie Shantz. "New Theatre North Playwrights Festival." *Canadian Theatre Review* 89 (Winter 1996): 78–80.

Nurse, Donna. "Writing Through Race: Black Writers on Being Edited, Published and Reviewed in Canada." *Quill & Quire* 66.5 (May 2000): 1, 18–19.

Olson, Michelle and Lisa C. Ravensbergen. *The Place Between.* Draft 3, unpublished. Toronto, 2003.

Quirt, Brian. Personal interview. 29 September 2003.

———. *The Whirlpool.* Adapted from the novel by Jane Urquhart. Toronto: Playwrights Canada, 2000.

Scott, Shelley. "Collective Creation and the Changing Mandate of Nightwood Theatre." *Theatre Research in Canada* 18.2 (1997): 191–207.

Sears, Djanet. "Introduction." *Testifyin': Contemporary African Canadian Drama.* Vol. 1. Ed. Djanet Sears. Toronto: Playwrights Canada, 2000. i–xii.

———. Personal interview. 19 November 2003.

——— and Pil Hansen. Email exchange (four messages). 15–17 November 2003.

———, Alison Sealy-Smith and Ric Knowles. "The Nike Method." *Canadian Theatre Review* 97 (Winter 1998): 24–30.

Sherman, Jason. *An Acre of Time.* Toronto: Playwrights Canada, 2001.

Shorty, Sharon. "Trickster Visits the Old Folks Home." *Staging the North: Twelve Canadian Plays.* Ed. Sherrill Grace, Eve D'Aeth and Lisa Chalykoff. Toronto: Playwrights Canada, 1999. 331–54.

Stanlake, Christy Lee. *Mapping the Web of Native American Dramaturgy.* Diss. Ohio State U, 2002.

Verdecchia, Guillermo. Personal interview. 11 September 2003.

———. *Fronteras Americanas.* Toronto: Coach House Press, 1993.

---

[1]   This article is a translated and revised version of Chapter 5 in the Danish PhD dissertation *Dramaturgi og Perception.* See Hansen.

[2]   The following are examples of sources reviewed: Appleford; Beaucage; Breon; *Canadian Theatre Review* 15; Cottreau; Grant; Haugo; Knowles, "The Heart", and "Marlon Brando"; Mendenhall; Nolan, "Selling Myself"; Nolan and Shantz; Nurse; Rudakoff and Thomson; Sears, Sealy-Smith, and Knowles.

[3]   The research project "Creative Spaces: New Play Development in English-Speaking Canada" at University of Toronto will examine whether or not assump-

tions or experiences such as these reflect actual practices. The study is headed by Bruce Barton and scheduled to be completed in 2009 (I am involved as a consultant).

[4]   Mojica intended to participate in the study, but ultimately was not able to.

[5]   This engagement can be considered discursively constituting in the following sources: Sears's introduction to *Testifyin': Contemporary African Canadian Drama* (i–ii); Mojica's contribution to a panel on "Women's Voices in Native American Theatre" at Miami University in 1997, quoted in the introduction to *Staging Coyote's Dream: An Anthology of First Nations Drama in English* (iv); Lushington's mission statement, Nightwood Theatre 1997 (Scott).

[6]   All direct quotations from the five participating dramaturgs are drawn from their interviews with me in 2003, unless otherwise indicated.

[7]   Nightswimming does not produce performances, but builds a network with the purpose of matching the works with established theatres that may produce them—a strategy that has been successful (Nightswimming, "Mandate and Mission").

[8]   During the work with Claudia Dey (2002), the cellist created a space of sound and the choreographer created phrases of movement that gave rise to a desire to let go of the text and work with singular words. The experiment did not lead to a manuscript, but to an investigative and instructive process.

[9]   Verdecchia delivers a discussion of the works as well as individual strategies in Harvie.

[10]   This question is asked as a closing point in Coulthard.

[11]   Lushington's concept *the contractual principle* can be mistaken for the *dramaturgical concept*. The most important differences are that the contract reaches from the audience relation into dramaturgical choices and it can be broken or renegotiated, while the dramaturgical concept is often consistent and concerns the aesthetic conception of an artwork.

[12]   Nolan, *Job's Wife*; *A Marginal Man*; *Annie Mae's Movement*; *Everybody's Business*.

[13]   Banks, Shorty, and Guno.

[14]   The troupe Chëyikwe Performance included the choreographer Michelle Olsen and the actor Lisa C. Ravensbergen. *The Place In Between* premiered in Vancouver, June 2004. The piece was in development in 2003.

"Snapshot": *Playwrights Atlantic Resource Centre*
by Jenny Munday

For members of the Playwrights Atlantic Resource Centre (PARC), and for me as the Artistic Director of PARC, one of the most significant and beneficial recent occurrences in play development has been the formation of what has become an informal network called the Playwrights' Development Centres of Canada (PDCCs) across the country. Initiated several years ago with support from the Canada Council's Flying Squad Program, the members of the PDCC have embarked on some joint projects, and representatives from at least some of the nine centres have arranged to meet on at least an annual basis.

Over the last two years, *Readings From the Centres*, an event created to showcase playwrights associated with each centre, has been hosted in Winnipeg and in Saskatoon, and plans are in the works for the annual gathering to happen in Halifax in the fall of 2007. Over the last two years, out of this series of readings and annual meetings—which has included representatives from the Manitoba Association of Playwrights (MAP), the Saskatchewan Playwrights Centre (SPC), the Alberta Playwrights Network (APN), PARC, and the Playwrights Theatre Centre (PTC)—have emerged opportunities for playwright exchanges and other cooperative activities.

MAP, APN, and SPC have each generously hosted PARC member playwrights at workshops and showcases in their jurisdictions. Robert Chafe and Michael Melski have both taken part in APN's PlayWorks Ink. Natasha MacLellan has been a guest at the SPC Spring Festival, Anthony Black has been a guest playwright at MAP, and Scott Burke has participated in MAP's Playwrights Colony. Michael Chiasson has been a dramaturge at that Colony and I have been a guest there. Only once has PARC, so far, been able to return the favour, by inviting Sharon Bajer to St. John's where a workshop of her play was hosted by PARC and RCA Theatre. We do plan over the next year to offer our Home Delivery dramaturgy service to playwrights from each of those centres and hope, in the future, to be able to invite playwrights from other parts of the country to take part in our Colony and Showcase Festival.

Through each of these exchange situations, playwrights have had the opportunity to meet with individual artists from other parts of the country and to work with dramaturges and actors who have brought new insights to Atlantic Canadian works. Connections made and showcases of works that have been part of these exchanges have led to productions, publications, and/or future working opportunities for all concerned. This kind of connection is proving to be one of our most effective means of both developing and exporting our members' work. This model that seems to be evolving, of sharing our resources and exchanging our artists and their works, appears to work to everyone's benefit. The work is being developed and promoted, horizons are being widened, and cooperation and mutual support are at the heart of it all.

This informal, mutually beneficial model should not be confused with the routine that sees plays being passed from one development centre or program to the other in a cycle of unending "development," which often amounts to the "everybody has had their hands all over this one" syndrome that has become all too familiar over the years.

That's not the same thing. That particular wheel of frustration sees playwrights, in desperate hope for a production, taking their new work from one development centre to another, from a development program at one producing theatre to another, in a hellish cycle that results in the play never being produced or being produced in a deadly hybrid of all the input from the various voices that have made a "contribution" but have never actually assisted in clarifying the playwright's vision and have often left little or no trace of the playwright's original ideas. Unfortunately, most of us can cite examples of the great play that "died on the operating table" under the hands of too many "specialists."

That kind of over-development or non-development doesn't make any meaningful contribution towards rectifying our main problem in the development of new works for the stage—that so few of them actually make it to the stage. And it isn't what the exchange that I'm describing involves. Rather, the mutual cooperation and support that some members of the informal network of Playwrights' Development Centres of Canada offer to each others' members involves exchanges of information and ideas on process, policies, and methodology that allow us all to improve our practice in play development and to serve the real needs of the playwrights we work with.

(2007)

"Snapshot": *Native Earth Performing Arts (Toronto)*
by Yvette Nolan

On the benefits of a long-term relationship.

At least we're not still trying to define *what is dramaturgy*. I think that is a step forward; we have stopped defending our very existence, and we are just doing the work. The work of the dramaturg is now valid, recognized by playwrights, artistic directors, actors, funders, designers, and a bunch of other practitioners involved in bringing a new piece to the stage.

What this means in the most practical terms is that the cost of paying a dramaturg is now a given in a grant application, a workshop budget, or a production.

What this means in philosophical terms is that the dramaturg can do her work with confidence, knowing that her work is integral to the success of the project. She is no longer a frill, an indulgence, a line item that can be cut in order to pay for more lumber or some recording time in the studio.

The validation of the role means that we can deepen the relationship between the playwright and the dramaturg. Once we make a good match, both players can settle in for the duration of the development of the play, whether that is until production, second production, publication, or some other imagined endpoint.

Let's say that the role of the dramaturg is to know the play, to truly know the play.

If she is one of its early readers, one of its interlocutors, then she is teasing out the meaning perhaps before the playwright herself is aware of the direction. As the play progresses through its process—reading, rewriting, reading, discussion, more writing, some excising—the ongoing relationship with the dramaturg deepens. The longer she spends with the play, the better she knows it. If we are blessed, if there is trust between the playwright and the dramaturg, as the dramaturg knows the play more intimately, the more she is empowered to speak for the play. Ay, there's the rub. Her primary allegiance is to the play. Not the playwright, not the producer, not the director, who may have a different vision of what this play will be. The dramaturg who knows the play is the advocate of the play, in the rehearsal hall, in the theatre.

I love making the good match. I love it when it works, when a pairing that I've put together really *takes* and the relationship continues on beyond the reading or the festival or the production. I have seen pairings that I have crafted shepherd a project through a year-long development process and into the first production. (Conversely, I have seen matches I have made go down in flames, where the dramaturg ends up throwing her hands in the air, and the playwright ends up going back to the script with which he entered the process). Sometimes the match is good enough that the pair move forward together on a new project, or a series of projects.

I have been the beneficiary of the good match as well. My current dramaturg was recommended to me by a friend and colleague who knew me, knew my work. We worked together on a piece that I had been stuck with for a number of years. Then last year, when I wanted to go back into a decade-old piece, I asked her to work with me again. This is where the trust pays off: I did not know how I would react to re-examining a piece that had already had two successful productions, did not know how precious I would be about the original idea of the play. Over nine months, in discussion with her, in response to her questions, I rewrote the play, and hallelujah, the play is better. Of course it is, of *course* it is, because we both wanted what was best for the play.

She may be my last dramaturg. She may not. I have found over the years that relationships evolve and change. I have split with a dramaturg because she was offended by my values. I have drifted away from another because her life became full of other things; we are still on good terms. For a time, I was promiscuous, spending time with one dramaturg after another. Thrilling, for a time, but ultimately not satisfying. I am happy to be in a stable, ongoing relationship. The benefits are plentiful: a shared vocabulary, a concomitant shorthand, the freedom to risk because she's got my back. It may not last, but I am enjoying it while it does.

(2007)

"Snapshot": *Nightswimming (Toronto)*
by Brian Quirt

From my perspective, two significant factors have had an impact on the field of play creation and development in Canada over the past decade. The first is the growth and evolution of new play festivals such as the Fringe, Summerworks, Rhubarb!, Groundswell, and CrossCurrents, to name the major events in Toronto each year. These festivals provide not only practical and supportive environments for playwrights to produce their new works, but they also offer work for freelance dramaturgs and opportunity for actors and other theatre artists to collaborate directly with writers. As well, these festivals give writers (and their creative teams) direct access to audiences, which is always the best and most productive element of any play development process. They also suggest a more expansive sense of collaboration in which the writer is empowered to be a central member of the creative team with responsibility for mounting the production. And they are an increasingly useful training ground for dramaturgs.

The other factor is LMDA Canada (Literary Managers and Dramaturgs of the Americas). The Canadian arm of this organization has, over the past ten years, presented three international conferences on dramaturgy and eight editions of its Mini-Conference on Dramaturgy, developed a substantial national network of dramaturgs and artists committed to the creation of new work, and brought Canadian dramaturgs into increased contact with our colleagues in the United States and beyond. The results of this type of network are always difficult to identify with any precision, but I believe that LMDA Canada has offered a forum for artists to express and explore a multitude of approaches to creating new plays. A more articulate conversation about this work has resulted.

I see four priorities ahead of us. The first is a continued focus on cultural diversity. We are in danger of falling far behind the cultural mixture of our cities, our audiences, and other media. There are more stories by a diverse body of artists drawing on more forms and traditions which we must cultivate by giving these artists access to the resources of theatre companies and festivals.

Play development programs must develop a more theatrical approach to creating new works by emphasizing on-the-feet workshops, presentations, and productions incorporating design, movement, sound, etc. Choreographers, performance artists, and visual artists must be welcomed into our theatres to remind us of the vitality of other disciplines and how much they can offer to the theatre. By insisting on presenting the work of our writers on-their-feet, we will, I hope, commit to play and plays rather than readings.

We must return play development to our theatres and get it out of rehearsal halls—or, in some theatres I have worked at, out of the hall to the bathroom. Working in a theatre space is different—it inspires different and more imaginative choices and reconnects us to our audience, even when they are not yet in the room.

Finally, play development will only ever be as good as 1) the plays, and 2) the directors who interpret them. Dramaturgs and new play development organizations must support director training and internships. This is a vital need. If the imaginative visions of our best playwrights are to truly flourish, we must have inspired, trained, and able directors to bring their works to life.

(2007)

"Snapshot": *Manitoba Association of Playwrights*
by Rory Runnells

The question asked is: "What, from your perspective, has been the most significant development (or developments) in new play dramaturgy in Canada over the past ten years?" That the question is necessary is perhaps the most significant development. This answer isn't to be flip, but rather to put in perspective the entire history of our dramaturgy. Ten years ago, about twenty-five years into the creation of a Canadian dramatic literature (not to ignore the singular efforts before that, but in terms of the clear burgeoning of the will to create a Canadian theatre consciousness), the question would have seemed too early. Can it be that we are now ready to embrace our history, and consider what may have been the most "significant"? Is it that we now have a literature but don't seem to know how we got it? I think the answer is "yes," but where did this literature come from? Several places, as it turns out: the theatres, the playwrights working outside the mainstream theatres, and the playwrights' development centres. The interaction between these, messy as it might appear, has wrought a flourishing but still struggling community of playwrights. Dramaturgy has followed suit, and done its part in various ways to bolster that community, but it is a servant of it, and must always be. The theatres use their dramaturges, usually directors; the centres try to connect the right people to create a play, which, let us emphasize until the cows not only come home but settle in the kitchen, should be aimed at production; and the playwrights, I find, seek their dramaturges. Whether in a one-on-one process, much like an editor with an author, or in a workshop with other voices striving to be heard, or in a group of their fellows, the dramaturge serves. Or should. The most significant development may be the simple recognition that whatever "develops" comes from the artist, with the unspoken recognition granted to the dramaturge.

As for the playwrights: the priorities haven't changed. The tools of the playwright are actors, directors, space itself, as well as dramaturges; these must be provided as much as film to the movie director or paint to the painter, to be able to create the play. The funding and commitment towards that must be in place. The theatres must continue to produce new plays and recognize that the local playwright is part of the national fabric. Each must make the playwright in its community a national force. The great struggle to create our current dramatic literature has made it, paradoxically, easier for the theatres to increasingly reduce their commitment to ongoing new work. After all, now they do Canadian plays all the time or, at least, don't deny that the creature, the Canadian playwright, is important. In any case, young playwrights (unlike the previous generation) won't wait for the theatres. They will create their own, or make the fringes their theatres (no space to go into the pros and cons of this)—but do it they must, if the theatres won't respond. The struggle for dramaturgy in all this is to remain prompt, aggressive, and completely on the side of the individual playwright. Someone else can define what the Canadian dramaturge is; perhaps the best thing is that the need defines the word when the playwright calls for input.

(2007)

"Snapshot": *Saskatchewan Playwrights Centre*
by Ben Henderson

I realize as I think of the questions posed to me by this project that part of my observations of the past ten years is coloured by a substantial change in my own relationship to play development, and part is coloured by fond memories of what preceded this past decade. Most of my career has been spent in the development of new plays as a director and artistic director. It is only in the last decade that I have shifted to the primary role of dramaturg, running the Saskatchewan Playwrights Centre.

From my new perspective I do perceive a number of shifts in the state of new Canadian theatre. I perhaps have a much better appreciation now for the work done by the play development centres across the country. These organizations share one essential thing in common. They all focus on the development of plays and not on the production of plays. For the most part they are also all organizations driven by the needs and desires of the playwrights rather than the aesthetics of an artistic director. I think as a result they have a real strength in encouraging diversity of work. A playwright is supported not because a work fits into a producible mandate but because the work deserves support. As a result, support is given to exciting works that might otherwise be dismissed too early as "not being our kind of thing."

If there is a downside to play development, it is that we all get into habitual ways of doing things that can begin to homogenize the kind of work we develop. The play development centres are just as prone to this disease, but perhaps because there is a desire to help each playwright according to their and their play's needs rather than any preconceived idea of what a play should look like, they are at least capable of wrestling with the problem. The play development centres have managed to find a home for the individual new voice.

It was as an artistic director that I first started using the play development centres in the mid-nineties. I had just taken over a theatre with a long history of developing and producing new work. It was one of the many companies at the time with a mandate to produce new plays. The company was in severe financial crisis and something had to go. I felt it was our responsibility to focus on the one thing that only we could do, which was to produce the work, and leave the development to the development centres.

I still very much believe in this model, but it has had a downside. The next step (after my time) was for the company to move away not just from developing new plays, but also from producing their premieres. If there is something that alarms me the most about the past decade, it has been the significant decline in the theatres willing to take the plunge into premiere productions. In Western Canada the only company left with a new play mandate is not producing this year for lack of funds. I have been told the situation is just as dire elsewhere. The result is that at a time when our playwrights are producing a growing volume of increasingly better and innovative work, the opportunities for production are dropping. Although companies are still doing well in producing Canadian works, the actual number of premieres appears to me to have dropped significantly. What we have is a very limited number of plays that get into the mainstream and then are produced in a kind of feeding frenzy across the country.

This is not to argue against the feeding frenzies. They mean that those writers lucky enough to get in the middle of one can actually make a decent penny from their work. But the lack of other premiere opportunities has a significant and negative effect on emerging younger writers. Production is a key part of developing both the play and the playwright. The various fringe festivals across the country are no substitute; they encourage the development of a very specific style of work.

I do not know if this has happened just because of the pressures to make increasingly safe choices at our producing theatres. Let's face it, premiere productions are high risk and companies are facing ever increasing financial stress. It is also possible that as companies have moved away from developing the writers themselves, we have inadvertently severed a connection between the theatre and the writer. Anecdotally, however, there are a fair number of theatres that have their own play development programs and the work being developed in them is just as disconnected from their producing stages.

I know the one thing that has not changed for me, as my role changed from artistic director to dramaturg, is a desire to see new plays by our country's writers produced on our stages. That is the ultimate objective for all of us. No matter how much strong work we develop, until we can ensure that the work can go the final stage into production we are still failing. Somehow, we must make a stronger link between the work being developed and the producing companies in a position to take the risk to produce it and move it forward.

Looking back it seems to me that we used to be much better at doing that. It was a time, however, when risk and the growth of our national voice was the objective. There was a huge desire to find and connect local voices to their communities and then to share those voices across the country. I do not think the need to do that has diminished, just the desire. The quality of the work being developed is as strong as ever; we must not lose our courage to take the grand risk or our theatre will slip back as quickly as it has emerged.

So where to next? We must continue to encourage diversity and inventive practice in the way we develop work. We must continue to create opportunities for our new voices to emerge and flourish. Most important, we must reconnect those voices to the producing stages of our country or all the efforts we have made over the past decades will be lost.

(2007)

APPENDIX 1: Works by Author

Barton, Bruce. "Navigating 'Turbulence': The Dramaturg in Physical Theatre." *Theatre Topics* 15:1 (March 2005): 103–19.

———. "Wrestling with Regionalism in Atlantic Canada: The Playwrights Atlantic Resource Centre." *Canadian Theatre Review* 114 (Spring 2003): 42–46.

Brown, Lois. "Power in the Performers' Hands." *Canadian Theatre Review* 87 (Summer 1996): 28–30.

Chan, Marty. "The Ethnic Playwright's Challenge." *Canadian Theatre Review* 110 (Spring 2002): 12–15.

Cottreau, Deborah. "Writing for a Playwright's Theatre: Urjo Kareda on Dramaturgy at Tarragon." *Canadian Theatre Review* 49 (Winter 1986): 5–8.

Danckert, Paula. "The Cartography of Drama: Dramaturg's Notes to Part Three, *The Swanne: Queen Victoria—The Seduction of Nemesis.*" Production program. 2004.

Ditor, Rachel. "Questioning the Text." *Theatre Topics* 13.1 (March 2003): 35–43.

Flaherty, Kathleen. "Table Stakes: Gambling with New Play Development." *Canadian Theatre Review* 71 (Summer 1992): 26–31.

Gilbert, Sky. "Dramaturgy for Radical Theatre." *Canadian Theatre Review* 87 (Summer 1996): 25–27.

Gómez, Mayte. "'Coming Together' in Lift Off! '93: Intercultural Theatre in Toronto and Canadian Multiculturalism." *Essays in Theatre* 13.1 (November 1994): 45–59.

Hansen, Pil. "Dramaturgical Strategies: Articulations from Five Toronto-Based Theatre Artists." First publication in English. (2006) 2009.

Hayes, Elliot. "Stasis: The Workshop Syndrome." *Canadian Theatre Review* 49 (Winter 1986): 36–40.

Herst, Beth. "Opting In: Theory, Practice and the Workshop as Alternative 'Process.'" *Canadian Theatre Review* 84 (Fall 1995): 5.

Henderson, Ben. "'Snapshot': Saskatchewan Playwrights Centre." First publication, 2009.

Hengen, Shannon. "The De-Ba-Jeh-Mu-Jig Method: Making Stories." *Canadian Theatre Review* 115 (Summer 2003): 35–38.

Hinton, Peter. "Dramaturgy: Forging Definition." *Canadian Theatre Review* 119 (Summer 2004): 5–7.

Hoffman, James. "Genre Contention at the New Play Centre." *Theatre Research in Canada* 16.1-2 (1995): 59–68.

Kugler, DD. "Learning to Hate the Bingo Scenario." *Canadian Theatre Review* 97 (Winter 1998): 48–51.

Munday, Jenny. "'Snapshot': Playwrights Atlantic Resource Centre." First publication, 2009.

Nolan, Yvette. "'Snapshot': Native Earth Performing Arts (Toronto)." First publication, 2009.

Quirt, Brian. "Pure Research." *Canadian Theatre Review* 119 (Summer 2004): 40–43.

———. "'Snapshot': Nightswimming (Toronto)." First publication, 2009.

Roberts, Diane. "Dramaturgy: A Nightwood Conversation." *Canadian Theatre Review* 87 (Summer 1996): 22–24.

Runnells, Rory. "'Snapshot': Manitoba Association of Playwrights." First publication, 2009.

Scott, Shelley. "A Fringe Odyssey: 20th Annual Edmonton Fringe Theatre Festival, August 16–26, 2001." *Theatre Research in Canada* 22.2 (Fall 2001): 229–34.

Sears, Djanet and Alison Sealy-Smith with Ric Knowles. "The Nike Method." *Canadian Theatre Review* 97 (Winter 1998): 24–30.

Selman, Jan. "Workshopping Plays." *Canadian Theatre Review* 49 (Winter 1986): 15–23.

Smith, Peter and Lise Ann Johnson. "240 Cups of Play Development." *Canadian Theatre Review* 87 (Summer 1996): 11–13.

Tomc, Sandra. "Carte Blanche: Toronto: The Laidlaw Report." *Canadian Theatre Review* 57 (Winter 1988): 78–81.

Wasserman, Jerry, and Denis Johnston. "The New Play Centre: Twenty Years On." *Canadian Theatre Review* 63 (Summer 1990): 25–28.

White, Bob. "The ATP Experience: Giving Good First Production in a Supportive Atmosphere." *Canadian Theatre Review* 87 (Summer 1996): 14–16.

APPENDIX 2: Works by Region

British Columbia

Questioning the Text
by Rachel Ditor

Genre Contention at the New Play Centre
by James Hoffman

Learning to Hate the Bingo Scenario
by DD Kugler

The New Play Centre: Twenty Years On
by Jerry Wasserman and Denis Johnston

Western Canada

"Snapshot": Saskatchewan Playwrights Centre
by Ben Henderson

"Snapshot": Manitoba Association of Playwrights
by Rory Runnells

A Fringe Odyssey: 20th Annual Edmonton Fringe Theatre Festival,
    August 16–26, 2001
by Shelley Scott

Workshopping Plays
by Jan Selman

The ATP Experience: Giving Good First Production in a Supportive
    Atmosphere
by Bob White

Ontario

Navigating "Turbulence": The Dramaturg in Physical Theatre
by Bruce Barton

The Ethnic Playwright's Challenge
by Marty Chan

Writing for a Playwright's Theatre: Urjo Kareda on Dramaturgy at Tarragon
by Deborah Cottreau

The Cartography of Drama: Dramaturg's Notes to Part Three, *The Swanne:
    Queen Victoria—The Seduction of Nemesis*
by Paula Danckert

Table Stakes: Gambling with New Play Development
by Kathleen Flaherty

Dramaturgy for Radical Theatre
by Sky Gilbert

Quebec

Atlantic Canada

APPENDIX 3: Works by Theme

i) Forging Definition(s)

Power in the Performers' Hands
by Lois Brown

The Cartography of Drama: Dramaturg's Notes to Part Three, *The Swanne: Queen Victoria—The Seduction of Nemesis*
by Paula Danckert

Dramaturgy: Forging Definition
by Peter Hinton

Learning to Hate the Bingo Scenario
by DD Kugler

Dramaturgy: A Nightwood Conversation
"re-imagined" by Diane Roberts

ii) Treating "Workshopitis"

The Ethnic Playwright's Challenge
by Marty Chan

Table Stakes: Gambling with New Play Development
by Kathleen Flaherty

Dramaturgy for Radical Theatre
by Sky Gilbert

Stasis: The Workshop Syndrome
by Elliot Hayes

Opting In: Theory, Practice and the Workshop as Alternative "Process"
by Beth Herst

Dramaturgy: Forging Definition
by Peter Hinton

Pure Research
by Brian Quirt

The Nike Method
by Djanet Sears and Alison Sealy-Smith with Ric Knowles

Workshopping Plays
by Jan Selman

240 Cups of Play Development
by Peter Smith and Lise Ann Johnson

The Laidlaw Report
by Sandra Tomc

Dramaturgy: A Nightwood Conversation
"re-imagined" by Diane Roberts

The Nike Method
by Djanet Sears and Alison Sealy-Smith with Ric Knowles

v) Beyond the Text—and Back Again

Navigating "Turbulence": The Dramaturg in Physical Theatre
by Bruce Barton

Questioning the Text
by Rachel Ditor

Dramaturgical Strategies: Articulations from Five Toronto-Based Theatre Artists
by Pil Hansen

Pure Research
by Brian Quirt

vi) Snapshots

"Snapshot": Playwrights Atlantic Resource Centre
by Jenny Munday

"Snapshot": Native Earth Performing Arts (Toronto)
by Yvette Nolan

"Snapshot": Nightswimming (Toronto)
by Brian Quirt

"Snapshot": Manitoba Association of Playwrights
by Rory Runnells

"Snapshot": Saskatchewan Playwrights Centre
by Ben Henderson

Suggested Further Reading

Barnett, Linda, Consulting Services. "Funding Play Creation: A Review of Canadian Theatre Productions 1996–2001 and An International Comparison of Funding Models." A Joint Study by Playwrights Union of Canada and the Professional Association of Canadian Theatres. Prepared May, 2001.

Brask, Per, ed. *Contemporary Issues in Canadian Drama.* Winnipeg: Blizzard Publishing, 1995.

———. "Dran Turgia." *Canadian Theatre Review* 49 (1986): 11–14.

Brennan, Brian. "The Banff Playwrights Colony: Finishing School." *Canadian Theatre Review* 49 (1986): 30–35.

Campbell, Naomi, Shauna Janssen, and J.P. Robichaud. "The Dramaturgy of Stage Management: A Constructed Conversation." *Canadian Theatre Review* 119 (2004): 20–23.

Cowan, Cindy. "Halifax: Towards an Atlantic Playwrights Colony." *Canadian Theatre Review* 49 (1986): 120–22.

Curtis, Ron. *A History of Playwrights Workshop Montreal 1963–1988.* Diss. McGill U, 1991. AAT MM67674.

Davis, Tracy, C. "Calgary: Rites and Wrongs in ATP's playRites '89." *Canadian Theatre Review* 60 (1989): 78–80.

De Boer, Deborah. "Victoria: The Canadian National Theatre Festival." *Canadian Theatre Review* 62 (1990): 77–78.

Ditor, Rachel. "Getting out of the Script Stack I." *Canadian Theatre Review* 114 (2003): 75–65.

———. "Getting out of the Script Stack II." *Canadian Theatre Review* 115 (2003): 57–61.

Duchesne, Scott and Jennifer Fletcher. "*Sled*: A Workshop Diary." *Canadian Theatre Review* 89 (1996): 33–38.

Dumas, Helene. "Triangular Play Development." *Canadian Theatre Review* 50 (1987): 66–69.

Filewod, Alan. *Performing Canada: The Nation Enacted in the Imagined Theatre.* Kamloops: *Textual Studies in Canada* Vol. 15, 2002.

———. "Performing Canada: The Nation Enacted in the Imagined Theatre." *Canadian Theatre Review* 114 (2003): 72–74.

———. "C:/Games/Dramaturgy: The Cybertheatre of Computer Games." *Canadian Theatre Review* 81 (1994): 24–28.

———. "Viewing Canadian Theatre/Canadian Theatre *Review-ing*." *Canadian Theatre Review* 79/80 (1994): 14–17.

————. "National Theatre/National Obsession." *Canadian Theatre Review* 62 (1990): 5–10.

————. "Erasing Historical Difference: The Alternative Orthodoxy in Canadian Theatre." *Theatre Journal* 41 (1989): 201–10.

Fitzsimmons Frey, Heather. "Dramaturgy and a Collective Theatre." *Canadian Theatre Review* 123 (2005): 73–78.

Flaherty, Kathleen and Deborah Hurford. "Journeys Without Maps: Dramaturgy of the Post-Modern." *Canadian Theatre Review* 87 (1996): 31–33.

Flather, Patti. "The Yukon Writers' Festival: Building a Northern Literary Voice." *Canadian Theatre Review* 73 (1992): 51–53.

Gass, Ken. "Toronto's Alternates: Changing Realities." *Canadian Theatre History*. Ed. Don Rubin. Toronto: Copp Clark, 1996. 404–10.

Goodwin, Jill Tomasson. "Private Voices/Public Forum: Morningside Drama as National Theater." *Canadian Theatre Review* 62 (1990): 19–23.

Grace, Sherrill, and Albert-Reiner Glaap, eds. *Performing National Identities: International Perspectives on Contemporary Canadian Theatre*. Vancouver: Talonbooks, 2003.

Hayes, Elliott. "The State of the Art vs. The Art of the State." *Canadian Theatre Review* 45 (1985): 19–28.

Healey, Michael. "Process, or How to Spend the Grant Money." *Canadian Theatre Review* 97 (1998): 5–7.

Heide, Christopher. "Wolfeville: Playwright-in-Residence, Horton District High." *Canadian Theatre Review* 48 (1986): 122–26.

Herzberg Lister, Rota. "Constructing a Canadian Theatrical Culture: The 1975 Conference of the Association for Canadian and Quebec Literature in Historical and Personal Perspective." Kamploops: *Textual Studies in Canada* Vol. 6, 1995. 22–32.

Hurley, Erin. "Theatre as National Export: on Being and Passing in the United States." In Grace & Glaap. 160–80.

Hollingsworth, Margaret. "Collaborators." *Canadian Theatre Review* 69 (1991): 15–19.

Hutcheon, Linda and Michael Hutcheon. "Opera and National Identity: New Canadian Opera." *Canadian Theatre Review* 96 (1998): 5–8.

Insell, Celeste. "Laying the Groundwork for Survival: African Canadian Theatre in Vancouver." *The International Review of African American Art* 10.1 (1992): 6.

Ives, L. Patricia. "*The Last Will and Testament of Lolita*: The Very Best Bad Girls Create…" *Canadian Theatre Review* 55 (1988): 30–33.

Johnson, Chris. "Wisdome Under a Ragged Coate: Canonicity and Canadian Drama." In Brask, *Contemporary*. 26–49.

Johnson, Kirsty. "Playwriting Madness: New Play and Playwright Development at Toronto's Workman Theatre Project." *Canadian Theatre Review* 115 (2003): 39–42.

Jordão, Aida. "Playwriting in Canadian Popular Theatre." *Canadian Theatre Review* 115 (2003): 62–65.

Kaplan, Jon. "Going for Broke." (Factory Theatre, Toronto) *Canadian Theatre Review* 44 (1985): 45–50.

Karastamatis, John. "Missed Stories: Has Inadequate Script Development Hampered the Success of Chinese Canadian Theatre in Toronto?" *Canadian Theatre Review* 110 (2002): 21–22.

Kareda, Urjo. "They Also Serve Who Only Stand and Wait for Rewrites…" *Canadian Theatre Review* 49 (1986): 6–11.

King-Odjig, Alanis. "To Keep the Seventh Fire Lit: Script Development at De-Ba-Jeh-Mu-Jig." *Canadian Theatre Review* 87 (1996): 17–18.

Knowles, Ric. *Reading the Material Theatre.* Cambridge and New York: Cambridge UP, 2004.

———. "Marlon Brando, Pocahontas and me." *Essays on Canadian Writing* 71 (2000): 48–60.

———. *The Theatre of Form and the Production of Meaning: Contemporary Canadian Dramaturgies.* Toronto: ECW, 1999.

———. "*CTR* and Canadian Theatre Criticism: Constructing the Discipline." *Canadian Theatre Review* 79/80 (1994): 10–13.

———. "Great lines are a dime a dozen: Judith Thompson's Greatest Cuts." *Canadian Theatre Review* 89 (1996): 8–18.

——— and Monique Mojica, eds. *Staging Coyote's Dream: An Anthology of First Nations Drama in English.* Toronto: Playwrights Canada, 2003.

Knowles, Richard Paul. "From Nationalist to Multinational: The Stratford Festival, Free Trade, and the Discourses of Intercultural Tourism." *Theatre Journal* 47.1 (1995): 19–41.

———. "The Dramaturgy of the Perverse." *Theatre Research International* 17:3 (1992): 226–35.

———. "Voices (off): Deconstructing the Modern English-Canadian Dramatic Canon." In Lecker. 91–111.

———, ed. *The Proceedings of the Theatre in Atlantic Canada Symposium, Mount Allison University.* Sackville: Centre for Canadian Studies, 1988.

Lazarus, John. "A Playwright's Guide to Workshop Survival. 2" *Canadian Theatre Review* 49 (1986): 27–29.

Lecker, Robert, ed. *Canadian Canons: Essays in Literary Value.* Toronto: U of Toronto P, 1991.

Leonard, Paul. "Rhubarb! Towards a new Dramaturgy." *Canadian Theatre Review* 49 (1986): 44–52.

McCaughna, David. "Playwrights Union of Canada." *Canadian Theatre Review* 45 (1985): 140–42.

McKinnie, Michael. "Legacies: Richard Rose's Vision of Tarragon Theatre." *Canadian Theatre Review* 113 (2003): 29–33.

Mendenhall, Marie Elaine Powell. *The playwright's path: an analysis of the Canadian play development process as practiced by the Saskatchewan Playwright's Centre 1982–2000*. Diss. U of Regina, 2001. AAT MQ65771.

Miller, Michael. "*Vocal Strain:* Playwright Michael Miller questions expectations and relationships between Black playwrights and the theatres that produce them (or don't)." *Performing Arts & Entertainment in Canada* 33.3 (2001): 19–21.

Munday, Jenny. "Brave New Words at Theatre New Brunswick." *Canadian Theatre Review* 87 (1996): 9–10.

Page, Malcolm. "Saskatoon: a Proliferation of Prairie Playwrights." *Canadian Theatre Review* 62 (1990): 75–76.

Peters, Helen. "The aboriginal presence in Canadian theatre and the evolution of being Canadian." *Theatre Research International* 18.3 (1993): 197–205.

Poteet, Susan. "New Play Development in Quebec: A Matter of Voice." *Canadian Theatre Review* 46 (1986): 28–35.

Quirt, Brian. "Dance and Dramaturgy." *The Dance Current.* 1.2 (June 1998). http://www.nightswimmingtheatre.com/.

Raby, Gyllian, P. Hawthorne, A. McInnes, R. Benedetti, J. Biros, and B. White. "The Role of the Director in New Play Development." *Canadian Theatre Review* 52 (Fall 1987): 7–13.

Rebeiro, Angela, ed. *Theatre in Society: Politics, Plays and Performances: Essays by Canadian Theatre Practitioners on the Occasion of the Canadian Theatre Conference.* Ottawa, 2002. Toronto: PUC Play Service, 2002.

Rioux, Monique. "Discovering the Inuit People." *Canadian Theatre Review* 46 (1986): 72–78.

Rivers, Paul. "Theatre Channel: Exploring the Dramaturgy of Juxtaposed Media." *Canadian Theatre Review* 127 (2006): 33–37.

Rudakoff, Judith. "Somewhere, Over the Rainbow: White-Female-Canadian Dramaturge in Cape Town." *The Drama Review* 48:1 (2004): 126–63.

———. "The Four Elements: New Models for a Subversive Dramaturgy." *Theatre Topics* 13.1 (2003): 143–52.

———. *Questionable Activities: Canadian Theatre Artists Interviewed by Canadian Theatre Students.* Vols. 1 & 2. Toronto: PUC Play Service, 1996. Toronto: Playwrights Canada Press, 2000.

———— and Rita Much. *Fair Play: 12 Women Speak: Conversations with Canadian Playwrights.* Toronto: Simon & Pierre, 1990.

———— and Lynn Thompson. *Between the Lines: The Process of Dramaturgy.* Toronto: Playwrights Canada Press, 2002.

Rossiter, Kate et al. "From Page to Stage: Dramaturgy and the Art of Interdisciplinary Translation." *Journal of Health Psychology* 13:2 (2008) 277–86.

Salter, Denis. "The Idea of a National Theatre." In Lecker. 71–90.

————. "Montreal: Intimate Universe." *Canadian Theatre Review* 64 (1990): 82–83.

Shantz, Valerie. *Yvette Nolan: Playwright in Context.* Diss. U of Alberta, 1998. AAT MQ28909.

Sherlow, Lois Juanita. *Towards Interculturalism: a critical history of contemporary drama in Canada.* Diss. U of Ottawa, 1996. AAT NN11602.

Smith, Mary Elizabeth. "On the Margins: Eastern Canadian Theatre as Post-colonialist Discourse." *Theatre Research International* 21.1 (1996): 41–51.

Springate, Michael. "A Deeper Questioning of Assumptions." *Canadian Theatre Review* 87 (1996): 34–35.

"Surviving the Nineties: A CTR Forum." *Canadian Theatre Review* 63 (Summer 1990): 34–42.

Taylor, Kate. "Shiny new stuff for the stage." *The Globe and Mail* (Toronto). 19 October 2002: R15.

Tihanyi, Deborah. "Theorizing New Play Development in Canada." *Canadian Theatre Review* 115 (2003): 26–28.

————. *New play development in English Canada 1970–1990: Defining the dramaturgical role.* Diss. U of Alberta, 1994. AAT MM94903.

Tompkins, Joanne. "Afterword." (National and Cultural Identity) *Modern Drama* 45:2 (2002): 298–301.

Wade, Bryan. "Down and Out in the CanLit Ghetto." *Canadian Theatre Review* 46 (1986): 106–09.

Walcott, Rinaldo. "Dramatic Instabilities: Diasporic Aesthetics as a Question for and about Nation." *Canadian Theatre Review* 118 (2004): 99–106.

Wallace, Robert. "Writing the Land Alive: The playwrights' vision in English Canada." *Contemporary Canadian Theatre: New World Visions.* Ed. Anton Wagner. Toronto: Simon and Pierre, 1985.

————. "Toward an Understanding of Theatrical Difference." *Canadian Theatre Review* 55 (1988): 5–14.

———— and Cynthia Zimmerman. *The Work: Conversations with English Canadian Playwrights.* Toronto: Coach House Press, 1982.

Weiss, Peter Eliot. "The Collective from a Playwright's Perspective." *Canadian Theatre Review* 49 (1987): 59–66.

Winsor, Chris. "Nationalism and Theatre in Quebec." (Interview with Alonzo LeBlanc). *Canadian Theatre Review* 62 (1990): 30–34.

Wylie, Betty Jane. "A Playwright's Guide to Workshop Survival. 1" *Canadian Theatre Review* 49 (1986): 24–26.

Zimmerman, Cynthia. "Maintaining the Alternative: an Interview with Urjo Kareda." In Grace and Glaap. 211–24.

DATE DUE	RETURNED

Bruce Barto
of Toronto.
periodicals a
Collective Cr
Texts from Ex
Imagination i
Marigraph (an
Current resear
material condi
English-speakin
physically-based
Current creative
multiple devised
interdisciplinary
playwright.

R